THE FIVE REPUBLICS OF
CENTRAL AMERICA

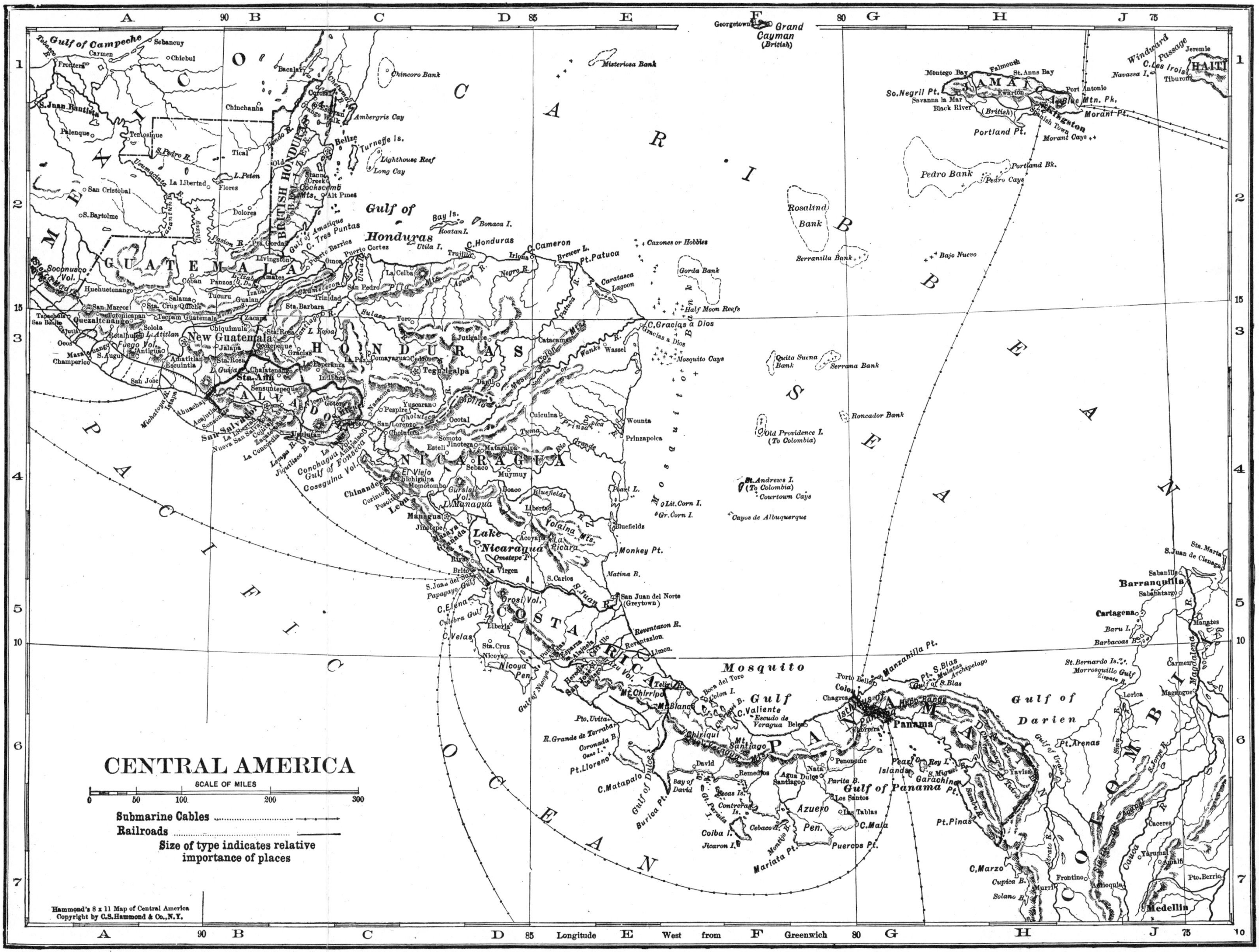

CENTRAL AMERICA
SCALE OF MILES
0 50 100 200 300
Submarine Cables
Railroads
Size of type indicates relative importance of places
Hammond's 8 x 11 Map of Central America
Copyright by C.S.Hammond & Co.,N.Y.
Longitude West from Greenwich
MEXICO
GUATEMALA
BRITISH HONDURAS
HONDURAS
SALVADOR
NICARAGUA
COSTA RICA
PANAMA
COLOMBIA
CARIBBEAN SEA
PACIFIC OCEAN
Gulf of Campeche
Gulf of Honduras
Gulf of Fonseca
Gulf of Panama
Gulf of Darien
Mosquito Gulf
Lake Nicaragua
Grand Cayman (British)
Jamaica (British)
Kingston
HAITI
Windward Passage
New Guatemala
Belize
Tegucigalpa
San Salvador
Managua
Leon
San Juan del Norte (Greytown)
Limon
Panama
Colon
Barranquilla
Cartagena
Medellin
Quezaltenango
Sta. Ana
Bluefields
Rosalind Bank
Pedro Bank
Serranilla Bank
Serrana Bank
Roncador Bank
Old Providence I. (To Colombia)
St. Andrews I. (To Colombia)
Cayos de Albuquerque
Mosquito Cays
C. Gracias a Dios
Bay Is.
Chincoro Bank
Misteriosa Bank
Azuero Pen.
Nicoya Pen.

THE FIVE REPUBLICS
OF
CENTRAL AMERICA

THEIR POLITICAL AND ECONOMIC DEVELOPMENT AND THEIR RELATIONS WITH THE UNITED STATES

By DANA G. MUNRO

EDITED BY
DAVID KINLEY
Professor of Political Economy in the University of Illinois

NEW YORK / RUSSELL & RUSSELL

FIRST PUBLISHED IN 1918 BY THE CARNEGIE ENDOWMENT
FOR INTERNATIONAL PEACE
REISSUED, 1967, BY RUSSELL & RUSSELL
A DIVISION OF ATHENEUM HOUSE, INC.
L. C. CATALOG CARD NO: 66-27128
PRINTED IN THE UNITED STATES OF AMERICA

INTRODUCTORY NOTE BY THE DIRECTOR

THE Division of Economics and History of the Carnegie Endowment for International Peace is organized to " promote a thorough and scientific investigation of the causes and results of war." In accordance with this purpose a conference of eminent statesmen, publicists, and economists was held in Berne, Switzerland, in August, 1911, at which a plan of investigation was formed and an extensive list of topics was prepared. It will be seen that an elaborate series of investigations was undertaken and, if the war had not intervened, the resulting reports might have been expected, before the present date, in printed form.

Of works so undertaken some aim to reveal direct and indirect consequences of warfare, and thus to furnish a basis for a judgment as to the reasonableness of the resort to it. If the evils are in reality larger and the benefits smaller than in the common view they appear to be, such studies should furnish convincing evidence of this fact and afford a basis for an enlightened policy whenever there is danger of international conflicts.

Studies of the causes of warfare reveal, in particular, those economic influences which in time of peace bring about clashing interests and mutual suspicion and hostility. They show what policies, as adopted by different nations, reduce the conflicts of interest, inure to the common benefit, and afford a basis for international confidence and good will. They tend, further, to reveal the natural economic influences which of themselves bring about more and more harmonious relations and tend to substitute general benefits for the mutual injuries that follow unintelligent self-seeking. Economic internationalism needs to be fortified by the mutual trust that just dealing creates; but just conduct itself may be favored by economic conditions. These, in turn, may be created partly by a natural evolution and partly by the conscious action of governments; and both evolution and public action are among the important subjects of investigation.

An appeal to reason is in order when excited feelings render armed conflicts imminent; but it is quite as surely called for when no excitement exists and when it may be forestalled and prevented from developing by sound national policies. To furnish a scientific basis for reasonable international policies is the purpose of some of the studies already in progress and of more that will hereafter be undertaken.

The war has interrupted work on rather more than a half of the studies that were in progress when it began, but it has itself furnished topics of immediate and transcendent importance. The costs, direct and indirect, of the conflict, the commercial policies induced by it and, especially, the direct control, which because of it, governments are now exercising in many spheres of economic activity where formerly competition and individual freedom held sway, are phenomena that call, before almost all others, for scientific study. It is expected that most of the interrupted work will ultimately be resumed and that, in the interim before this occurs, studies of even greater importance will be undertaken and will be pushed rapidly toward completion.

The publications of the Division of Economics and History are under the direction of a Committee of Research, the membership of which includes the statesmen, publicists, and economists who participated in the Conference at Berne in 1911, and two who have since been added. The list of members at present is as follows:

INTRODUCTORY NOTE

EUGÈNE BOREL, Professor of Public and International Law in the University of Geneva.

LUJO BRENTANO,[1] Professor of Economics in the University of Munich; Member of the Royal Bavarian Academy of Sciences.

CHARLES GIDE, Professor of Comparative Social Economics in the University of Paris.

H. B. GREVEN, Professor of Political Economy and Statistics in the University of Leiden.

FRANCIS W. HIRST, London.

DAVID KINLEY, Professor of Political Economy in the University of Illinois.

HENRI LA FONTAINE, Senator of Belgium.

His Excellency LUIGI LUZZATTI, Professor of Constitutional Law in the University of Rome; Secretary of the Treasury, 1891-3; Prime Minister of Italy, 1908-11.

GOTARO OGAWA, Professor of Finance at the University of Kioto, Japan.

Sir GEORGE PAISH, Joint Editor of *The Statist*, London.

MAFFEO PANTALEONI, Professor of Political Economy in the University of Rome.

EUGEN PHILIPPOVICH VON PHILIPPSBERG,[2] Professor of Political Economy in the University of Vienna; Member of the Austrian Herrenhaus, Hofrat.

PAUL S. REINSCH, United States Minister to China.

His Excellency BARON Y. SAKATANI, recently Minister of Finance; Present Mayor of Tokio.

THEODOR SCHIEMANN,[1] Professor of the History of Eastern Europe in the University of Berlin.

HARALD WESTERGAARD, Professor of Political Science and Statistics in the University of Copenhagen.

---

[1] Membership ceased April 6, 1917, by reason of the declaration of a state of war between the United States and the Imperial German Government.
[2] Died, June, 1917.

INTRODUCTORY NOTE

FRIEDRICH, FREIHERR VON WIESER, Professor of Political Economy at the University of Vienna.

The function of members of this Committee is to select collaborators competent to conduct investigations and present reports in the form of books or monographs; to consult with these writers as to plans of study; to read the completed manuscripts, and to inform the officers of the Endowment whether they merit publication in its series. This editorial function does not commit the members of the Committee to any opinions expressed by the writers. Like other editors, they are asked to vouch for the usefulness of the works, their scientific and literary merit, and the advisability of issuing them. In like manner the publication of the monographs does not commit the Endowment as a body or any of its officers to the opinions which may be expressed in them. The standing and attainments of the writers selected afford a guarantee of thoroughness of research and accuracy in the statement of facts, and the character of many of the works will be such that facts, statistical, historical, and descriptive, will constitute nearly the whole of their content. In so far as the opinions of the writers are revealed, they are neither approved nor condemned by the fact that the Endowment causes them to be published. For example, the publication of a work describing the attitude of various socialistic bodies on the subject of peace and war implies nothing as to the views of the officers of the Endowment on the subject of socialism; neither will the issuing of a work, describing the attitude of business classes toward peace and war, imply any agreement or disagreement on the part of the officers of the Endowment with the views of men of these classes as to a protective policy, the control of monopoly, or the regulation of banking and currency. It is necessary to know how such men generally think and feel on the great issue of war, and it is one of the purposes of the Endowment to promote studies which will accurately reveal their atti-

INTRODUCTORY NOTE

tude. Neither it nor its Committee of Research vouches for more than that the works issued by them contain such facts; that their statements concerning them may generally be trusted, and that the works are, in a scientific way, of a quality that entitles them to a reading.

JOHN BATES CLARK,
Director.

EDITOR'S PREFACE

THIS volume by Dr. Dana G. Munro on the history and economic conditions of the five Central American Republics was undertaken for the Carnegie Endowment for International Peace as one of a series of studies intended to present similar conditions in others of the Latin American Republics. The general purpose of the studies is to acquaint our own people with conditions as interpreted by a student and critic from among ourselves, in order that we may get a better and more sympathetic understanding of the ideals and conditions of life of our Central and South American neighbors. It is our hope also that such presentation may be helpful to the peoples of these countries themselves as a sympathetic attempt by friends to understand them and to let them see how things appear through the eyes of friendly outsiders.

Dr. Munro's volume is the result of several months of study on the ground. He traveled by all the usual means of locomotion through the countries he describes, getting his information, as far as possible, at first hand. His account may be relied on as a correct presentation of the life of the people as seen by an outsider.

Nothing is more desirable in American international relations than a better understanding and closer coöperation among the peoples of the western hemisphere. The more we know about one another's difficulties, sympathies, and ideals, the better friends we shall all be, the more ready to make allowances for one another's shortcomings, and the better able to appreciate one another.

DAVID KINLEY,
Editor.

AUTHOR'S PREFACE

BY many persons in the United States, Central America is conceived of chiefly as a land of revolutions, bankrupt governments, and absconding presidents, and a haven for fugitives from justice from more settled countries. The progress of the people of the Isthmus since their declaration of independence, and the significance of this progress in view of the difficulties with which they have had to contend, are rarely recognized. The fact is too frequently overlooked that the greater part of the people of the five republics, except in Costa Rica, are descendants of the semi-civilized aboriginal tribes whom the *Conquistadores* enslaved in the sixteenth century, and that these Indians still remain, for the most part, in a condition of dense ignorance and economic dependence. Even the white upper classes were prevented for three centuries from making any advance in civilization by the restriction of intercourse with other countries and the centralization of authority in the hands of foreign officials under the Spanish colonial system; and they were unable to set up a stable political system when they obtained their independence, because of their lack of experience in self-government, and because of the absence of political institutions upon which a stable system of government could be based.

When we take these facts into consideration, and when we see the advances which some of the Central American Republics have been able to make despite these handicaps, we shall be less ready to conclude that their people are inherently unfit for self-government. Our own race is removed from the disorderly conditions which characterize the more turbulent parts of the Isthmus only by a few hundred years, and in the United States we are not unfamiliar today with evils similar to some of the worst evils of Central American political life. There is no reason to suppose that all of the five republics will not eventually develop stable governments, as some of them have already done. Although conditions in many parts of the Isthmus are still very bad, they are gradually being overcome by the efforts of the better elements among the ruling classes and by the gradual progress of the common people. Since the Washington Conference of 1907, moreover, the preservation of internal and international peace in the Isthmus has been powerfully aided by the influence of the United States.

That the economic and political conditions of Central America and the other countries of the Caribbean should be understood by the American government and the American people is of the utmost importance. The policy of the United States, more perhaps than any other factor either external or internal, will determine the course of the development of the five republics during the next few decades, and if this policy is to be beneficial, it must be based on knowledge and must be controlled by an intelligent public opinion. Only injustice can result from the publication of works like many of the recent superficial descriptions of Central America, whether they portray the five countries as foci of continual disorder, constitutionally incapable of self-government, and hence destined to absorption by a stronger power, or paint a ridiculously laudatory picture, based on official reports and on the utterances of the authorities rather than on critical observation. It is the purpose of this study to describe conditions simply as they appeared to the author during a sojourn of two years in the Isthmus, with the object of setting forth what the people of Central America have achieved since their declaration of independence and what problems confront them in their present stage of development.

AUTHOR'S PREFACE

The difficulties in the way of a careful study of the history and the economic and political conditions of the five republics are very great, because there is so little trustworthy written material. Historical works are especially unsatisfactory. The colonial period is ably treated in two or three books by Central American authors, but the development of the community since its separation from Spain, and the far-reaching economic and political changes which have taken place during the last century, have apparently never been studied by anyone who was equipped by historical training and by a knowledge of the country to interpret them. In attempting to obtain material for sketching the historical development of the Isthmus, therefore, I have been forced to rely on the very inadequate histories which do exist, which are little more than lists of presidents and revolutions, and upon a large number of political pamphlets, government documents, and memoirs of Central American leaders and of early travelers in the Isthmus. Much of this material is all but worthless because of the ignorance or the ulterior motives of the writers, but there is enough of value to reveal certain broad tendencies of economic and political development.

It is equally difficult to secure data concerning the condition of the country at present. Official publications can rarely be accepted as reliable because of the carelessness with which records are kept and statistical data are gathered by most of the departments, and because official statements about the material progress of the country and the activities of the authorities too often represent patriotic aspirations rather than accomplished facts. The differences in the use of terms and in standards of public service, moreover, are so great that it is difficult for a foreigner to obtain an idea of the actual situation in one of the countries merely by conversation with the authorities and other persons in the capital. The writer found it extremely helpful to supplement such conversations with trips to the provincial towns and through the rural districts. An acquaintance with the life and the character of the people outside the somewhat Europeanized cities, and an observation of the actual working of the political machinery, did much to make clear many things which otherwise might have been difficult to understand.

The courtesy of the officials of the five governments, and the hospitality extended to the traveler by all classes of the people, make a journey through Central America an experience upon which one can always look back with keen pleasure. It would be impossible here to thank individually the many friends who helped to make my stay in the Isthmus both pleasant and profitable. Nevertheless, I wish to express especially my appreciation of the assistance which I have received from Dr. L. S. Rowe, Mr. John M. Keith, Señor Luís Anderson, Señor Manuel Aragón, Mr. Boaz Long, Mr. and Mrs. Arthur Jones, General Luís Mena, Mr. and Mrs. William Owen, Professor Philip M. Brown, Señor Francisco Castro and Doña Fidelina de Castro, Dr. Escolástico Lara, Dr. Juan B. Sacasa, Dr. Louis Schapiro, and General José María Moncada. Without their assistance, it would have been impossible to secure the information upon which this study is based.

CONTENTS

CHAPTER		PAGE
I.	THE COUNTRY AND THE PEOPLE	1
II.	CENTRAL AMERICAN POLITICAL INSTITUTIONS	24
III.	GUATEMALA	50
IV.	NICARAGUA	72
V.	SALVADOR	99
VI.	HONDURAS	119
VII.	COSTA RICA	138
VIII.	THE ESTABLISHMENT OF A CENTRAL AMERICAN FEDERATION	164
IX.	THE CAUSES OF CENTRAL AMERICAN REVOLUTIONS	185
X.	THE WASHINGTON CONFERENCE OF 1907	204
XI.	THE INTERVENTION OF THE UNITED STATES IN NICARAGUA	227
XII.	COMMERCE	265
XIII.	CENTRAL AMERICAN PUBLIC FINANCE	284
XIV.	THE INFLUENCE OF THE UNITED STATES IN CENTRAL AMERICA	303
	BIBLIOGRAPHY	321
	INDEX	327

CHAPTER I

THE COUNTRY AND THE PEOPLE

Physical Features—Character of the Population—The Land-owning and Laboring Classes: Their Mode of Life and Personal Characteristics—Factors Which Have Retarded Economic Development—Agricultural Products—Foreign Immigration and Investments.

GUATEMALA, Salvador, Nicaragua, Honduras, and Costa Rica, the five Republics of Central America, occupy a narrow strip of land between the Atlantic and Pacific Oceans, extending East and South from Mexico to the Isthmus of Panama. Although their combined area is smaller than that of the state of California,[1] they comprise many regions of strikingly different climatic conditions, for the mountains which occupy the greater part of their territory cause variations in the distribution of rainfall, and also provide plateaus and high valleys where the tropical heat is less intense because of the altitude. Along the shore of the Caribbean Sea there is a broad strip of country but little above sea level. This has remained almost uninhabited until recently because of its intense humidity and suffocating temperature, but within the last twenty-five years it has become of great economic importance, at least to the outside world, through its exports of bananas. The lowlands extend inland to the Central American *Cordillera,* a series of ranges which

[1] The estimated area and population of the five countries, as given in the Statesman's Year Book for 1916, are:

	Area.		Population.
Guatemala	48,290	square miles.	2,003,579. (1915)
El Salvador	7,225	" "	1,225,835. (1914)
Nicaragua	49,200	" "	703,540. (1914)
Honduras	44,275	" "	562,000. (1914)
Costa Rica	23,000	" "	420,179. (1915)
	171,990		4,915,133

grow higher and higher as they approach the Pacific Ocean, until they culminate in a great chain of volcanic peaks which traverses the Isthmus from the Mexican boundary to that of Panama. It is near these peaks, where the decomposed lava from past eruptions has created a marvelously fertile soil, and where the climate, with copious but not excessive rains during six months of the year, is healthful and favorable to agriculture, that the great majority of the people of Central America live. Almost all of the more important cities and towns are situated either in the mountain valleys, at an altitude of from two to seven thousand feet, where the temperature rarely exceeds eighty degrees Fahrenheit, or in the hot, but dry and therefore comparatively healthful plain between the base of the volcanoes and the Pacific Ocean.

Populous and partially civilized Indian communities had existed in this part of America for centuries before the Spanish conquest, and their descendants form the bulk of the population of the five republics. Although the original inhabitants were almost exterminated in many districts by the oppression and mistreatment of the early colonists, enough remained to become the predominant racial element in the conglomerate population, Spanish in language and religion but Indian in civilization and standards of living, which arose from the fusion of the invaders, the aborigines, and the negroes who were brought in as slaves or escaped to the mainland from the West Indies. This was especially true of the three central countries of the Isthmus, and the development of these has therefore been somewhat different from that of Costa Rica, where the white stock predominates even among the common people, and from that of Guatemala, where the pure-blooded Indians are still a distinct and separate race.

Although the Central American countries are theoretically democracies, there is in each a small, powerful upper class, consisting of the so-called " principal families."

These are for the most part descendants of the prominent creole[1] families of colonial days, and are therefore in many cases of pure or almost pure Spanish descent. A large proportion,—perhaps the majority,—however, have more or less Indian and even negro blood in their veins. This class has been able to maintain its dominant position in the community, partly because of its command of the government, which it assumed when the republican institutions which the Isthmian patriots attempted to introduce after the declaration of independence were found to be unworkable because of the ignorance of the mass of the people, but more especially because of its control over agriculture. At the time of the conquest, the land, like everything else in the invaded territory, was treated as the property of the crown, and that in the neighborhood of the Spanish settlements was divided among the colonists by the royal governors. Further large allotments were made from time to time during the colonial period. After the declaration of independence, the governments of the several republics continued to regard as state property all land not already specifically granted, and sold or gave away large tracts of it to rich natives or foreigners, notwithstanding the fact that much of the public domain was already occupied by peasants who had always considered the patches which they cultivated as their own. The number of large holdings has been further increased in some of the republics by the division of the common lands formerly held by each village among the village's inhabitants; for the beneficiaries have often sold their shares to their wealthier neighbors. At the present time a comparatively small number of persons own a very large amount of agricultural property, and employ the majority of the other inhabitants of the Isthmus as workmen on their plantations. The economic and political power of this class would manifestly be very

[1] The word creole is used in the Spanish-American sense, to signify a person of Spanish descent born in America.

great even if it were not supported by their prestige as the descendants of the conquering race.

Although their wealth is entirely agricultural, the "principal families" invariably reside in the cities. They make frequent visits to their plantations, which they intrust to the care of overseers, but the majority of them show a marked aversion both to country life and to rural pursuits. As a whole they are neither very enterprising nor very energetic. Those who do not inherit a plantation which produces an income sufficient to support them turn to one of the already overcrowded learned professions rather than to the development of the natural resources of their countries, in the exploitation of which foreigners are daily making fortunes before their eyes. Nearly every member of the upper class, moreover, is actively engaged in politics, often to the exclusion or to the detriment of his other occupations.

The wealthier families live in one or two story houses of adobe or concrete, which cover a surprisingly large extent of ground but have little pretension to architectural beauty or to comfort. These are built around two, and often three, courtyards or *patios*. The front *patio,* upon which open the *sala,* or parlor, and the bedrooms, generally contains an attractive garden surrounded by an open *corredor,* which serves as living room and dining room. At the rear are the kitchen, stable, and servants' quarters. The standard of living, especially in the less advanced countries, is still rather primitive. Furniture and food are of a very simple character, and the servants, of whom each family employs a large number, are untrained and inefficient. The band concerts three or four times a week, the cinematographs, and occasional cheap operettas offer almost the only opportunity for diversion, except on the very unusual occasions when a government subsidy makes possible a short season of opera or drama. Social events are comparatively few. In every city there are two or three civic *fiestas* during the year, when the native society abandons itself to a round of dancing, horse-racing, and other gayeties, but at other times the capitals of the Isthmus are decidedly dull. Life in them has, however, a peculiar charm for the foreigner, because of the kindliness and friendliness of the people.

Since the building of the railways and the increase of commerce have brought the Central American countries into closer touch with the outside world, there has been a great change in customs and ways of living in such places as Guatemala, San Salvador, and San José de Costa Rica. The high price of coffee during the last decade of the nineteenth century brought about an era of prosperity such as the rather backward communities of the Isthmus had never before known. Elaborate private residences and costly public buildings were erected in the national capitals, and pianos, window glass, modern furniture, and other articles which had formerly been little used, were imported from Europe in great quantities. After the reaction which set in when the value of coffee in the world's markets declined, the new standard of living remained, and even the poorer members of the upper classes now enjoy most of the comforts and many of the luxuries of modern civilization. The tendency to adopt European and North American customs is greatly furthered by the young people, who in increasing numbers are sent abroad to school and college, for they return with new tastes and new ways of thinking even when they do not acquire a great amount of learning.

Although the members of the upper class are for the most part descendants of the *conquistadores,* social and political prominence is today no longer entirely a matter of birth. The old creole families formed a narrow and exclusive circle until the latter part of the nineteenth century, but as a result of factional wars among themselves and against other portions of the community, they have now become generally impoverished and almost exterminated. A new element, recruited from the more intelligent and ambitious members of the lower classes, has meanwhile achieved a large amount of political power, and has perforce been admitted to a position almost of equality with the old aristocracy. At the present time, humble birth in itself is no obstacle to advancement, although educational opportunities are so limited, and the part played by family influence and favoritism is so great, that only the most capable and energetic boys from the lower classes can hold their own with those to whom the accident of birth has given powerful friends and greater opportunities for study.

The half-breeds, known as *ladinos* or *mestizos,* occupy an intermediate position between the white aristocracy and the great mass of the laboring population, in which the Indian blood predominates. For the most part these are artisans, or skilled laborers, in the towns. They are generally clever workmen, enterprising and quick to learn, but without the capacity to work steadily and diligently for any one object. They occupy practically all of the positions which call for manual dexterity or special training. Many become more prominent than the persons of pure Spanish descent in the public schools and universities, and not a few rise to high positions in the government or in the learned professions.

In each of the five republics there are some small farmers, who are for the most part descendants of the early Spanish colonists. These are the leading citizens of the smaller towns and villages. They do not always have property of their own, but often cultivate fields allotted to them by the municipalities of which they are citizens. The new settlements which were founded from time to time during the colonial period were given tracts of land, usually a league square, to be used in common by their inhabitants, one part as pasture, another as forest, and a third to be apportioned each year among the members of the community. Similar grants were made to many of the Indian villages and tribes, which in some cases received a title to much larger tracts than their white neighbors. These common lands still exist in all of the republics, but the number of villages which hold them has been greatly reduced because some of the governments, as in Costa Rica and Guatemala, have enacted laws dividing them among the inhabitants, in the hope of stimulating private enterprise. The property thus apportioned, as we have stated above, was frequently sold to the rich planters, especially in the districts where the climate was suited to the cultivation of coffee, and the former owners became part of the class of landless laborers. Even where this has not occurred, the smaller villages have in most places decayed because of the emigration of their inhabitants to the cities and to the coffee-growing centers. The small-scale agriculturist has ceased to be an economic factor of importance, except in Costa Rica and in some parts of Salvador; and today there are few places more lifeless and more depressing than the once prosperous settlements in the more remote country districts.

The household servants and the common laborers, who form the poorest classes, are descendants of the native tribes whom the *conquistadores* overcame and enslaved early in the sixteenth century. The first settlers everywhere forced the Indians to work for them, either by declaring them slaves, as a punishment for rebellion, or by establishing the *encomienda* system, under which influential Spaniards were intrusted with the religious instruction of the inhabitants of certain villages, and in return for the benefits thus conferred were allowed to demand a certain amount of labor from their spiritual charges. These *encomiendas,* or *repartimientos,* were the principal source of income among the early colonists. The unfortunate aborigines were compelled to work in mines or plantations or to bring in tribute to their masters, and they were treated with the most revolting cruelty when they failed to do so. After the Spanish government became aware of the grave abuses which the system involved, it ordered its suppression, but the *encomiendas* were finally abolished only after a long struggle with the colonists, who were secretly aided by the royal governors in maintaining their privileges. The Indians never entirely regained their economic independence, for their descendants, with the exception of a few thousands who live an isolated, half-savage life in clearings in the forest, are to the present day dependent upon employment on the plantations of the white families.

Whether in the cities or in the country, the laboring classes live in one or two room huts of adobe or wood, with dirt floors and thatched roofs. A crude table and two or three chairs, one or more beds of rawhide or wood, and often a shrine, with a small image of the Virgin or of some saint, comprise the entire furniture. The walls are decorated with colored prints and advertisements, which are much prized by those fortunate enough to secure them from some passing traveler or from friends in the city. There is usually a loft in one end of the hut, in which the stock of corn and beans, if there is any, and a few of the more bulky family possessions are kept, while the small tools and utensils and the contents of the larder are suspended from the walls. Water, which is often brought by the women on their heads from some little distance, is contained in large earthenware jars and dipped out in gourds, which serve not only as cups but as washbasins. Cooking is performed over an open fire on a brick platform, where there is sometimes a primitive oven. The family livestock is represented by a few pigs and chickens, which associate on friendly terms, inside and outside of the house, with the lean dogs and naked children.

Under such conditions, the Central American laborer

lives contentedly and without worry, for he requires few clothes and but a small amount of inexpensive food. Corn, prepared in the form of *tortillas,* beans and rice cooked with lard, and coffee form the diet of the average family day after day. Plantains are also eaten in great quantities in some parts of the Isthmus, and eggs can frequently be secured. Meat can be had only occasionally outside of the cities, and vegetables, although easily grown, are little cultivated. The same is true of the innumerable and delicious tropical fruits, which grow up where accident dictates, without care or protection.

Because of the primitive living conditions, there is a considerable amount of disease and a high death rate, especially among the children. Malarial fever and typhoid are common, and intestinal parasites are omnipresent. The hookworm, especially, has done incalculable harm. The eradication of this disease has recently been undertaken by the governments of several of the five republics, with the aid of the International Health Commission of the Rockefeller Foundation, which has contributed large sums of money and lent trained men for the prosecution of the work. The prevalence of the hookworm, which perhaps contributes as much as any other factor to the poor physical condition of most tropical races, is indicated by the fact that of the persons examined by the representatives of the Commission in 1915, 60.1 per cent were found to be infected in Costa Rica, 58.6 per cent in Guatemala, and 49.4 per cent in Nicaragua.[1] Notable results have already been obtained, not only in curing sufferers, but in educating the people and their governments to appreciate the need for improvements in sanitation and the need for closer attention to the public health in general. When the principles of hygiene are better understood in the Isthmus, and when better systems of sewers and water supply are

[1] These figures are compiled from the Second Annual Report of the International Health Commission, 1915.

provided, the Central American cities should be as healthful as any in the temperate zones, for their moderate climate and the porousness of the volcanic soil upon which they are situated should do much to prevent the diseases common in other parts of the tropics.

In the country villages, life is extremely uneventful and deadening. The women spend a large amount of time in visiting one another and in attending church services or prayer meetings. The men work, where there is work, on week days, and get drunk on *aguardiente,* or sugar-cane rum, on Sunday. The fiestas and fairs, which are held at least once a year in every village, are mainly an occasion for gambling and debauchery, so far as the common people are concerned. There are few other recreations. The monotony of such an existence, which leads the rural laborers to embark on any adventure offering promise of excitement and prospects for loot, is one of the factors which makes it easy to raise a revolutionary army in many of the Central American States.

Except in Guatemala, where there exists a peonage system which will be described later, the wages of the working man are not very low, considering the fact that his services are of far less value to the employer than would be those of one who was more energetic and intelligent. They range in general from the equivalent of fifteen cents United States currency a day with food and lodging to thirty, forty, or even fifty cents a day without it, and in some places are still higher. The workmen are neither conscientious nor physically strong, and the amount which they accomplish in a day is small. On many plantations, payment is made by the task, and the employees work intermittently, frequently failing to appear for days at a time. This is in part due to the prevalence of drunkenness and disease, and in part simply to an indisposition to work more than is necessary to provide a bare subsistence.

There is little pretense of equality in the treatment by the government of the upper and lower classes. The laborers and country people are forced to bear the entire burden of the military service which is theoretically required of all, and to perform work on the roads and other public undertakings from which the wealthy families are practically exempt; and they are everywhere taxed heavily, although by indirect means, for the benefit of the professional politicians who occupy posts in the government. The petty local officials exercise an almost irresponsible authority over them, and frequently use their power for their own personal advantage or for that of their friends. The poor man enjoys little security in his personal or property rights, and thus has little incentive to better his position.

Education, however, has done much in the last twenty-five years to improve the situation of the masses in the more advanced republics, for the laboring man who learns to read and write has in his hands a powerful weapon both for his own protection and for the advancement of his political and economic interests. In Costa Rica, where public schools have been established everywhere and the percentage of illiteracy is comparatively insignificant, the peasants are assuming a more influential place in the community. Salvador, Nicaragua, and Honduras have been prevented by internal disorder and lack of resources from raising their educational systems to the level of that of their more tranquil neighbor, but their rulers have taken a very real interest in popular instruction, and have made it possible for a very large part of the people to acquire a knowledge of reading and writing. In Guatemala alone the great majority of the inhabitants are at present illiterate. This is not entirely the fault of the government, which has instituted a large number of schools and has legislated for the establishment of others by the owners of plantations, but is due rather to the indifference of the Indians themselves, who as a rule do not care even to learn to speak Spanish.

Public and private morality have been rather disastrously affected by the social conditions arising from the conquest of a half-civilized race by adventurers who in too many cases belonged to the lowest and worst classes in Spain. The Indians who continued to form the bulk of the population were deprived of their own religious and moral customs, and were given in their place a Christianity which was imposed upon them by force, and of which, because of the cruelty and licentiousness of their conquerors, they saw only the worst side. The oppression and violence which characterized the communities of the Isthmus during their early history long prevented their social life from acquiring stability, and made brute force, rather than conscience or public opinion, the ruling principle in private as well as in public affairs. Even at present, in some of the five countries, political and social conditions tend to militate against public spirit and altruism in public life and personal honesty in private life. Social conditions also leave much to be desired. With the men of the upper classes, ideas of morality are generally rather loose, and it is not unusual to see a respected citizen bringing up a number of children by other women side by side with those of his lawful wife. The community not only does not censure his careless observance of the marital tie, but even receives the illegitimate offspring on practically the same footing as the legitimate. With the half-breed laborers, marriage is an institution which finds little favor, not, as is sometimes said, because of the expense which the ceremony involves, but because both the men and the women dislike the obligations and ties which a formal union creates, and prefer a relation which, although generally fairly permanent, can be broken off by either party at will.

This low morality is to a very great extent due to

the lack of religious restraints. At one time, the Catholic Church, to which all of the people nominally belong, was very powerful throughout the Isthmus, and the clergy and the numerous monasteries exercised a strong social and political influence. A few years after the declaration of independence, however, the Liberal leaders, who had been opposed by the clerical party in their struggle to regain power during the years 1826-29, expelled the archbishop and many of the other priests, and suppressed all of the convents. The religious orders were never revived, except in Guatemala after the Conservative victory of 1839. There they continued to exercise a dominant influence until the revolution of 1871, after which the government again suppressed them and took radical measures to destroy the influence of the secular clergy. In the other countries, the priests continued to play a small part in politics, usually as the allies of the Conservative party, but at present their influence can hardly be said to be important. In spiritual as well as in temporal affairs the Church has now almost entirely lost its hold on the people. Many of the women are still very devout, but the men, especially among the upper classes, are for the most part frankly irreligious. In the country districts, few of the churches can support a priest, and religious observances are confined to prayer meetings, led and participated in by the women, and to the rather licentious celebration of holy days. Among the priests, many of whom are foreigners, there are some who lead an irreproachable life, but many others, especially in the poorer countries, do much to harm the Church by their scandalous conduct. There are a few missionaries from England and the United States, but Protestantism is so utterly unsuited to the temperament of the people that they have made few converts.

The Central American has, nevertheless, many good qualities. He is good-natured, affable, profoundly attached to his friends and the members of his family, and deeply susceptible to lofty ideals and patriotic impulses. In every city there are a number of men who are distinguished for their personal integrity and their scrupulous honesty, whose influence and example do much to offset the demoralizing effects of conspicuous political corruption and commercial dishonesty. Even among the most brutal and the most ignorant of the men who have been in power in the various republics, there have been few who have not done what they could, in spite of the difficulties presented by armed opposition and administrative disorganization, to promote the social and economic progress of their countries.

The backwardness of the five republics is in large part due to the isolation in which they were kept by Spain during the three centuries of their existence as colonies. Their development was restricted until the beginning of the nineteenth century by a misguided policy which made progress almost impossible. Agriculture and industry were hampered by burdensome regulations and taxes which not only prevented the cultivation of many products for which the country was admirably suited, but also made difficult, if not impossible, the exportation of those which could be grown. The prohibition of commercial intercourse with foreign countries and the restriction of that with Spain, combined with other obstacles to transportation to and from Europe, practically shut off Central America from the rest of the world during the entire colonial period. Even the declaration of independence in 1821 made little immediate change in this respect, for the new republics had still no direct means of communication with Europe and North America. They all faced the Pacific rather than the Atlantic Ocean. Guatemala City, San Salvador, and the other capitals were not only nearer to the West than to the East Coast, but they were separated from the latter by mountainous country and pestiferous jungles through which traveling was difficult and dangerous. It was not until the construction of the Panama and Tehuantepec Railways brought the West Coast ports within comparatively easy reach of the centers of the world's trade that they could export their products profitably. More recently the construction of railways across Guatemala and Costa Rica has given those countries an outlet upon the Atlantic.

Even after the main obstacles to communication with the outside world had been removed, the economic development of the five republics was held back by internal conditions, for the political disturbances which characterized their first half century under republican institutions, and which are still prevalent in some of them, made large scale agriculture difficult and unprofitable, and discouraged commerce. The civil wars often drew the laborers away from the plantations at the time when their services were most needed, and caused a periodic destruction of property and a laying waste of planted fields. In Guatemala, Costa Rica, and Salvador, where revolutions have been less common during the last generation, the wealthier classes have become very prosperous through the production and exportation of coffee, but Honduras and Nicaragua, because of the almost continuous fighting between rival factions, are today but little better off than in 1821.

All of the five Central American countries are still purely agricultural communities. Manufacturing has never advanced beyond the point of providing a few primitive articles for home consumption, and the native industries have declined since the increase of commercial relations with the outside world has made it more profitable to import many things, such as textiles, furniture, and leather goods, than to make them with the crude tools of the local craftsman. There are a few small factories in each city which produce *aguardiente,* cigars and cigarettes, cloth, candles, and other articles, but in none of them is there employed a great amount of capital or a great number of laborers. The most important agricultural products, from the native point of view, are the staple food crops, among which corn, which is cultivated by every farmer in every part of the Isthmus, holds first place. Beans, rice, sugar cane, and plantains are also found everywhere where they will grow. Potatoes, cacao, and countless varieties of fruits and vegetables from the temperate zone as well as from the tropics are raised here and there in the climates suited to them, but comparatively little interest is shown in their cultivation, and they are surprisingly hard to obtain except in the markets of the larger towns. Agricultural methods have changed little since the Spanish conquest. Except in the most thickly settled regions, the old Indian system of planting is still employed. A patch of forest is cleared by cutting down the larger trees and burning off the undergrowth and branches, and the seed is sown among the charred trunks in holes made with a pointed stick. After being used for one year, the land is planted with grass for pasture or allowed to return to its original condition, and is not cultivated again for from three to five seasons. In the regions where the density of the population makes it necessary to plant the fields year after year, a crude form of wooden plow is used, but fertilizers and modern agricultural implements are little known. The *machete,* a long heavy knife which each laborer carries at his belt, serves as axe, hoe, and trowel. The soil is so rich, however, that it produces two and in some places even three crops each season without apparently becoming impoverished.

In Nicaragua and Honduras, and in the low country along the Pacific Coast of the other republics, a large part of the land is devoted to cattle *haciendas.* The stock as a rule is not of a very fine type. Except on a few ranches no attempt has been made to improve the race of the herds by the importation of animals from abroad, and the native stock seems to have degenerated somewhat as the result of centuries of life in a hot climate. The cattle receive little attention from their owners, and in some regions die by thousands in dry years for lack of food and water. Practically all of the meat is consumed in Central America, for the surplus product of Honduras and Nicaragua is bought by their more densely populated neighbors. The hides and horns are exported to the United States and Europe, but the occasional attempts which have been made in recent years to do the same with a few thousand head of live cattle have not been very successful. Dairy products play but a small part in Central American domestic economy. The native cows produce little milk, and the cheese which is made in large quantities is commonly of a very inferior quality.

Until several years after the declaration of independence practically the only exports of Central America were the forest products of the East Coast and small amounts of indigo, cochineal, and cacao from the communities on the Pacific side of the Isthmus. The five republics had very little commerce, and for this reason had little intercourse with the outside world. This state of affairs was completely changed when the coffee plant was introduced from the West Indies in the second quarter of the last century. As the soil and climate on the slopes of the volcanoes along the western coast were found to be admirably suited to this valuable crop, and the product of Central America from the first commanded a high price in the European markets, the number of plantations increased rapidly, and the new industry soon became the chief interest of the landed proprietors in Guatemala, Costa Rica, and Salvador, and to a less extent in Nicaragua. The cultivation of coffee was in fact carried to a point where it seriously affected the production of the staple food crops, for land formerly planted with corn and beans was turned into *cafetales,* and the inhabitants of the rural districts, who formerly raised enough food to supply their own wants and to sell a small amount in the cities, were led by the greater earnings or were forced by official pressure to become laborers on the coffee plantations. Food prices have consequently risen, and it has become necessary to import flour, rice, and sometimes even beans and corn from other countries. When land has once been planted with coffee trees, which require from three to five years to come into bearing and thus represent a large amount of fixed capital, it is difficult to return it to its original uses, or to release the laborers from the plantation to engage in other occupations, even though in eras of low coffee prices the production of other crops might be more profitable.

Coffee is most advantageously grown on a large scale, as its preparation for the market requires the removal of the pulp of the berry and of the two skins of the bean itself by rather expensive and complicated machinery. The better plantations in Central America produce from 200,000 to 1,000,000 pounds of cleaned coffee each year,[1] and have their own *beneficios,* or cleaning mills. The farmers who operate on a smaller scale, or who for some reason have not found it profitable to install a cleaning mill, send their coffee to *beneficios* in important shipping centers, where the work is performed at so much per bag. Before the war the greater part of the product was exported to Germany, England, or France, but the partial closing of the market in Europe has caused increasing amounts to be sent to the United States since 1914.[2]

The rapid development of the export trade and the corresponding increase in the imports of the five re-

---

[1] In Guatemala there are three or four plantations which produce much more than this.

[2] For a more complete account of the coffee trade, see Chapter XII.

publics would not have been possible without the improvement in means of transportation which has taken place during the last half century. There has been a remarkable betterment, especially in the facilities for travel between Central America and the United States. On the Atlantic side, the United Fruit Company, and, in times of peace, the Hamburg-American line, as well as a number of smaller companies, provide an ample freight and passenger service between all of the important ports and New Orleans and New York. From Puerto Barrios and Puerto Limon, the termini of the transisthmian railroads, there are several boats each week. The conditions on the West Coast are much less satisfactory, for the Pacific Mail Steamship Company, which has almost a monopoly since the German Cosmos Line was forced to withdraw by the war, provides a very irregular and rather expensive service. Even there, however, conditions are immeasurably better than at the time of the opening of the Panama Railway in 1855.

Internal communications have also been improved. Fifty years ago, there were practically no railways in the entire Isthmus, but at the present time each of the national capitals, except Tegucigalpa, is connected with one or more seaports by daily train service. Other forms of transportation and travel, however, are still in a rather primitive state. Some of the republics have spent large amounts of money in constructing roads for bringing the products of the country to the cities or to the railway stations, but as a rule the impecunious governments have not been able to make much headway against the difficulties presented by the mountainous character of the country and the torrential rains of the wet season. There are few highways which are suitable for any vehicle more elaborate than the slow-going oxcart, and in many places even these have to give way to the pack mule.

20 THE FIVE REPUBLICS

One of the forces which has been most potent in bringing Central America into closer contact with the outside world has been the cultivation of bananas by North American enterprise along the low, densely wooded Atlantic Coast. Until recently almost the only inhabitants of this region were scattered, uncivilized tribes descended from Indians and runaway West Indian negroes, who lived in an extremely primitive way in clearings along the shore or on the banks of the rivers. There were one or two struggling ports and a few settlements of woodcutters who traded in mahogany, logwood, and Spanish cedar, but these had little intercourse with the civilized communities of the interior. Within little more than a quarter century, this unpleasant and unhealthful but marvelously fertile region has been transformed. Great banana farms have been created in the formerly impassable jungle, and a net of railways has been built to carry the perishable fruit to the ports, from which it is shipped in fast steamers to the United States and Europe. This is the work of one American corporation, the United Fruit Company, which controls the banana trade not only of Central America, but of the West Indies as well. As the plantations and the transportation lines are managed principally by North Americans and the manual labor is performed by negroes from the British West Indies, English is the predominant language of the new towns which have sprung up. To the native Central American, the Coast is almost a foreign country. The Caribbean ports of Honduras and Nicaragua are in fact for all practical purposes farther from Tegucigalpa and Managua than from New Orleans, and even in those countries where there are better means of transportation from the interior to the fruit ports the banana country has developed in its own way, influenced little, economically or politically, by the communities of the interior. The interior towns, however, have been profoundly affected by the changes on the East Coast. The fruit trade is mainly responsible for the improvement of the steamship service; and in Guatemala and Costa Rica the railways built originally for the transportation of bananas have been extended to the capitals of the two republics, so that the journey from Europe and North America to those cities, and through them to other parts of the Isthmus, has been shortened by several days.

In the interior of several of the republics, the last fifty years have seen a considerable immigration of foreign business men and planters, among whom Germans and North Americans have been the most numerous, although there have also been many Frenchmen, Englishmen, and Italians. The newcomers have obtained almost complete control over the foreign trade of the Isthmus, and even the retail trade at the present time is largely in the hands of Spanish, Chinese, and Armenian shopkeepers. Mercantile pursuits were at one time one of the chief occupations of the creole families, but most of the easy-going Central American merchants, accustomed to the routine created by three centuries of isolation, have been unable to hold their own under changed conditions. The same is true, though to a less extent, in agriculture. Many of the finest plantations were developed in the first place by foreigners, and others are constantly passing into their hands. The majority of those still belonging to natives are heavily mortgaged, for the Central American planter apparently cannot resist the temptation to borrow money, notwithstanding the high rates of interest and the ruinous conditions on which he secures it. There are several European firms whose business it is to make loans secured by plantations and crops. These eventually take over the properties which fall under their control, either reselling them or operating them on their own account.

There are also several small and not very scrupulous

banks, of which the majority have been established, in part at least, with foreign capital. In some of the republics these have co-operated effectively with the officials in the disorganization of the currency and of the government finances. Large investments have been made by North American interests in railways and mines. The total amount of foreign capital in the country is, however, comparatively small, because internal disorders and the slowness with which the country has been opened up have until lately discouraged investments. There is still an immense field for foreign enterprise in the exploitation of Central America's natural resources, which include not only land suitable for the production of almost every kind of agricultural product, but also great forests of valuable woods and as yet untouched mineral deposits.

In some respects, the relations between Central America and the outside world have not been entirely beneficial to the communities of the Isthmus. Many of the foreigners, especially among the Americans, have been fugitives from justice in their own countries who have used their talents to the disadvantage of the natives, or adventurers who have mixed in the politics of the country for their own profit. Unscrupulous corporations or individuals have exploited the inexperience or cupidity of the local governments to obtain valuable concessions without making any adequate return for the favors received, and have not even hesitated to incite or to assist revolutions when they thought that their interests would be furthered by doing so. Too many of the foreign business men have done what they could to make worse the already low standards of commercial morality and have shown themselves more unprincipled than their native competitors. In spite of the distrust generated by hard experiences, however, the Central Americans do not seem to dislike the newcomers or greatly to resent their intrusion. Many

North Americans and Europeans have become respected and influential residents of the communities in which they have settled, and marriages between foreigners and natives of the better class, which have been generally welcomed by the creole families, are gradually giving rise to a half-foreign element which is becoming more and more prominent in each of the five republics.

Closer contact with the outside world has thus brought about entirely new conditions throughout the Isthmus. What the final result of the present changes will be, it is difficult to say. The native families are now more and more losing their hold on the economic life of the country, for commerce, banking, mining, and to an increasingly greater extent agriculture, are controlled by foreigners. They are therefore being forced into the learned professions, which afford a very poor livelihood for any but the most able, and into politics. Their influence is becoming less and less, and the time seems not far distant when the dominant place in the community will be assumed by the foreigners and their descendants, who will probably be assimilated to a great extent into the native population. Some of the more energetic and intelligent native families will doubtless be able to maintain their present wealth and influence, although they will be forced to change their customs and habits completely, as many of them are already doing in the more advanced countries. Whether political and social conditions will be improved or made worse by these developments it is still too early to say, but it is inevitable that both the character of the governments and the conditions of the people as a whole should be profoundly affected.

CHAPTER II

CENTRAL AMERICAN POLITICAL INSTITUTIONS

Early Political History of the Isthmus—Difficulty of Establishing a Stable Government—Annexation to Mexico—Establishment and Dissolution of the Central American Federal Republic—Strife Between Liberals and Conservatives—Description of Central American Governments at Present—Importance of the President—Political Parties, Patronage, and Graft—Revolutions.

ON September 15, 1821, the principal civil and ecclesiastical personages of Guatemala City, with many of the royal authorities and the more prominent creoles, met in convention to proclaim the independence of the five provinces of the Viceroyalty of Guatemala, which had until that time been a dependency of the Spanish crown. The existing administrative machinery was not for the moment abolished, for many of the officials had approved of and had taken a prominent part in the action of the separatist party. The Governor General, Brigadier Gainza, continued to exercise the executive power, and the local governors in Salvador, Honduras, Nicaragua, and Costa Rica were instructed to do the same. In the capital, a committee of influential natives, called the *Junta Consultiva,* was appointed to assist the former royal authorities until a new form of government should be decided upon. There was no armed resistance to this action on the part of the mother country, for the latter, engaged in a prolonged struggle with her more important colonies in the South, was in no position to send troops to subjugate the inaccessible and relatively insignificant communities of Central America.

The prospect which confronted the provinces thus

thrown upon their own resources was far from bright. They were ill equipped for existence as an independent nation. The creole aristocrats, who had led the movement for separation from Spain, and who now assumed control of the government, had had little training to fit them for the exercise of their new responsibilities, for few had received more than the most rudimentary education at home, and fewer still had traveled in foreign countries. None had had any practical experience in political affairs, for it had always been the policy of the royal authorities to fill official positions exclusively with Peninsular Spaniards,[1] thus excluding the natives of the colonies from all share in the administration. There were a half-score of brilliant leaders in the councils of the new nation, but they were notable rather for their exalted but impractical ideals than for any grasp of the concrete situation with which they had to deal at home. Their patriotism was of a high order, but their statesmanship left much to be desired. Among the common people, the great majority were ignorant and superstitious Indians, with a small admixture of Spanish blood and a thin veneer of Spanish civilization. They were scattered through a strip of land eight hundred miles in length, in isolated valleys, separated from one another by mountain ranges and pestilential jungles, where rough mule trails afforded the only means of communication. Throughout the greater part of the Isthmus, the people of each village, having little commerce with their neighbors or with the outside world, depended for subsistence almost entirely upon their own products. A few favored sections produced indigo, cochineal, or precious metals for export, but the expense of shipping these articles from the Pacific Coast to Spain, the only country with which the colonists were allowed to trade, was so great that the planters derived little profit from them. Standards of

[1] By Peninsular Spaniard is meant a native of European Spain.

living were therefore little higher, even in the cities, than they had been three hundred years before.

The Central American nation was divided within itself from the very first. In Guatemala there was a bitter jealousy, created by the special privileges and the pretensions of the more favored classes, between the Peninsular officials and the creole great families on the one hand and between the latter and the merchants and professional men of less aristocratic origin on the other; and this feeling was intensified by radical differences of opinion about religious and economic questions. Besides the dissensions within the group which assumed the control of political affairs in the capital, there were factional conflicts and local civil wars in almost every part of the Isthmus. The provinces, which had long felt that their interests were sacrificed by the royal authorities to those of Guatemala, showed an inclination to dispute the authority of the new central government, and their insubordination was encouraged by the ambitious local governors, who desired to enjoy independent authority, and by the not inconsiderable party which still remained loyal to Spain. San Salvador, Comayagua, Leon, and Cartago, the seats of the provincial governments, were soon the centers of more or less open revolts against Gainza and the *Junta Consultiva,* while other towns, actuated on their side by jealousy of the local capitals, allied themselves to the party in control in Guatemala. The result was a condition of anarchy which throttled agriculture and commerce, and almost put an end to all semblance of organized government.

The inexperience of the creole leaders, and the conflicts between jealous social classes and rival towns, were the more disastrous because the Central American communities possessed no political institutions which could be used as the basis for the establishment of an independent government. In this respect they were in a situation very different from that of the United States in 1783, for in that country the state and local organizations had remained almost unchanged despite the revolution, and the creation of a new central authority had been made comparatively easy by the inherent political capacity derived from centuries of racial experience in self-government. In Central America, the country had been ruled for three hundred years by officials and laws imposed by an outside force, and when this force was withdrawn the old order fell to pieces, leaving nothing to take its place. The self-appointed revolutionary committees had little hold on the loyalty of the people, and little power to make their commands respected. The only political institution which may be said to have survived the change was the municipality. Even in colonial times, the wealthier creoles had been able to purchase positions in the *ayuntamientos,* or governing boards of the cities, and had thus had a voice in the management of certain purely local affairs. After the declaration of independence, the *ayuntamientos* were in many places almost the only respected authority, and they played a large part both in maintaining order and in organizing the *juntas* which took charge of provincial affairs. But they never formed a real basis for the formation of state and national governments, because their independence and authority, which had been small under Spanish rule, was taken from them early in the revolutionary era by the military despots who obtained control of affairs. Their prominence during the transitional period after 1821 contributed little to the establishment of orderly government, for they were the foci of the local jealousies which did more than anything else to keep the country in a state of anarchy.

The organization of a permanent government, to take the place of the provisional revolutionary committees, consequently presented a difficult problem. There was from the first a strong party which favored the establishment of a federal republic, but the majority of the wealthy classes, who had supported the declaration of independence only because of their jealousy of the Peninsular Spaniards who monopolized the official positions and because they realized that the mother country was no longer in a position to protect her colonies from outside aggression and internal disorder, doubted the ability of the people of the Isthmus to rule themselves under republican institutions, and advocated the union of the five provinces with Iturbide's Mexican empire. This party soon grew very strong as the result of disorders which broke out in Honduras and Nicaragua, and on January 25, 1822, the *Junta Consultiva* voted in favor of the annexation. General Filísola, the representative of the Emperor, reached the capital a few months later, and proceeded at once with an army against the people of San Salvador, who had refused to recognize his authority. He had barely overcome the resistance of the republicans there when news arrived that Iturbide had fallen.

Filísola, returning to the capital, called together a congress of representatives from each of the five provinces, to which he turned over his power. This body, assuming the title of National Constituent Assembly, declared the former Central American colonies a federal republic, and appointed a provisional executive committee of three men, who exercised a precarious authority, subject to constant interference by the Assembly, for two years. During this time, the Assembly framed an elaborate constitution, modeled on that of the United States, establishing a federal government in Guatemala City, and state governments in each of the five provinces. A president and five *Jefes de Estado,* chosen by the people through electoral colleges, took the place of the Captain General and the royal provincial governors, and the law-making power was placed in the hands of a Congress of one chamber. The system of checks and balances in the American constitution was taken over and made more intricate by elaborate provisions for the maintenance of the independence of the legislative, executive, and judicial departments and for the prevention of abuses of power.

The Assembly also adopted much progressive legislation, which did away with many of the worst features of the Spanish regime. From the first, however, its sessions were disturbed by irreconcilable differences of opinion between the radical members, who were in the majority, and the clergy and many of the rich landowners and merchants, who disapproved of the proposed reforms. As a result of this conflict, two parties were formed, which called themselves "Liberals" and "Conservatives." The Liberals controlled the first constitutional congress, which met in 1825, and elected their candidate, Manuel José Arce, President of the Republic. The latter, however, soon quarreled with his own party, dissolved the congress, and even overthrew and reorganized the state government of Guatemala, with the aid of the Conservatives. These arbitrary acts caused revolts in many parts of the Isthmus, and especially in Salvador. The people of that state had always been peculiarly jealous of the control of their affairs from Guatemala, and their hostility towards the capital had been increased by the opposition of the federal authorities to the creation of a new diocese in their territory. Under the leadership of Father Delgado, who aspired to the bishopric, they united with the disaffected party in Honduras and Guatemala in a two years' war against Arce, and finally succeeded in overthrowing him (1829).

Francisco Morazán of Honduras, the leader of the victorious army, was proclaimed President of the Federation in 1830. The Guatemala state authorities who had been expelled by Arce were reinstated, and Liberal supremacy was established by force of arms throughout the Isthmus. There were frequent Conservative revolts, however, and even the people of Salvador, who had played the principal part in Morazán's triumph, showed their former jealousy of domination from Guatemala by turning against him. Their resistance was overcome by force in 1831, but it was thought politic to transfer the seat of the federal government to San Salvador. After this, Morazán's prestige waned rapidly. His efforts to repress disorder were unavailing, and the Conservatives gradually regained control of many of the state governments. The last federal congress, which adjourned in 1838, declared the states free to govern themselves independently; and in 1839, when Morazán's second term came to an end, his authority was recognized nowhere outside of Salvador. He was expelled from Central America in the following year by an army from Honduras, Nicaragua, and Guatemala.

The breakdown of the federal system was inevitable. Even those responsible for the adoption of the constitution of the United States as a model had little idea how that constitution really worked, and had no conception of the spirit of compromise and of mutual respect for legal rights which alone made the existence of a government such as they wished to establish possible. Many of the state governors refused to obey the federal officials, and were overthrown by the latter and replaced by adherents of the faction in power in the capital. The Congress, attempting to tie the hands of the executive, was reduced to impotence by the use of the army. The President himself succumbed before the end of his term to a revolution in which all of the disaffected elements took part. Even a better organized government would probably have been unable long to maintain order in a country where distances were so great, means of communication so inadequate, and sectional jealousies so intense as in Central America.

Equally inevitable was the breakdown of the democratic institutions which the leaders of the constituent assembly had sought to create. The elections soon became a farce because of the ignorance and indifference of the great mass of the people. The history of the Central Americans had never taught them respect for the will of the majority, and there was consequently little inclination from the first to accept an unsatisfactory verdict at the polls in good faith. The authorities gradually learned to bring pressure to bear upon the voters in the interests of the party in power, and as time went on assumed a more and more complete control of the balloting, until candidates opposed by the government ceased to have any chance of success. At the same time the members of the opposition party were restrained or expelled from the country, to prevent their intriguing or revolting against the government. Within a few years authority established and upheld by force was the only authority which was recognized or respected, and there was no means of changing the officials in power, and consequently no recourse against bad government, except revolution. Civil war had thus become an indispensable part of the political system.

For some years after 1839, there was intermittent internal and international strife, with hardly an interval of real peace, in nearly every state of the Isthmus. Costa Rica alone, because of her peculiar social conditions, which will be described in a subsequent chapter, led a comparatively tranquil existence in her isolated valley. Elsewhere the establishment of stable governments seemed impossible. Conflicting ambitions, mutual persecutions, and sectional jealousy, as well as differences over religious and economic questions, divided the political leaders of the community into vindictively hostile factions, which had no means of settling their disputes except by an appeal to arms. The state governments, resting upon the outcome of revolutions, had little claim to legality or to the respect of the community, and they were compelled to maintain their position, where they maintained it at all, by force and by tyrannical repression of attempts to overthrow them. Besides the opposition of disaffected classes at home, they faced also the constant danger of intervention by neighboring state governments which were in the hands of the opposite party, for the solidarity created by mutual action in federal affairs led the Conservatives and Liberals in each state to assist their former brothers in arms in other states even after all formal political connection had been broken. This solidarity was strengthened by the ambition of a large section of the Liberal party to re-establish the old federal union by force, under the leadership of the followers of Morazán, and by the opposition to this plan on the part of the Conservatives.

During the greater part of the period from 1839 to 1871, the Conservatives, under the leadership of the aristocratic-clerical party in Guatemala, were dominant throughout the Isthmus. The Liberals secured control for short terms at different times in Salvador, Honduras, and Nicaragua, but in almost every case they were overthrown by the intervention of Rafael Carrera, the President of Guatemala. These Conservative governments, although usually controlled by the wealthiest and most respectable classes in the community, did little to improve the desperate political and economic situation into which the continual civil war had plunged the new republics, partly because of frequent changes in the personnel of the governments and frequent dissensions within the ruling class, and partly because of the inherent weakness of administrations established and upheld by the force of a foreign government.

In 1871-72 the Liberals returned to power as the result of a concerted movement in Guatemala, Honduras, and Salvador. This revolution effected far more than a mere change of presidents; it marked the destruction of the old aristocratic-clerical party as the dominant force in politics. In Guatemala, where the Conservative leaders were exiled or imprisoned, and both the great families and the Church were deprived of a great part of their property and influence, the old regime has never been restored. Its disappearance greatly weakened the position of its allies in Honduras and Salvador. A very similar though almost bloodless revolution occurred in Costa Rica in 1870, when General Tomás Guardia overthrew the "principal families" which had hitherto controlled the government. In Nicaragua, where party divisions were based rather on local rivalries than on class distinctions, the change from the old order to the new was neither so sudden nor so complete, and the Granada aristocracy was able to maintain itself in power until 1893.

The Conservative party continued, indeed, to exist as a political force, but it was no longer a social group which stood for definite principles and points of view so much as mere organization of professional politicians. The influence of the great families became less and less, and the leadership in the party was assumed by military chiefs whose objects and ambitions were little different from those of their opponents. Since 1871, party lines have tended to disappear, and it has made little difference in political conditions whether an administration was controlled by one faction or the other. In Honduras and Salvador, in fact, even the party names have almost ceased to be used, and in Nicaragua they denote merely the adherents of rival cities. It is difficult to say how strong the old aristocracy still is in Guatemala because of the ruthless suppression of all manifestations of political opinion by the government.

Since 1871, the republics of the Isthmus have been governed for the most part by strong, absolute rulers, who have concentrated all power in their own hands and who have on the whole been more successful in maintaining order than the frequently changing and less centralized administrations controlled by the Conservative oligarchy. Revolutions and revolts still occur, but they are less often victorious than formerly, for the relative power of the government has greatly increased. The agricultural development of recent years has made the wealthy classes, who have capital invested in coffee and sugar plantations, inclined to frown on attempts to plunge the country into civil war; and the improvement and the increased cost of artillery and other military material have made it more difficult to equip a revolution strong enough to overcome the regular army. Individual presidents, supported by strong military forces, have thus been able to hold the supreme authority for long terms of years, and to establish highly centralized, comparatively efficient administrations, which have done much to encourage the development of the country. Whatever may be the disadvantages of the exercise of irresponsible power by one man, there can be no doubt that the Central American countries have made more progress under governments of this kind than they did under the constantly changing administrations of their early history, which had neither the prestige nor the military power necessary to maintain order. Until the other departments, and especially the legislatures, had been reduced to subjection by the executive, the action of the latter was often almost completely paralyzed, and more than one president was forced to resign by petty disputes arising purely from personal jealousy. Under such conditions it was of course impossible to pursue any definite and coherent policy.

The majority of the Central American governments at the present time are republican only on paper, although the forms of the various constitutions are still observed. Elections are held regularly in all of the five republics, but they are controlled by the administration, which almost invariably secures the triumph of the official ticket. The extent to which this control is exercised varies with the character and the strength of the President. In most cases, opposition candidacies are simply not permitted, and anyone engaging in propaganda unfavorable to the government's party is severely dealt with. At other times, only known adherents of the President are allowed to cast their votes, and the ballots, if necessary, are fraudulently counted. Even in Costa Rica, where comparative freedom prevails, the citizens are sometimes intimidated or coerced, and the authorities are able to bring pressure to bear in many ways, by promises of favors or by petty persecutions. Such practices are made easier by the fact that the voting is open and public, as the Australian ballot is unknown. One or two real elections, in which the government has not desired or has not dared to impose its will on the country, have been held in each of the five republics, but they have usually not been participated in by a large part of the people outside of the cities, and they are looked back upon for generations as events far out of the ordinary. As a rule changes in the presidency come about only when the chief magistrate voluntarily relinquishes his office to a member of his own party, or when the opposition is victorious in a civil war.

So long as he can maintain himself in office and suppress revolts against his authority, a Central American president is an absolute ruler, who dominates all other departments of the government. He appoints and removes every administrative official, and through his ministers directly supervises every branch of the public service. The revenues are collected and expended under his orders with a more or less perfunctory regard for the budget voted by the legislature, and with little pretense of making an accounting for them. He not only executes, but also makes and unmakes the laws, either through his control of the Congress, or simply by executive decree. The army and the police are under his absolute command. Even the courts usually decide the more important cases which come before them in accordance with his wishes. His power is curbed only by the fear of losing the support of his followers or of being overthrown by a popular revolt, and neither of these dangers is ordinarily very great so long as he retains the loyalty of his friends by gifts of offices and money, and prevents political agitation by an effective use of the army and police.

The national legislatures, in spite of the constitutional provisions aiming to make them independent and co-ordinate departments of the government, have in practice little authority of their own. Except in Nicaragua, where the bi-cameral system now prevails, each of the republics has a Congress of one chamber. The members of these are theoretically elected by the people for a term of two or four years, but they are in reality chosen by the administration like other officials, and are therefore little more than a mouthpiece of the president. Any attempt on the part of the Congress to oppose the wishes of the executive, in fact, is discouraged by the use of force or by minor persecutions, such as the withholding of salaries or the molestation of the delegates by the police. Not infrequently differences of opinion arise in regard to matters of little significance, but in matters of serious importance the Congress rarely attempts to assert its own will.

With the judicial department, the case is much the same. The Supreme Court, elected for a fixed term either by the Congress or by the people, usually appoints and removes all minor judges and judicial employees. This system has worked well in Costa Rica, where the tribunals are generally independent and honest, but in the other republics political considerations are apt to play a large part not only in the selection of judges but in the decision of cases. The courts are subjected to much the same kind of pressure as the legislature, and there are few of them which would dare to oppose themselves to the expressed wishes of the president. They therefore do little or nothing to protect private citizens against abuses of power by the executive authorities or by the minor officials.

The president is assisted by ministers whom he appoints and who are responsible to him alone. The most important portfolios are those for War, Public Works, Finance and Public Credit, and Government. The minor departments—Justice, Public Instruction, Charities, etc. —are generally placed in charge of subsecretaries. The heads of the departments are rarely more than advisors and aids to the president, who directs their policy and passes on practically all of their acts. They have no independent authority, and as a rule no real influence over the conduct of affairs when the chief executive is a man of strong character.

The local administration is under the direction of the Department of Government, which has a representative subject to the orders of the minister, and through him responsible to the president, in every town and village throughout the country. Each republic is divided into from seven to twenty-three departments, under governors who are at the same time military commanders, " *jefes políticos y comandantes de armas.*" [1] These officials, who are appointed by the president, enforce the laws, collect the taxes, and control the expenditure of government funds in their jurisdictions, and for these purposes have under their orders practically all of the subordinate national authorities. The departments are subdivided into " municipalities "—districts which include a town or village with the surrounding country— where the central authority is represented by a minor official commonly called *comandante*,[2] who commands a few soldiers and is intrusted with the duty of maintaining order and enforcing the laws. These de-

[1] In Costa Rica, the departments are called provinces, and their administrative heads, *gobernadores.*

[2] This is not the official designation, which differs from country to country. In Guatemala, they are called *comisionado político y comandante militar,* in Nicaragua, *agente de policía,* in Costa Rica, *jefe político,* etc.

partmental and local authorities are too frequently petty tyrants, who show little respect for the private rights or the property of the inhabitants of the districts under their jurisdiction. As they are subject to little real restraint in their own sphere of action, they are able to exploit the people of the lower classes practically as they please, and even persons of wealth and social position are not free from their persecutions unless they can protect themselves by the exercise of political influence. Redress against abuses of power is difficult to secure, because the courts usually cannot or dare not interfere, and the higher authorities, more concerned with the loyalty than with the official virtue of their subordinates, take little interest in protecting the rights of common citizens.

In each municipal district, there is a local government, or *municipalidad,* consisting of one or more *alcaldes,* or executive officers, and a board of *regidores,* or aldermen. This body, which has wide jurisdiction over matters of purely local interest, such as the repairing and lighting of streets, the building of roads and bridges, and the enforcement of sanitary regulations, is elected by popular vote and is theoretically independent of the local representatives of the department of government. In practice, however, the latter dominate its actions, and prevent the *alcaldes* from carrying out any action of which they do not approve. The members of the *municipalidad* themselves, moreover, are in most places nominated by the central government, which controls their election as it does that of other officials. In any event they are prevented from playing a very prominent part in the promotion of local interests by the lack of funds. Their revenues, which are derived mainly from taxes on business establishments and fees for water and other public services, rarely suffice to carry out any very important improvements, and their credit is very poor. As a result, the central government is forced to construct and administer all of the more expensive public works, and to exercise many of the other functions which are assigned to the local boards by law.

It can be readily seen that in a political organization such as has just been described the character of the administration will depend almost entirely upon the capacity and disposition of the man at its head. An able president, in a Caribbean Republic, exercises an absolute power for which it would be difficult to find a parallel anywhere in the civilized world.[1] He is not restrained, like the absolute monarchs of Europe and Asia, by dynastic traditions or religious considerations, and he has little need to consider public opinion so long as he retains the good will of the army and of the office holders who owe their positions to him. He can often re-elect himself for term after term, and he is responsible to no one for the exercise of his authority or for his management of the public revenues. The country is so small that he can, and does, extend his control to matters of minor and purely local importance, even interfering with his fellow-citizens' personal affairs and family relations, without regard for the most sacred rights of the individual. It is in his power to exile, imprison, or put to death his enemies, and to confiscate their property, while at the same time he can enrich and advance his friends. The ever-present possibility of revolution, it is true, prevents too great an abuse of power in some of the more enlightened republics, but in the others centuries of misgovernment and of the

[1] It should be stated that the description of Central American governments in this chapter does not apply in all its details to Costa Rica. In that country, although the written constitution and the framework of the government are the same as in the other countries, political conditions are, in fact, very different. The President comes into office, in most cases at least, by a free election rather than a revolution, and exercises a far less absolute power than elsewhere on the Isthmus. The peculiar conditions existing in Costa Rica will be described in a subsequent chapter.

oppression of one class by another have done away with respect for individual rights to such an extent that the cruelest and most arbitrary rulers are tolerated because the people feel that they would only risk their lives and property, without improving their condition, by revolt

Only an exceptionally able man, however, can exercise such despotic power for a long period. A chief executive of less force of character will generally find it impossible to maintain his position or will be dominated by his political associates. Often a military leader or a powerful minister is the real ruler. It is frequently said that a strong, autocratic government is that which is best suited to the peculiar conditions of tropical America, because it affords the greatest security to agriculture and commerce and the best protection to foreign investments. Many Central American presidents, however, inspired by patriotism and by republican ideals, have refused to exercise dictatorial powers, allowing the other departments of the government a measure of independence, and relinquishing their offices to a more or less freely elected successor at the end of their legal term. These have not always been so successful in maintaining order and in carrying out public improvements as their less scrupulous contemporaries, because they have been unable to act with the same decisiveness and effectiveness which are possible where all authority is concentrated in the hands of one man; but such administrations at least provide an opportunity for the people to gain some experience in self-government, and make for a more healthy national political life than can be found where the expression of opinion in the press and even in conversation is curbed by a military despotism. When a long-standing and strongly established dictatorship breaks down, moreover, there is too frequently a period of disorder which destroys all of the advances made during years of peace. The entire organization of the government, built around one commanding figure, goes to pieces when the leader, either through death or incapacity, is compelled to relax his hold; and it is very rarely that a new man is at once found who is capable of keeping the administrative machine together. In those countries, such as Costa Rica, where the presidency is a position of less influence and profit, and where the custom of rotation in office prevails, it is comparatively easy to settle the question of the succession peaceably, in accordance with the law or by an agreement between the political leaders; but where all parties have been subjected for years to the autocratic rule of one man, and compelled humbly to obey his commands, none of the factional chiefs can tolerate the thought that a personal rival may succeed to the same position. For this reason, the fall of a Central American dictator is generally followed by a more or less prolonged civil war, which only ends when one group of men succeed in imposing their will upon the others.

It would be impossible for a single individual, who can rely neither upon the loyalty due to an hereditary sovereign nor upon the prestige enjoyed by a chief magistrate chosen by a majority of the people, to impose his absolute authority upon the whole nation, were it not for the peculiar political conditions existing in Central America. In all of the five republics, the common people show little hostility to despotism as such and little disposition to attempt to influence the selection or to guide the policy of their rulers. Neither the illiterate and oppressed Indian *mozo* of Guatemala nor the prosperous and conservative *concho* of Costa Rica has any real conception of the meaning or of the possibilities of democratic institutions, and both are willing to leave the conduct of political affairs to their superiors. For them, the government, with the forced military service and the compulsory labor on public works which it demands, is simply a necessary evil, and attempts to change its personnel by civil war arouse more dismay than enthusiasm. Few among the lower classes enter into revolutionary uprisings voluntarily. The upper classes, on the other hand, are interested in politics not so much for the sake of principles or policies, as because they wish to secure a share of the offices and spoils which provide many of them with a comfortable living at the expense of the rest of the community. There are among them many professional politicians and military leaders who have no other lucrative occupation, and the number of these has been swelled considerably in recent years by the fact that the commerce and to a less extent the large scale agriculture of the five republics have fallen under the control of foreigners, leaving many formerly wealthy native families impoverished. By the use of offices and money, therefore, the government can always secure adherents and build up a strong following, the members of which are deeply interested in its remaining in power because their positions depend upon it. It is upon a political organization of this kind, and upon the army, that the president must rely for holding in subjection his personal enemies and the mass of the ignorant and indifferent common people.

The military force is the chief support of the government. The highest officers in this are usually influential and trusted members of the president's party, for the very existence of the administration depends upon their loyalty. The standing army itself is composed of a few thousands of ragged, barefooted conscripts of the most ignorant type, commanded by professional soldiers of little education or social position, who have in many cases risen from the ranks themselves. Theoretically every male citizen is liable to military service, but in practice all but the poorest classes secure exemption in one way or another. There is little fairness or system in recruiting. When additional soldiers are needed, the required number of peasants or laborers are simply seized, taken to the *cuartels,* and forced to enlist for a longer or shorter period, whether they have already performed their legal service or not. When news is received that troops are being raised in a given vicinity, every able-bodied man goes into hiding; and in certain capitals, one frequently sees small parties of "volunteers," bound with rope and under a heavy guard, being brought in from the country to augment the garrison. Since soldiers of this type think little for themselves, and follow blindly the commands of their leaders, it is the latter who really control the army. In spite of the immense power which they might exert, however, these officers are usually merely the tools of the civilian politicians, who secure their support by giving them money and conferring military honors upon them. Although each republic has been governed at times during its history by men who were professional soldiers, the number of real military dictators has been surprisingly small.

Although the great historic political parties have disintegrated, and in some states have disappeared altogether, there is always a more or less open and organized opposition to the government, made up of the rivals of the men in power and of the discontented elements which have not received their share of the offices and spoils. These factions, in the main, simply represent personal and local jealousies and ambitions. Their members are held together by ties of blood and of friendship, always potent in a Latin American country, but especially so in these little republics, whose people have until recently had comparatively little intercourse with the outside world and have become closely related by continual intermarriage. Enmities between prominent families become especially bitter in such communities, as does also the jealousy between different towns and villages, which, though but a few miles apart, have little commercial or social intercourse with one another. Questions of national policy, and plans for the development of the national resources play a small part in political contests. The prominent leaders are not so much the representatives of theories or tendencies as men who have won the confidence and loyalty of the people of their towns and villages, or who are the heads of powerful family connections, and the intrigues and the struggles for power between such men and their followings are the principal motive of the civil wars which are still so frequent in many of the five republics. The factions which dispute the control of the government in the four northern republics still call themselves Liberals and Conservatives, but there is at the present time little difference in their policies or in the character of their membership. They are in reality mere combinations between the ambitious leaders of smaller groups, each of whom is striving to advance his own fortunes and those of his friends.

The animosities created by former civil wars, however, as well as the bitterness of the struggles for office at the present time, still make the feeling between the different factions very intense. In some of the republics, each group of men which has secured control of the government has endeavored to consolidate its power, and to avenge its members for past injuries at the hands of the party which it has overthrown, by severe and often utterly unjustifiable treatment of its defeated enemies. The latter are frequently reduced to a point where they find life in their own country almost intolerable. The more influential leaders of the opposition are exiled or imprisoned, and sometimes deprived of their property by confiscation or forced loans, and the rank and file of the party are subjected to all of the persecutions which the greed or the vindictiveness of the new authorities may suggest. Many of the measures taken are really necessary, especially when there is danger of a counter revolution; but they do much to keep alive a bitter personal hatred between the rival groups of politicians.

Within the last few years, the realization of this fact has led the governments of many of the republics to adopt a more humane and civilized policy, but the customs formed during a century of civil war have made the execution of such a policy very difficult.

The fact that the control of the government is seized and held by each succeeding administration by force naturally inclines the victorious party to treat it as the spoils of war. A sweeping change of employees, from cabinet ministers to janitors, takes place upon the accession of each new president, and causes a demoralization of the public service which can easily be imagined. Not only are inexperienced and inefficient men given official positions, but the pay roll is loaded down with salaries to useless or purely ornamental functionaries, appointed as a reward for political services. The schools and certain other governmental activities, such as the telegraphs, are to a slight extent saved from the general disorganization by the fact that the small salaries paid and the special abilities required in them make the positions unattractive to the sinecure-hunting professional politicians; but even in these, the experienced and faithful employee has no chance against the man who has powerful friends.

Favoritism in appointments is not, however, so grave an evil as the graft which is more or less prevalent in the governments of all of the five republics. This corruption is due partly to the tendency to regard official positions as the fruits of a temporary victory, from which as much profit as possible is to be secured while the domination of the party in power lasts, and partly to the fact that it is impossible for many of the employees to live on their ridiculously inadequate and often irregularly paid salaries. In some of the countries, where there have been long periods of despotic government by one man, who has subordinated every other consideration to the maintenance of his personal following and the consolidation of his power, conditions are almost incredibly bad. From the postal clerk who steals illustrated reviews out of the mail boxes, to the high official who mysteriously becomes the owner of large amounts of property during his tenure of office, the servants of the nation rob their fellow-citizens by an infinite variety of methods. The President and the ministers derive profits from the granting of concessions and contracts; the local officials exact tribute from those who depend on them for protection; and every other employee who has regulations to enforce or favors to dispense endeavors to secure small sums from those who are affected by his performance of his duties. Under these military dictatorships, the irresponsible authority enjoyed by the officials, and their continual abuse of their position, result eventually in a deplorable vitiation of political ideals and official morality among the members of all parties, for the opponents of such an administration, on coming into power in their turn, are too often unable to resist the temptation to follow the example of their predecessors, and to avenge and indemnify themselves for their sufferings at the hands of their enemies.

The most harmful corruption is that which exists in the courts. Cases are too often decided with regard only to the influence of the persons involved or to the inducements which they hold out, and political considerations play a very large part wherever they arise. In some countries, in fact, the President has often intervened openly in judicial questions, forcing the magistrates to decide them as he desired. Where the evidence makes impossible or ridiculous the verdict which the court would like to render, cases are very likely to be held up indefinitely by the loss of necessary documents, or the decision is purposely made invalid by allowing technical defects in the procedure. A magistrate who attempts to perform his work conscientiously frequently has his decisions reversed by the upper courts or left unexecuted by administrative officials, and is himself not unlikely to be deprived of his position.

Such corruption, however, has reached its extreme development only in a few cases, where particularly unscrupulous men have obtained absolute control of the government. In the majority of the five republics, graft flourishes to an alarming extent, but is neither so universal nor so disastrous to the public morals. Ideas of official virtue are rather lax among most of the professional politicians, but there are nevertheless comparatively few who do not show a sincere desire to carry out the duties of their offices faithfully and efficiently, even though profiting at the same time from their position in ways which an Anglo-Saxon official would consider illegitimate. In Costa Rica, as we shall see, the employees of the government receive fairly adequate salaries, which under normal conditions are regularly paid, and, in consequence perhaps of this fact, perform their duties as honestly and efficiently as the officials of the average North American state. In each of the other governments, there are officials whose integrity is above suspicion. These, however, are the exception rather than the rule, and graft will apparently always be one of the most salient characteristics of Central American administration so long as the moral standards and political conditions of the Isthmus remain what they are.

The execution of the criminal laws is usually lax and sometimes corrupt. The members of the upper classes can generally evade punishment, or at least escape with light penalties, even when they have committed a serious offense, provided the offense be not political. There is none of the five countries in which atrocious murders have not been committed with impunity, and frauds of a disgraceful character carried out without fear of justice, by persons of social prominence, within very recent years. Where the lower classes are involved, the laws are enforced rather more severely, but in an irregular manner, and criminals frequently escape punishment through the venality or the carelessness of the courts or of their jailers, when there are no special circumstances to make the government anxious to hold them. Those who are convicted and sentenced are usually employed under a heavy guard on public works, and receive in return for their labor a small amount of money with which they can buy food. The death penalty is very rarely enforced for any non-political crime, although it is said that it is the custom of the military officials in some of the countries to shoot suspects at the time of their arrest, in order to avoid the trouble and expense of trying them. Notwithstanding the inactivity of the officials, however, there is not a large amount of brigandage in Central America, and deeds of personal violence, if we except the bloody encounters which occur every Sunday under the influence of *aguardiente,* are comparatively few. The people seem to be peaceable and law-abiding by nature, even in places where there is no organized force to hold criminals in check.

The worst features of the Central American governments are due chiefly to the fact that the officials are subject to so little control by public opinion. Those who benefit by the acts of the administration support it whatever its defects, while those who do not, oppose it regardless of its merits. The sentiment of the ruling class as a whole may influence the government in non-political matters, but in taking measures to strengthen their own position the president and his advisors are rarely deterred by considerations of legality, popularity, or morality. An administration does not weaken itself so much by the violation of rights guaranteed by the constitution as by failing to provide offices and other rewards for its own supporters. The press, as a means for shaping public opinion, has little political importance, for even in those countries where it is not subject to a close censorship, the majority of the newspapers are too partisan or too venal to command general respect.

The only remedy against bad government is revolution. This, unfortunately, almost invariably proves worse than the evil which it seeks to cure. The civil wars of the last ninety-six years have wrought incalculable harm in all of the five republics except Costa Rica, not only by the destruction of lives and property, but by making force the only basis of authority, and by placing men of military ability rather than constructive statesmen in positions of power. The numerous Central American patriots who have worked with all their will and energy for the establishment of efficient administration and the economic progress of their countries have found their efforts nullified by the continual disorder which has made peaceful evolution impossible. Time after time, by an outbreak of civil war, all classes of the population have been forced to suspend their regular occupations, and crops, livestock, and other property have been carried off for provisions or for loot. Under such conditions there is little incentive for the natives to develop their agricultural properties or for foreigners to invest money in railways or in mines. The resources and energies of the governments, wasted in maintaining their military supremacy over their enemies, have not been available for the construction of the much needed roads and railways or for the execution of the sanitary measures which are all but indispensable in a tropical country. As the result of these conditions some of the republics of the Isthmus have made little progress since their declaration of independence, although those which have enjoyed comparative peace have advanced rapidly in prosperity and civilization. The first requisite for the improvement of the economic and political conditions of Central America is the substitution of some peaceful means of changing the personnel of the governments for the costly and destructive method of revolution.

CHAPTER III

GUATEMALA

Political History—The Government—The Indian Population—The Contract Labor System—Production of Coffee and Other Crops on the South Coast—Means of Transportation—Outlying Sections of the Country.

GUATEMALA is the most important of the five Central American republics. Her two millions of people form about forty per cent of the entire population of the Isthmus, and her commerce is greater than that of any of the other four countries. Although in many respects less advanced than Costa Rica and Salvador, her wealth and her strongly organized government, supported by a formidable army, have always enabled her rulers to play the leading part in the international politics of the Isthmus, and even to exert a decisive influence in the internal affairs of her neighbors.

The people of the Republic live for the most part on the plateaus along the Pacific Coast, not far from a chain of lofty volcanic peaks which fringe the interior tableland on the south, and on their farther side slope abruptly down to the low coastal plain. Of the many populous towns in this region, by far the greater number were prosperous and rather highly civilized communities centuries before Columbus discovered America. They are still inhabited mainly by Indians, although in each place there is now an upper class of white merchants, planters, and professional men.

For several years after the declaration of independence, the history of Guatemala, as we have seen, was closely connected with that of the federal government. The Liberal state administration, which Morazán had installed, maintained itself in office until 1838. It was overthrown by a revolt among the bigoted and ignorant *ladinos* east of the capital, who were persuaded by the priests that an outbreak of cholera in the preceding year was due to the poisoning of the rivers by the authorities. The Liberals retired to the western city of Quezaltenango, where they attempted to set up an independent state, but they were completely defeated by the Conservative army in 1840. Rafael Carrera, a half-breed peasant who had led the popular uprising, was for a generation the most powerful personage of Central America. Becoming president in 1844, he retained this office during the greater part of the period from then until his death in 1865, although the difficulties arising from renewed Liberal revolts caused him to resign twice for short intervals. In 1854, he was made president for life. Carrera was an absolute despot, fond of the trappings of supreme power, but in political matters somewhat subject to the control of the leaders of the Conservative party and the ecclesiastical authorities. The policy of his government was therefore shaped by the great families and by the Church, and the more liberal and progressive elements in the community were not allowed to express their opinions or to take part in public affairs.

One of the early acts of the Conservative administration was the repudiation of the federal union. The wealthy classes of the capital had suffered so much from the disturbances attending that ill-starred experiment, and had been put to so much expense in organizing expeditions to uphold the authority of the federation in the other states and in defending the central authorities against attacks from outside, that it is not surprising that they preferred to sever all connection with their turbulent neighbors. During their entire tenure of power, it was their policy to discourage the restoration of the union, not only by refusing to accede to any proposals tending to this end, but also by intervening by intrigue and even by force in the internal affairs of their neighbors when the plans of the unionist party could not be frustrated in any other way.

After the death of Carrera, and during the administration of Vicente Cerna, his successor, the Liberals renewed their activities in opposition to the government, and finally succeeded in 1871 in overthrowing it by revolution. The first president under the new regime was Miguel García Granados. He was succeeded in 1873 by the real leader of the party, General Justo Rufino Barrios, under whose masterful leadership the Conservatives were completely crushed. The religious orders, which had been very powerful, were expelled from the country and deprived of their property, and a similar fate overtook the heads of the old aristocratic families. Liberal reforms of all kinds were introduced in theory if not always in practice, and provision was made for the building of railways, the encouragement of agriculture, and the establishment of schools. Barrios' great ambition was the restoration of the Central American union, but his efforts to secure the co-operation of the other governments of the Isthmus for this purpose met with little success. It was in an attempt to accomplish this object by force that he met his death, for he was killed in a battle against the army of Salvador in 1885.

Manuel Lisandro Barillas, one of the *designados,* or vice-presidents, succeeded Barrios and held office until 1892. At the expiration of his term, not having the strength nor the desire to remain in power, Barillas held the only comparatively free election in the history of the Republic, and José María Reyna Barrios, a young nephew of the great Liberal leader, became President. Although capable and energetic, this ruler was so extravagant in his expenditure of the public revenues that his death by assassination in 1898 left the Republic in a very serious financial condition. This was intensified by the political difficulties which confronted the first *designado,* Manuel

Estrada Cabrera, when the latter took control of the administration. After a few months of tension, however, the new chief executive succeeded in establishing the legal authority and in overcoming some of the problems confronting the national treasury. He is still at the head of the state, after nineteen years of service.

The dense ignorance and the oppressed condition of the masses of the people, combined with the bitter factional strife among the upper classes, where party hatred has probably been stronger than in any of the other Central American countries, have caused the government of Guatemala to became a military despotism, more absolute than any other on the Isthmus. The administration firmly maintains its authority by means of a large standing army and police force, and promptly and mercilessly checks the slightest manifestation of popular dissatisfaction. An elaborate secret service attempts, with a large measure of success, to inform itself fully of everything which occurs in the Republic. Supposed enemies of the party in power are closely watched, through their neighbors, their servants, and even through the members of their own families, and foreigners coming to the country often find themselves shadowed until the details of their business are discovered. It is dangerous to express an opinion on political matters even in private conversation. Much of the mail, and especially that coming from abroad, is opened and read in the post office. The formation of social clubs is discouraged because of possible political results, and it is impossible for a man prominent in official circles to have many friends without arousing distrust. Persons who fall under suspicion are imprisoned or restricted in their liberty, or even mysteriously disappear. The ruthless execution of large numbers of persons, many of whom were probably innocent, have followed attempts to revolt or to assassinate the President. This reign of terror is approved by many influential natives and by the majority of the foreigners in the country on the ground that only a very strong government can prevent revolution and maintain order; and there is no doubt that the life and property of foreigners, at least, has been safer in Guatemala than in some of the other Central American countries. The omnipresent spy system, however, and the cruel treatment meted out to those who incur the displeasure of the authorities, have created an atmosphere of mutual suspicion and fear, especially in the capital, which has noticeably sapped the spirit and the self-respect of the people. Patriotism and national pride have to a great extent been destroyed by the ban on the discussion of important national questions, and the country has thus probably become less rather than more fit for self-government during the last two decades.

Although the presidents, almost without exception, have shown great force of character and marked administrative ability, the subordinate officials are very frequently inefficient and corrupt. Official morality seems to be growing worse rather than better, apparently as a direct result of the depreciation of the currency, which has not been accompanied by a corresponding increase in salaries. The highest employees, such as the ministers and the judges of the Supreme Court, receive the equivalent of about fifty dollars a month, and the remuneration of minor functionaries varies from one dollar to twenty dollars. Posts in the government, consequently, have little attraction except for those who desire them because of the opportunities which they afford for graft, and respectable persons, who are often appointed to professorships in the schools or to other positions requiring special knowledge and experience, accept only because they are practically compelled to. The great majority of the administrative and judicial officials are men of a rather low type, and bribery, theft, and oppression are consequently very prevalent. The fact that the superior authorities do not punish or discourage even the most flagrant corruption gives rise to the suspicion that they are willing to have their subordinates recompense themselves in this way, in order not to be forced to pay them salaries out of the national treasury adequate for their support.

Notwithstanding the corruption in the government and the exploitation of the people for the benefit of the official class, there is at least a pretense of public-spirited administration. Humanitarian laws are put on the statute books and praised in the newspapers; the cities are beautified by laying out parks and erecting monuments; magnificent buildings for schools, hospitals, and other public institutions are constructed; and the progressiveness and benevolence of the administration are heralded by subsidized writers, not only in Central America, but even in the United States and Europe. The motives of the government are no doubt praiseworthy, but the actual good accomplished has not been great. The execution of the reforms has been left to officials who had no understanding of their spirit and who were in many cases deterred by their own interests from carrying out their provisions; and the schools and other public institutions have never been properly equipped or provided with adequate teaching staffs because of the failure to appropriate money for these purposes.

Although all power is centered in the hands of one man, the forms of the constitution are still observed and elections are held regularly in accordance with the law. They are, moreover, participated in, not by a few chosen voters, as in some other Central American countries, but by the entire body of citizens. In a presidential election, especially, all classes of the population are rounded up by the military and taken to the polls, where they exercise a right of suffrage restricted only by the fact that they are not permitted to vote for any but the official candidates. The number of votes for the re-election of the president thus equals, when it does not exceed, the total number of adult males in the Republic.

Since the breakdown of the Central American federation, Guatemala has suffered from fewer successful revolutions than any other state of the Isthmus. The Republic has been by no means free from internal disorder, but at least it has not been subjected to the continual demoralizing changes of regime which have occurred so frequently in its neighbors. This comparative stability has been in part due to the strong organization which the government inherited from its Spanish predecessors. The Captain General and the royal *audiencia* in Guatemala City had naturally enjoyed more prestige and had possessed more means of making their authority respected than had the subordinate governors in the provinces in colonial days, and the old administrative machinery and traditions were maintained to some extent after the declaration of independence. Moreover, the country has had a series of able rulers, holding office generally for life, who have crushed all opposition with little regard for constitutional provisions or public opinion, and who have almost always been able to defeat attempts at revolution and to arrange for the succession of a president of their own choosing. There are, of course, turbulent elements which make occasional attempts to overthrow the government, but their influence has been much less than in Honduras, Nicaragua, or Salvador because of Guatemala's racial and economic conditions.

Among the upper classes, although they are divided among themselves by bitter political feuds, and although there are many powerful families which have suffered indescribable outrages at the hands of governments of opposite political faith, the revolutionary spirit seems at present to be conspicuously absent. The majority of the white families who own plantations upon which they employ Indian labor are more interested in the maintenance of peace than in obtaining offices for themselves by a revolt which would cause their workmen to be recruited into the army and would perhaps lead to the destruction of their properties. The difficulty of overthrowing the government, with its large standing army and its superior military equipment, and the terrible consequences which follow an unsuccessful attempt to do so, deter those who have anything to lose from engaging in political agitation.

The half-breed middle class, which is usually a cause of disturbance in the neighboring republics, plays but a small part in politics. The *ladinos,* as they are called, occupy an economic and social position between that of the Indian laboring population and the landed proprietors, being employed as artisans, small tradesmen, and minor public officials in the towns, and as carpenters, mule drivers, and skilled laborers in the country. In the districts east of the capital, where there are few full-blooded Indians, the *ladinos* work on the plantations or on their own small patches of ground. Many of the more intelligent rise from humble origins to high positions, but the majority are ignorant, dishonest, and vicious, and form one of the least desirable elements in the community. Their importance, however, is small, as compared with that of the other classes.

The great majority of the inhabitants of the Republic are docile and ignorant pure-blooded Indians. These have never shown any liking or capacity for war since the first small force of Spanish invaders conquered their populous kingdoms at the beginning of the sixteenth century. Political agitators have rarely been able to incite them to resistance to the authorities, for whom they have a deep-rooted respect and fear; and for this reason the organization of a revolutionary army among them is more difficult than among the turbulent half-breeds of the other Central American countries. For the government, on the other hand, they make patient and obedient, if not very intelligent, soldiers. Many of them are raised to high military offices, for their lack of interest in political affairs makes them more dependable than the white or *ladino* officials. They are on the whole, therefore, an influence on the side of peace.

Guatemala is the only one of the Central American countries where the aboriginal population still maintains its identity as a distinct race. In other parts of the Isthmus the Indians were exterminated by thousands during the first century of Spanish rule, and those who survived were assimilated into the European communities to such an extent that they adopted the language and customs of their conquerors everywhere except in a few outlying districts. In Guatemala this did not take place, partly because the population was more compact and more civilized at the time of the conquest, and partly because the natives received more protection in their rights from the Spanish authorities in the capital than in the provinces. The Indians were of course subjected to the *encomienda* system just as were those of Honduras and Nicaragua, but the *repartimientos* worked less harm among them than in those countries because their great number made the exploitation of the whole population by the small groups of Spaniards impossible. The Indians are still sharply set apart as a class from the half-breed and white population. In many places they are almost entirely unacquainted with Spanish, although their native languages, of which it is said that there are nineteen spoken in the Republic, are becoming more and more contaminated by Castilian words and phrases. The inhabitants of each village still maintain the distinctive costumes and in some places retain traces of the religious observances of pre-Spanish days; and wherever they have been left to themselves they still carry on agriculture and their primitive household industries in much the same way as before the conquest.

The failure of the Indians to assimilate with the white population caused them to remain in the position of a subject race. Even after the abolition of the *encomiendas* they were still compelled to labor for little or no remuneration on the plantations of the white landowners, for it became the practice for the authorities to recruit a number of them by force and to send them anywhere where their services were needed, either as a special favor to the beneficiary or for a money consideration paid into the treasury. These *mandamientos,* as they were called, were the chief means by which agricultural laborers were secured until nearly the end of the nineteenth century. After the establishment of the large coffee plantations, however, they were found to be entirely inadequate for providing the large and regular supply of labor which was necessary for the new industry, and the system has been to a great extent superseded, although not entirely done away with by the present *Ley de Trabajadores,* enacted in 1894.

This law defines two classes of laborers or *mozos: colonos,* who reside permanently on the plantation, and *jornaleros,* who sell their services for a longer or shorter period by contract. The former usually work for the employer only a part of each month in return for the land which he allows them to cultivate. This system is most common in the Alta Verapaz, where the plantations have great amounts of land unsuitable for coffee cultivation, and where the Indians, who until a short time ago had lived a life of complete freedom in the forest, are less amenable to control than on the South Coast. The laborers there are for the most part natives who lived upon the land before it was purchased by the present owner, and who had no recourse, after the establishment of the plantation, but to accept their new status or to leave their homes. They are on the whole better off than the *jornaleros* because they enjoy more independence and are able to work part of the time for themselves.

The *jornaleros,* or day laborers, are held on the plantations under a peonage system. Theoretically the Indian is perfectly free to contract himself or not as he pleases, but when he has once done so, he may not leave his employer's service until he has completed the time for which he agreed to work and has repaid any money which the *patron* may have lent him. If he attempts to escape, he is hunted down by the authorities and returned to the plantation; and the entire expense of capturing him and bringing him back is debited in his account. If, on the other hand, he refuses to work, he may be imprisoned until he is in a more reasonable frame of mind. Those who still prove obstinate, after fifteen days in jail, may be sent at the request of the employer to the convict labor squads, where fifty per cent of the returns of their labor are set aside for the benefit of their creditors. The whole system depends upon keeping the *mozo* in debt. For this purpose, he is allowed a limited amount of credit at the plantation store and is even loaned small sums of money from time to time if necessary. Few are sufficiently energetic or ambitious to make a serious effort to free themselves from these obligations. They have in fact little incentive to do so, for those who leave the plantation can only look forward to similar employment elsewhere, or what is much worse, to impressment into the army, from which *mozos* working on large coffee, sugar-cane, banana, or cacao plantations are legally exempt.

The law imposes on the employers certain obligations which are more or less faithfully observed. In most cases, huts are provided for *mozos* of both classes, and food is dealt out to them when the supplies of food which they themselves raise are exhausted. The *jor-*

naleros, in fact, are fed almost entirely by their employers, although they are frequently given small patches of ground for gardens and are allowed three or four weeks during the year in which to cultivate them. The planter distributes medicines and even furnishes amateur medical advice when it is needed. Free schools, required on all by law, are maintained on some plantations, although as a rule they are attended only by the children of the *ladino* employees, for the Indians do not care about educating their children and are generally not compelled to do so. The owner of the plantation is responsible for the maintenance of order, and is empowered to imprison criminals and fugitives from labor until the local authorities can take charge of them. In these duties he is assisted on the larger plantations by an *alcalde auxiliar,* an official appointed by the municipal *alcalde* from a list of names submitted by the owner. This functionary, who nominally represents the authority of the government, but is in reality an employee of the planter, is an invaluable aid to the latter in maintaining his control over the laborers.

The wages paid to laborers are at the present time extremely low, for they have risen little in spite of the rapid depreciation of the national currency. The *jornalero* or *colono* on the average plantation, in addition to a limited amount of very simple food, receives from two to three *pesos* (from five to eight cents in United States currency) a day, whereas voluntary laborers, upon whom the planter has no hold, receive from five to seven *pesos* for precisely the same work. It is customary in most places to pay by the task, so that those who are most efficient may earn slightly more than this sum, while those who are weak or incapable will receive less. Considering that the Indian enters the service of the planter owing the fifty or one hundred *pesos* which it is customary to advance to him when he is contracted, it is not surprising that he is unable to free himself from debt, especially as the few articles which he must buy—clothes, tools, and candles for the church or chapel—are relatively very expensive. The combined earnings of the whole family, for the women and children are usually given tasks as well as the men, are in fact hardly sufficient to supply the necessities of life without an occasional extra loan from the employer.

This peonage system, in itself pernicious, is subject to the gravest abuses. The short-sighted and improvident Indians are easily persuaded to accept advances of money when they have some immediate occasion, such as a baptism or a funeral, for spending it, without realizing apparently the onerous conditions under which they must make repayment. The professional *habilitadores,* or contractors of labor, and the agents whom many of the planters maintain in the native villages, take advantage of this fact and of the other weaknesses of the Indians' character to obtain a hold upon them. This is made much easier by the aborigines' fondness for liquor and by their helplessness when drunk. The Indians are often induced to sign contracts by misrepresentations or even actual violence, for the corrupt and unscrupulous local authorities not infrequently bring pressure to bear upon them by threats of arbitrary imprisonment or of impressment into the army. Many of the representatives of the government derive a large income from considerations paid them for service of this kind and from tributes which they exact every month or every year from the planters in their districts as the price of official support in disputes with their laborers. That the contracts are rarely entered into voluntarily and with a full appreciation of their terms is evident from the great difference in the wages received by those who work under them and the wages earned by the so-called voluntary laborers. The government has made half-hearted attempts to check the worst features of the system, but its decrees enjoining strict respect for personal liberty and stipulating minimum wages for contracts made in the future have for the most part been left unexecuted by the local officials.

The contract labor system is defended in Guatemala on the ground that the cultivation of coffee, upon which the prosperity and the commerce of the country depend, could not be carried on without it. The Indian, it is said, would never work for more than a few days in the year unless he were compelled to, as he is perfectly contented with a few possessions which he can obtain for himself by cultivating a small patch of ground in the woods. The planters complain of a scarcity of labor even at the present time, and often find it difficult to cultivate their properties and harvest the crops. This argument explains, but hardly justifies, the system. An institution which subjects the masses of the people to a degrading bondage, and which prevents these masses from progressing or becoming more fit for the self-government which they are nominally supposed to exercise, must in the long run be extremely harmful to the country as a whole. The development of agriculture and commerce, which has been beneficial chiefly to foreign investors, can hardly be said to be desirable if it has made social and political conditions within the country worse. While the Indians are practically serfs, living under the most primitive conditions and deprived of any opportunity to better their position, it will be impossible to educate them or to raise their standard of living.

There is, moreover, no conclusive proof that the Indians would refuse to work if they were not forced to by the labor laws and the tyranny of the officials. They naturally do everything they can to escape employment under the present conditions, where they receive in return for their labor nothing but the bare necessities of life. These they could obtain for themselves, almost without working, if they were left in their original condition in the forest. There is no reason to suppose, however, that they would refuse employment at wages which were really worth their while. They are certainly not a more lazy race than their half-breed neighbors, and they would doubtless improve their standards of living, which are today no lower than those of the *ladinos* in the more backward parts of Honduras and Nicaragua, if they were given an opportunity to do so. Nor would the cost of coffee growing be so increased as to make it prohibitive. In Costa Rica and Salvador, where the wages are from four to eight hundred per cent higher than in Guatemala, the planters are prosperous and make large profits. Under the present system, the underfed and ill-treated Indians are unwilling and inefficient workers, and their services involve a great extra expense to the employer in the form of sums to be paid to *habilitadores* and local officials in return for aid in contracting them. This money would be saved, and the value of the Indians as laborers would certainly be greatly increased, if the peonage system were done away with and the workers were freely employed at fair wages.

There are some thousands of Indians, especially in the less developed parts of the Republic, who still cultivate their own properties or a share in the common lands of their villages, raising not only the corn and beans with which they feed their families, but also a small surplus which they carry long distances to sell in the markets in the towns. They seem to delight in the free life of the mountain trails, where the traveler continually passes long lines of them, in their picturesque local costumes, carrying vegetables, home-made cloth, baskets, and grass mats—the men with heavy burdens in the peculiar square frames on their backs, and the women with baskets or bundles poised on their heads. Many of them come to the capital from places several days' journey distant, camping by the side of the road at night, and reach their destination nearly as quickly as more aristocratic travelers do on mule back. Besides those who market their own products in this way, there are large numbers of professional *cargadores,* who spend their lives on the roads, taking goods from one place to another for hire or as a commercial speculation. They are said to cover as much as thirty miles a day with a load of one hundred pounds, and they form one of the most important factors in the internal transportation of the country.

These free Indians work only part of the time or not at all on the plantations. When they do work, it is usually as "volunteers" at the time of the harvest. Their number, however, is constantly diminishing. As the extension of the coffee plantations has made the demand for laborers more and more insistent, it has become increasingly difficult for the Indians to escape from the snares of the *habilitadores* and the pressure exerted by the local officials, so that those in the more developed agricultural districts have with few exceptions been persuaded or forced into service on the plantations. Many of the Indians who lived on the public domain have been forced to work for the foreigners who purchased from the government the land which they had formerly cultivated, for it has been the regular practice in some parts of the country to secure new *mozos* in this way. Even those who once owned land of their own have often sold it to their wealthier neighbors.

At the present time the situation of the Indians is probably worse than it was fifty years ago, and it is certainly worse than that of the lowest classes in the other republics. The development of the peonage system has deprived them of even the small measure of economic and political liberty which they once enjoyed, and by taking them away from their homes has almost entirely destroyed their old community life. The native municipalities, which exist side by side with the *ladino* municipal boards in many of the towns, and which formerly managed the internal affairs of the native community, have been powerless to protect the members of the latter from the operations of the *habilitadores* and the tyranny of the representatives of the central government. Many of the Indian villages which once enjoyed a sort of independence of their white neighbors are now completely at the mercy of brutal local officials, who are not content to exact money from the people under them by every conceivable pretext, but even make a regular practice of virtually selling into slavery those who are intrusted to their government.

Their own vices, meanwhile, have reduced the native race to a pitiable condition in those districts where they have longest been in contact with civilization. The cheap and poisonous *aguardiente,* the sale of which is encouraged by the government because of the revenue which it produces, is consumed in great quantities by the laboring classes, and there are drinking places everywhere, not only in the towns and villages, but even along the country roads. The liquor is much inferior to that produced in the other Central American countries, and is sold at a price equivalent to less than ten cents a quart. Its effects are appalling. To it are due the greater part of the crimes committed in the country, for drunkenness makes the usually peaceable Indians quarrelsome and unruly, and causes Sundays and holidays to be marked everywhere by a great number of murders and robberies. There is a very evident degeneration, due to this one vice, among the Indians in the southern part of the country.

The coffee plantations, which have within fifty years become the most important enterprises in the country, are for the most part situated on the southern slopes of the volcanoes along the Pacific Coast, not far from the populous towns and villages of the interior plateau. They are on the average larger than in the other countries of the Isthmus, and as a rule have their own cleaning mills. The coffee of Guatemala is the best in Central America, with the possible exception of that of Costa Rica, and is hardly excelled in any part of the world. The largest and best plantations are owned and managed by Germans, who either set them out in the first place or acquired them from their former native owners; and many of those which still belong to citizens of Guatemala are for all practical purposes under the control of foreign concerns which hold mortgages on them. Not only production, but also marketing, which is mainly in the hands of German export firms, have been highly systematized.

The production of coffee overshadows all other agricultural enterprises on the South Coast, but there are nevertheless many other crops which deserve to be mentioned because of their local importance. In the plateau above the coffee plantations, not only the typical Central American foods, like corn and beans, but also many temperate zone fruits and vegetables, and even wheat, are cultivated successfully. On the coastal plain to the South, there are large cattle ranches and cane plantations, which, in part at least, supply the home demand for meat, sugar, and *aguardiente*. Sheep in the highlands, and cotton in the lowlands, supply the raw material for the clothes still woven by the Indians on hand looms in their huts. There is a regular exchange of foodstuffs, carried for the most part on the backs of men, between the settlements in the plateau and the more tropical districts of the coast plain. The traveler cannot fail to be impressed with the great variety of products which differences in the altitude and in the distribution of rainfall make possible, for in the markets of the capital one can see almost every kind of temperate and tropical zone fruits and vegetables, brought from one point or another of the steep slope between the plateau and the coast. Little attempt has been made, however, to cultivate for export any of the valuable native plants, with the exception of coffee, or even, in the case of some of them, to raise enough to supply the local demand. Flour, for instance, is brought from the United States in large amounts, although there is no apparent reason why a quantity of wheat sufficient to supply the whole country should not be harvested on the plateaus west of the capital. Cotton also flourishes, but most of the cloth used is imported or is manufactured in the country from imported yarn. As in the other countries of the Isthmus, the production of the one great export has consumed the capital and energies of the inhabitants of the Republic to such an extent that other forms of agriculture have been seriously neglected.

The economic development of the southern part of the country has been greatly accelerated in recent years by the improvement in means of transportation. The Northern Railway, which connects the capital and the South Coast with Puerto Barrios on the Caribbean Sea, was completed in 1908 after great expense and many difficulties. Another road runs from Guatemala City to the Pacific ports of San José, Champerico, and Ocós, crossing the southern part of the country to the Mexican frontier, where it is separated by only a few hundred yards from the Pan American Railway of that Republic. With the exception of the capital, however, most of the important towns still depend upon more primitive forms of transportation, as they are situated in the high plateaus, several miles above the railway line which runs along the South Coast. The same is true of the majority of the coffee plantations. The highways which connect the towns and *fincas* with the stations and with each other are chiefly mule paths, although there are cart roads, and even in some cases carriage and automobile roads, between the largest cities.

The railway system is under the control of an American-owned corporation which is closely allied to the United Fruit Company. The freight rates are high and very inequitable, as they have been arranged with a view to giving Puerto Barrios, which is served by the Fruit Company steamers, every possible advantage over the Pacific Coast ports, through which a large part of the foreign commerce of the country is still carried on. According to the schedule in force in the fall of 1915, for example, the company charged $0.70 gold [1] to haul a bag of coffee from the station of Candelaria to Barrios, a distance of 331 miles; $1.48 from Guatemala City to Barrios, or 196 miles; and $0.64 from Los Amates to Barrios, which is sixty miles. To the Pacific ports, on the other hand, the rates were proportionately much higher, for that from Candelaria to Champerico, twenty-two miles away, was $0.22, and that for the seventy-five mile haul from Guatemala to San José was $1.00.

The policy of the railway company has to a great extent counteracted the benefits which the Republic might have received from the opening of the Panama Canal, because it has discouraged the shipping of imports and exports by way of the Pacific Coast. The western departments have profited somewhat by receiving lower rates to Barrios, but it still costs them more to send their coffee by that route than if they had a fair rate to the southern ports. In other parts of the country, the railroad is forced to charge higher rates than would otherwise be necessary, in order to maintain its total revenues. The loss to the country as a whole from having its commerce deflected to a more expensive route than that which it would otherwise have taken is considerable. Although the Pacific Coast ports are mere open roadsteads, where the irregular steamship service cannot be

[1] When the expression "gold" is used in regard to sums of money, United States currency is meant.

compared with that provided by the Fruit Company at the safe harbor of Puerto Barrios, they are nevertheless the logical outlet for the commerce of the more populous part of Guatemala, because they are so much nearer to the coffee plantations. The difference in the ocean freights from Barrios to New York and from the Pacific ports via Tehuantepec or Panama to New York —between forty and fifty cents on each one-hundred pound bag of coffee—is not in reality enough to offset the actual cost of the long railroad haul across the mountains.

Although it is on the South Coast that the great majority of the people of Guatemala live, there are several other districts of economic importance. The exploitation of the natural resources of these has been left almost entirely to foreigners. Beyond the arid and unproductive interior districts immediately north of the volcanic region, there is another coffee belt in the Department of Alta Verapaz, the product of which, known to the trade by the name of the departmental capital, "Coban," is of an unusually fine quality. The owners of the plantations are for the most part Germans. The coffee, which amounts to about ten per cent of the total exported from the Republic, is shipped from the port of Livingston, with which the plantations are connected by a short railway and a regular line of launches on Lake Izabal and the Rio Dulce. East of the Alta Verapaz, along the lower part of the railway line from the capital to Puerto Barrios, the United Fruit Company has established a number of banana plantations. These are not so extensive as those of Costa Rica or Honduras, but they furnish a continually increasing export, which is now second in value only to that of coffee. The low, unhealthful plain of Peten in the North, which comprises almost a third of the area of the Republic, is rich in mahogany, Spanish cedar, and other valuable trees, but the lack of means of transportation and the deadly climate have so far prevented the increase of the population there and have discouraged the development of the natural resources.

Guatemala has been gifted by nature with a delightful and healthful climate and a marvelously fertile soil which ought to make her one of the richest countries in tropical America. She can never attain real prosperity, however, until her rulers make a determined effort to improve the situation of the masses of the people by doing away with the worst features of her social organization. Among the lower classes, the contract labor system and the unrestricted sale of *aguardiente* are today causing a steady degeneration, which eventually, if not checked, will cause the community as a whole to sink farther and farther into a condition of semi-barbarism. These evils will be very difficult to remedy. Legislative action to secure the independence of the Indians will be obstructed by the interest which the ruling classes have in the *status quo,* and the education of the laborers to a point where they will be able to protect their own interests will be a matter of generations and perhaps of centuries. Upon a gradual raising of the social and economic status of the aborigines, however, rather than upon the development of agriculture and the exploitation of the natural resources of the country, the future of Guatemala depends.

CHAPTER IV

NICARAGUA

Points of Resemblance Between Nicaragua, Salvador, and Honduras—Peculiar Geographical Situation of Nicaragua—Factors Which Have Caused Disorder There—Rivalry Between Leon and Granada—History of the Republic—Economic Conditions—Means of Transportation—Relations with the United States.

NICARAGUA, Salvador, and Honduras strongly resemble one another in many of their characteristics. They differ from the two other republics of the Isthmus in that there has been more mixture of races among their people than in those countries. The Indians did not remain a distinct ethnic entity, as in Guatemala, and were not exterminated, as in Costa Rica, but fused with the invaders into a fairly homogeneous half-breed population which adopted the language and religion of the Spaniards but in most places retained the Indian ways of living and cultivating the soil. The upper classes, especially in Nicaragua and Salvador, are for the most part of European ancestry, and the laboring population, although there is but a small part of it which does not also show an admixture of Spanish blood, is distinctly Indian in features and customs; but only in a few places is there a sharp line between either of these classes and the half-breed, or *mestizo,* element, which is perhaps the most numerous of the three. Social distinctions seem to some extent to coincide with, but they can hardly be said to depend upon, racial lines.

There is thus more homogeneity in the population and less inequality between the classes than there is in Guatemala. Although the greater part of the people are laborers on the plantations of the aristocracy which owns all of the best agricultural properties, they are free laborers, who receive fair wages and are not compelled to work unless they wish to. There is, furthermore, a somewhat wider distribution of land than in the northern Republic, and the rights of the small farmer are better protected than are those of the Guatemalan Indian.

The government, although in no sense democratic, is nevertheless dependent to some extent upon public opinion, for the lower classes are all too prone to revolt and overthrow a president with whom they are discontented. The political parties are led and directed by a wealthy and educated minority, but their sanguinary contests with one another are usually decided by the support of the common people, and especially of the people of the cities. Several causes lead artisans and laborers who otherwise have no interest in politics to take part in these civil wars. One of the most important is the rivalry between different towns and villages, the spirit of *localismo,* and another, which, however, is rapidly becoming less prominent, is the traditional division, based on no real opposition in principles or policy, into " Conservatives " and " Liberals." Still a third is the disposition to be " against the government," whatever its merits—a disposition which is by no means peculiar to the Hispano-Indian race. It is upon these factors that the political parties are built up. Each chief endeavors to secure a following among the artisans and laborers of his district by cultivating friendly personal relations with them and by playing on their prejudices, and to carry his followers with him in whatever line of action best suits his personal interests. The groups thus formed consequently represent petty prejudices and loyalty to individuals rather than political principles.

The presidents of these countries are therefore less absolute rulers than the chief executive of Guatemala usually is. Instead of an easily controlled army of ignorant Indians, who have little disposition to do anything but obey the commands of their officers, the government must depend on soldiers who, to some extent at any rate, think for themselves and take an interest in political affairs. It must not only retain the good will of its followers, but it must refrain from arousing hostility in the community at large, where the opposition is usually too numerous and too well-organized to be rendered harmless by killing or exiling its leaders and repressing its agitation. There is no public opinion sufficiently strong to prevent the party in power from dealing severely with its most conspicuous enemies, or from misusing its control of the machinery of the administration for the benefit of the officials and their friends, but there is at least an ever-present danger of revolution to make it cautious about alienating the sympathies of too large a proportion of the people at large.

Republican institutions cannot be said to flourish in any of the central republics, but there is a far more hopeful prospect of their eventually becoming a reality there than in Guatemala. It would be impossible, among the factious half-breeds of the Nicaraguan towns, to round up all classes of the population by military action and lead them to the polls to vote for the president, as was done when President Estrada Cabrera was unanimously re-elected in 1916, but it is not very difficult to control the election by other means. Under ordinary circumstances, there is no chance for any but the official ticket. The opponents of the government, and even those who are suspected of being lukewarm in their support of it, are excluded from the official lists of voters, with or without a perfunctory excuse, and opposition candidacies are discouraged by the imprisonment or the expulsion from the country of the rival leaders and of their chief supporters. Fraud and intimidation are generously employed to increase the government's majority. The measures taken are usually sufficient to secure a result satisfactory to the faction in power, but occasionally they are unavailing because the opposition is strong enough to wring a compromise from the administration or to overthrow it by revolution. Elections, therefore, are often accompanied by more or less disorder and uncertainty, and a too violent attempt to impose an unpopular candidate on the people has not infrequently been followed by civil war. With the spread of popular education at the present time, there are grounds for hoping that elections will in the not very distant future become more nearly a real expression of the will of the people—a character which they have already assumed in Costa Rica.

The political and economic development of Nicaragua has been determined by forces similar to, but more marked than, those which have affected Salvador and Honduras, and a study of her history and institutions will therefore make it easier to understand the situation of the other two republics.

Nicaragua has always been an object of interest to the outside world because of her geographical situation. In her territory, the Central American *Cordillera* is broken by a depression which extends across the Isthmus, forming the basin of the two great lakes and of the San Juan River, their outlet to the Atlantic. Lake Nicaragua, which is only 110 feet higher than the ocean, is separated from the Pacific by a range of small hills, the lowest passes of which are said to be but twenty-five or twenty-six feet above its surface and thus only 135 above that of the sea.[1] At the narrowest place this strip of land is less than thirteen miles wide. North of Lake Nicaragua, and connected with it by a small river, is Lake Managua, between which and the Pacific there is a distance of about thirty miles across the low plain of Leon. In colonial times, the route

[1] Elisée Reclus, *North America*, Vol. II, pp. 274, 279.

across the Isthmus through Leon to Granada on Lake Nicaragua, and from thence by water, was commonly used for the transportation of products from all parts of Central America to Spain; and much more recently it was one of the most popular ways of reaching California from the East Coast of the United States. It early attracted the attention of those who were interested in transisthmian canal projects, and came to be considered by many as the most practicable route for an interoceanic waterway. Diplomatic controversies for the control of the proposed canal, and the machinations of corporations desiring to secure concessions for its construction, which it would be impossible even to sketch here, have played a large part in the international relations of the Republic, and at times have not been without effect on her internal political conditions.

The people of Nicaragua, more than those of any of the other countries of the Isthmus, are dwellers in cities. About a fourth of all her inhabitants live in six important towns in the lake plains.[1] The Spaniards established their principal settlements in this region at the time of the conquest, in spite of the hot climate, in order the more easily to hold in subjection and to utilize the labor of the large Indian communities which had long since grown up there because of the fertility of the soil and the plentiful water supply. The concentration of the population in a few centers has intensified all of the conditions which have worked against peace in Central America, and has made Nicaragua the most turbulent of the five republics. The inhabitants of cities, since the beginning of history, have been more inclined to disorder and revolt than their brothers in

[1] There are no very reliable figures for the population of the cities or for the total population of the Republic, but the best estimates agree that the Republic has about 600,000 inhabitants, while the population of the cities mentioned may be stated approximately as follows: Leon, 62,000; Managua, 35,000; Granada, 17,000; Chinandega, 10,000; Masaya, 13,000; Rivas, 8,000.

the country, and this is especially true in Central America, because both *personalismo* and *localismo,* with all their attendant evils, reach their most complete development in large communities, where the contact between individuals is closer and the number of persons interested in politics is greater than in rural districts. The *mestizo* artisans, who are relatively more numerous and more influential in Nicaragua than anywhere else in the Isthmus, are always ready to drop their work and take up arms in the interests of their faction or of their *patron,* and even the ordinary laborers, in the towns at least, are Liberals or Conservatives, and followers of this or that chief. The common people are but little interested in the principles involved in the contests between the two great traditional political parties, but they follow their leaders partly from personal devotion and partly because they are united to them by the old local hatreds which have kept these parties alive in Nicaragua after they have become little more than names in other parts of the Isthmus.

This rivalry between different towns has caused bloodshed at one time or another in each of the Central American republics, but in all except Nicaragua it has to a great extent died out at the present time, because the capitals have become more important than any of their rivals, and have drawn to themselves many of the wealthier and more influential provincial families. In Nicaragua, neither of the two cities established by the Spaniards at the beginning of the sixteenth century has been able to establish its supremacy, and the history of the country from the very beginning has been one long struggle, made more bitter by radical differences in the ideals and interests of their people, for the control of the government and the direction of the affairs of the nation.

Granada, at the western end of the Great Lake, has always been primarily a commercial center, since the days when it was the chief port for the trade between Central America and Spain by way of the San Juan River. Her leading citizens are not only landed proprietors, but merchants, who sell goods in person over the counters of their stores. Her great families form a coherent and powerful group, which has always been able, because of its wealth and social prestige, to exert an influence far out of proportion to its numbers, not only in its own city but in the country at large. The greater part of the fifteen or twenty thousand other inhabitants depend upon them as servants or employees, for the artisan class is small and relatively unimportant. There are few professional men of social prominence and few small landholders, for the rural districts roundabout are mostly given over to large, carelessly managed cattle ranches. The Chamorros, Lacayos, and Cuadras, with their relatives, have always considered themselves a sort of creole aristocracy, and even in colonial times they were restive under the control of the Spanish authorities at Leon. After the declaration of independence, they naturally joined the great families of Guatemala in the Conservative party, and they have since retained the name, if not the principles, of that organization.

The Liberal party, on the other hand, has its center in Leon, the capital of the province in colonial times, and today, with sixty or seventy thousand inhabitants, the largest city of the Republic. There, the domination of political and social affairs until 1821 by officials sent over from Spain prevented the rise of a strong creole aristocracy, and the constant infusion of Spanish blood during colonial times, as well as the presence of many Peninsular Spaniards even after the declaration of independence, somewhat retarded the changes wrought in the white stock in other places by nearly four centuries of life in the torrid climate of the lake plains. The people of Leon have always shown an inclination towards intellectual and professional pursuits which is noticeably absent in Granada, and take great pride in their schools and their university. The most prominent lawyers and physicians of the Republic, even in Managua and the other cities, are for the most part *Leoneses,* just as the majority of the leading native merchants are related to the Granada families. Leon has a large and aggressive body of artisans and many small landholders, for the wide plain around the city is divided into a large number of little properties, worked either by the owner in person or under his immediate supervision. There are few families of great wealth. It was inevitable that such a community should take the side of the Liberals in the struggles which marked the early years of the Central American federation, for the character of its population made it radical just as the position of the great families of Granada made them conservative.

The other towns of the Republic, none of which until within recent years could compare in wealth or population with either of the two chief cities, are divided between these in their sympathies. Those which are dependent geographically upon one of the rivals have naturally followed it in politics. Others are split within themselves by feuds between their leading citizens and between different elements in their population. Since the development of the coffee industry has caused a great increase in the importance of Managua, Matagalpa, and some of the other towns, these places have of course acquired much political influence, but the various groups among their people have rather allied themselves to the already existing factions than formed new ones of their own. The Conservative and Liberal leaders in Granada and Leon still dominate the party councils, although their authority is sometimes questioned by their allies in the newer centers.

The jealousy between Granada and Leon found expression in armed conflict as soon as the authority of the mother country was removed. After the declaration of independence, the Spanish governor in Leon, like the authorities in many of the other provinces, refused to recognizè the authority of Gainza, while the Granadinos joyfully accepted the new central government in Guatemala in preference to that of the mother country. As the result of this situation, an intermittent war began which lasted until General Morazán, on becoming president of the Federation, sent Dionisio de Herrera, as *jefe de estado,* to restore order. Under him the Liberal party was firmly intrenched in power. He was succeeded by a series of *jefes* of the same faction, most of them under the control of a military leader named Casto Fonseca, who was *comandante de armas.* The destruction of the Liberal governments in the other republics, however, made the position of the authorities in Nicaragua precarious; and in 1845 their administration was overthrown by a Conservative uprising aided by armies from Honduras and Salvador, which wished to punish Leon for the asylum afforded there to the defeated followers of Morazán. After sacking the capital and slaughtering a large part of its inhabitants, the invaders moved the capital to Masaya and later to Managua, both small towns near Granada. A Conservative government, made up of the great families of the latter city, endeavored to establish order and repair the damage wrought by the civil wars which had continued almost without interruption ever since the federal government had grown too weak to maintain peace, but their efforts were of little avail. The new *comandante de armas,* Trinidad Muñoz, kept the country in a state of continual disturbance, by intrigue and conspiracy, in order to increase his own influence, and finally betrayed the party which had placed him in office and used the force intrusted to him to bring about the re-establishment of the capital at Leon. A new Conservative uprising aided by Honduras and Costa Rica overthrew him in 1851, and the seat of the government was again transferred to Managua. The Conservatives made a sincere effort to establish harmony between the two parties, but after their attempts to conciliate their opponents by giving them a place in the cabinet had proved a failure, they endeavored equally unsuccessfully to maintain order by severe measures which only made the Liberals the more bitter.

In 1854, the people of Leon, under the lead of Máximo Jeréz and Francisco Castellón, drove the forces of the government out of their city and attacked Granada. The Conservatives, who received timely aid from Guatemala, resisted determinedly. By the end of the year they were apparently gaining the upper hand, when the Liberals, in their attempts to turn the tide, called in the support of a band of North American filibusters. This was the origin of the "National War," one of the most remarkable and most romantic events in the history of the Isthmus.

On June 16, 1855, William Walker landed at the port of Realejo, with fifty-seven other adventurers, ostensibly for the purpose of aiding the Liberal government at Leon, which had invited him to come to Nicaragua, but in reality with the intention of obtaining control of the entire country for himself. This he succeeded within a few months in doing. Carrying his force to San Juan del Sur by sea, he evaded a Conservative army sent to attack him there, sailed up the lake to Granada, and on October 13 occupied that city with little resistance. The force of the Conservative leaders was unimpaired, but they feared to attack the foreigners, who held their families as hostages. Corral, the head of the government forces, agreed therefore to a treaty of peace, signed on October 23, by which Patricio Rivas, a moderate Conservative, became president, Corral himself secretary of war, and Walker commander of the army. The native troops were for the most part disbanded, and the filibusters, or the "American Phalanx," as they called themselves, were practically the only military force in the Republic.

Walker desired to establish a coalition government, under his own control, in which the leaders of both great parties should be represented. This proved impossible, because the native chiefs from the first showed signs of disaffection. Corral was discovered to be holding treasonable correspondence with the presidents of the other Central American republics, and was shot only a short time after the signature of the treaty of peace. Rivas, the new president, and Jeréz, the leader of the Liberals, deserted Walker in the following June, and began a revolution against him in Leon and the western departments. Walker thereupon had himself elected President of the Republic (June 29, 1856).

The adventure of the filibusters had meanwhile attracted much interest and sympathy in the United States, where the control of Nicaragua by an American was regarded as an offset to the encroachments of Great Britain on the eastern end of the proposed route of the interoceanic canal. The control exercised by that power over Greytown, at the mouth of the San Juan River, had not yet been given up, in spite of the provisions of the Clayton-Bulwer Treaty. The people of the South, moreover, who favored expansion in tropical countries in order to maintain the relative influence of the slave states in the Union, believed that they saw in the measures which Walker adopted early in his administration to aid Americans in acquiring land in Nicaragua, and to open the way for the introduction there of negro slavery, indications that his ultimate object was the annexation of the country to the United States as a new slave-holding commonwealth. This belief appears to have been erroneous, for Walker himself more than once expressed the intention of creating an independent nation, with himself at its head as military dictator;[1] but it at least gained for the adventurer a large amount of assistance.

It was therefore easy for Walker's friends to secure large amounts of supplies and many recruits for his cause in the United States. The original force of fifty-eight was soon increased to several hundred, and the immense losses caused by disease and by fighting were made up with little difficulty. It is said that 2,500 men in all joined the "phalanx," of whom more than one thousand died of wounds or of disease.[2] The government of the United States attempted to stop the recruiting of men and the fitting out of expeditions within its jurisdiction, but it was able to accomplish very little because of the deficiencies of its neutrality laws and the strong popular feeling in favor of the filibusters, which often prevented the federal officials from carrying out the orders of their superiors. The President and the Department of State themselves were by no means unfriendly to Walker's enterprise while it still offered a prospect of success. The American minister in Nicaragua had throughout exerted his influence in favor of Walker, although in so doing he had greatly exceeded his instructions, and the Rivas government had been officially recognized by President Pierce on May 14, 1856. This recognition was not, however, extended to Walker after the latter had become president.

The most useful friends and the most dangerous enemies of Walker's regime were the American financiers interested in the Accessory Transit Company, a concern which was at that time transporting many thousands of Americans each month from New York

[1] See William O. Scroggs, *Filibusters and Financiers,* which gives a very complete account of Walker's career, and upon which the foregoing sketch is to a great extent based. Walker himself wrote a book about his campaigns, entitled *The War in Nicaragua,* and many of his followers also left accounts of their adventures.

[2] Scroggs, op. cit. p. 305.

to San Francisco by way of the San Juan River, crossing from the Great Lake to the Pacific by a macadamized road from La Virgen to San Juan del Sur. When the filibusters arrived in Nicaragua, a contest was in progress in this company in which Morgan and Garrison, the agents at New York and San Francisco respectively, were striving to wrest the control from Cornelius Vanderbilt. Failing to achieve their purpose, Morgan and Garrison determined to make use of Walker to turn the tables upon their successful rival. They did much to aid him in securing control of the Nicaraguan government by supplying him with money and arms and by bringing him large numbers of recruits in their steamers from New York and San Francisco; and in return for these favors they prevailed upon him to revoke the concession of the old company and to grant a new concession to them. This action brought Walker into a conflict with Vanderbilt, who from that time on used every means to compass the filibuster's destruction.

In July, 1856, Walker was practically supreme in southwestern Nicaragua, and had complete control of the Transit route. An army sent against him by Costa Rica a few months before had won two or three battles, but had soon been forced to withdraw by an epidemic of cholera. The hostile elements in Nicaragua itself, and the armies of Guatemala, Salvador, and Honduras, were however gathering at Leon, for all Central America had risen in arms against the foreign invader. In September the allies advanced on Masaya, where they inflicted a heavy defeat on a small force of Americans. In November they took Granada, the seat of Walker's government, which the filibusters evacuated and destroyed on their approach. Walker then moved his army by water to the Transit road, which was the chief avenue by which he received supplies and recruits from the outside world.

The allies had thus far been unable to inflict a decisive defeat on the American leader. Although they had faced him for five months with forces which must have outnumbered his little command at least three to one, the quarrels between their leaders had made effective action impossible, and the diseases which had decimated both camps had disheartened them far more than they had the intrepid "phalanx." It is probable that they would soon have abandoned the campaign had not Costa Rica, instigated by Vanderbilt and encouraged by the government of Great Britain, again taken the field and struck Walker a decisive blow at his weakest point. In December a force from that country, directed by one of Vanderbilt's agents, had descended the San Carlos River and seized the steamers on the San Juan and the Great Lake, thus cutting off Walker's communications with New York, whence he had received the greatest part of his reinforcements. They then joined the allies who were confronting the filibuster force at Rivas. Walker was now no longer able to replenish his supplies or to fill the gaps in his ranks with new recruits. Although in desperate straits, he held out for several months, beating off the attacks of the Central American troops with great loss. The melting away of his small force through disease and desertion, however, finally made his position untenable. On May 1, 1857, he surrendered to Commander Davis of the U. S. S. St. Mary's, who had interposed his mediation to put an end to the hostilities.

At the conclusion of the war there were six armies in Nicaragua, representing the four other Central American republics and the two factions in the country itself. Most of the foreign contingents were withdrawn by their respective governments, after some slight difficulties, but neither the Conservatives under General Tomás Martínez nor the Liberals under Jeréz were willing to allow the other party to take possession of the government. Another civil war would probably have been the result, had not the Republic suddenly been menaced by a new danger from without. Costa Rica, attempting to take advantage of the exhaustion of her neighbor, declined to evacuate the territory which she had occupied on the south bank of the San Juan River, and demanded the surrender of certain military posts there which would give her control of the greater part of the route of the proposed canal. As soon as the intentions of President Mora became evident, Jeréz and Martínez assumed a joint dictatorship and prepared for war. Hostilities were only averted by the sudden return of Walker, which forced the two countries to settle their differences and to prepare to resist a new invasion. Costa Rica had already withdrawn her claims when news arrived that the filibuster had been taken prisoner by the captain of an American warship on the East Coast before he had had time to reach the interior.[1]

Meanwhile the capital had been definitely and permanently established at Managua, and Tomás Martínez had taken charge of the presidency as the result of an election. With his accession began the first, and up to the present time the only, era of relatively stable and comparatively efficient government in the history of the Republic. Martínez held office until 1867, suppressing a Liberal revolt led by Jeréz in 1863, and was succeeded by a series of capable and honorable presidents belonging to the Conservative party.[2] These men were the leaders of a strongly organized and homogeneous group, which was able to maintain itself in office until 1893 because of its unity and its moderate and sagacious

[1] Walker was eventually captured and shot while attempting a third invasion of Central America on the North Coast of Honduras in 1860.

[2] These were: Fernando Guzmán, 1867-71; Vicente Cuadra, 1871-75; Pedro Joaquín Chamorro, 1875-79; Joaquín Zavala, 1879-83; Adán Cárdenas, 1883-87; Evaristo Carazo, 1887-89; David Osorno, 1889; and Roberto Sacasa, 1889-93.

policy. Although thoroughly conservative in ideas as well as in name, striving to maintain the existing social order and the influence of the Church, the administrations of the "thirty years" nevertheless did much to promote the economic and social progress of the country. A railway was built from the Pacific port of Corinto to Leon and Lake Managua, and another from the city of Managua to Granada; agriculture was encouraged in many ways; and even the school system was enlarged and improved. Their most important achievement was the maintenance of peace during so long a period. There were few revolts of importance, and not one successful revolution between 1863 and 1893, notwithstanding the fact that the prolonged tenure of power by one political group, which allowed no real freedom of elections, was naturally distasteful to the opposition.

The methods by which the Conservatives were able to sustain their authority for so long should afford a valuable lesson for their successors. In the first place, the government was that of a group of men, rather than that of one absolute ruler. As each president at the end of his term turned over his office to one of his associates, instead of bringing about his own re-election, there was little jealousy between the leaders, and each in turn had the support of a united party. So long as there was no treachery within the administration itself, and so long as friendly relations were cultivated with the neighboring states, the government, with its control of the army and the forts, had little to fear from its enemies. The Liberals, on their side, showed little inclination to recommence the civil wars which had devastated the country from 1821 to 1863, for they profited by the maintenance of order, and were treated with far more fairness and generosity than usually falls to the lot of the opposition party in Central America. At the present time, after a quarter century of renewed party strife and mutual persecution, many members of both parties look back on the "thirty years" as the happiest period of the Republic's history.

There were, however, dissatisfied elements which only awaited an opportunity to overthrow the Conservative regime. The Leon leaders were far from accepting the rule of their traditional rivals complacently, and they could rely upon the support of increasingly numerous groups of young men of the middle and lower classes in other parts of the country, who were beginning to take a prominent part in political agitation. The "Principal Families" were losing their prestige as they had already lost it in Guatemala and Costa Rica, and their political power was destroyed when the first serious dissension appeared in their ranks. In 1889 President Carazo died in the middle of his term, and was succeeded by Roberto Sacasa, one of the few Conservatives from Leon. When the new president attempted to give the people of his own city some of the more important public offices, the extreme partisans of Granada overthrew him in 1893. This act, which broke the unity of the Conservative party and thus weakened the government, was followed by a successful Liberal uprising in Leon some months later.

As the result of this revolution, the presidency was given to a young man from Managua, who was prominent among the younger generation of Liberals. José Santos Zelaya was the absolute ruler of Nicaragua for sixteen years. He was supported at first by the leaders at Leon, but in 1896, when it became evident that he intended to force his re-election for a second term, the western city rose against him. The administration was saved only by the intervention of the allied government of Honduras and by the aid of the Conservatives of Granada, who were willing to support even a Liberal president against their traditional enemies. This episode illustrates one of the chief sources of Zelaya's power—

his skill in playing off the members of the different factions against one another. When it became evident that it was impossible to overthrow him, the Leon chiefs again associated themselves with him, and even some of the wealthy *Granadinos* accepted positions and favors from him.

During the Liberal administration, the railway system and the steamer service on the lakes were extended and improved, the development of the coffee districts was stimulated by generous subsidies, and the capital, Zelaya's birthplace, was transformed from a rather primitive small town to the most progressive city of the Republic, which at the present time is ahead of Granada, and but little behind Leon, in population. Marked progress was made in the matter of public instruction, for schools were opened in all parts of the country, and many young men of special ability were sent abroad to study. It is to be regretted that the Conservative administrations which succeeded Zelaya have fallen far behind the Liberal dictator in this respect, and have abandoned many of the educational institutions which he opened.

Despite his progressive policy, however, Zelaya was a brutal and unscrupulous tyrant, who exploited the country for his own personal profit on a scale unprecedented in the history of the Isthmus. He and his ministers established monopolies of all sorts, and sold valuable concessions to foreigners or acquired them themselves, until there were few forms of agriculture or industry which did not pay a heavy tribute to some favored person. The silver currency disappeared before large issues of irredeemable paper money, and the requisitions of the government were paid for, not with cash, but with receipts which could be negotiated only at a loss and through the aid of persons having influence with the treasury department. Private persons enjoyed little protection in their property and personal liberty against abuses of power by the local and military officials, and the enemies of the government suffered not only exile and the confiscation of their property, but even torture and sometimes death in the prisons. The rich families of Granada, who were with some reason held responsible for the revolts which occurred almost every year, were treated with great brutality. The avarice and cruelty of the men in power, however, were felt most severely only by their irreconcilable enemies. The friends of the government prospered, and the people as a whole suffered comparatively little. In the country at large, in fact, the inflow of money resulting from the reckless sale of concessions created a sort of prosperity, for which the country has had to pay since Zelaya's fall.

Zelaya raised Nicaragua to a position of influence in Central America which she had never before enjoyed. He fomented revolutions in all of the other four republics, and even in countries so far distant as Colombia and Ecuador, until by 1909 the only one of his neighbors who did not hate and fear him was the president of Honduras, whom he himself had placed in office by his invasion of that state in 1907. During the last three years of his administration, his attempts to re-establish the old federal union, with himself at its head, plunged all Central America into turmoil. His warlike activities and his systematic opposition to American influence in the Isthmus finally brought about an open rupture with the government of the United States, and did much to cause his downfall. The history of the revolution of 1909, and the history of the Republic since that date will be treated in Chapter XI.

Ninety-five years of rarely interrupted civil strife have left Nicaragua in a condition which offers little hope for the early re-establishment of peace and good government. The advances made along these lines between 1863 and 1893 were to a great extent nullified during the Liberal regime, when the continual attempts at revolution, followed usually by barbarous treatment of the people of Granada and other Conservative centers, not only revived and intensified the old localistic spirit, but aroused a turbulent spirit and a strong taste for factional strife among the people of all classes. Within a few years after 1893, it would have been impossible for either party to acquiesce in the rule of the other as the Liberals had acquiesced in the Conservative regime of the "thirty years," for the subordination of any sense of justice to political considerations in the conduct of the government and in the courts made the opponents of the party in power so insecure in their property and in their personal liberty that they were ready to support almost any revolutionary movement which promised an alleviation of their condition. The only creed of public officials and professional politicians seemed to be the promotion of the interests of their faction and the abuse and subjugation of their political enemies. These conditions were little changed by the advent of the Conservatives to power in 1910, because the new authorities, who had grown up under the oppression of Zelaya, with the worst features of his administration constantly before their eyes, apparently could not resist the temptation to avenge themselves upon their former rulers on the one hand and to attempt to recoup their losses at the expense of the nation on the other. The political morality of all parties had been so debased that a restoration of the clean and moderate regime of the "thirty years," of which many of the older generation in Granada had dreamed, was no longer possible.

The fertile lake plains, laid waste time after time by revolutionary armies, are no longer the "Mahomet's Paradise" which travelers had described in glowing terms in colonial times. After the declaration of independence, the energies of the ruling class in each section of the country were entirely occupied in endeavors to maintain themselves in power or to overthrow administrations controlled by their enemies. The harassed landholders continued to cultivate their plantations as well as they could in the intervals between civil wars, but the political situation of the country soon became so hopeless that there was little incentive for them to attempt to repair the damage wrought by each successive outbreak or to engage in new agricultural enterprises. The indigo plantations which had made the people of the province wealthy under the rule of Spain were abandoned some time before the invention of aniline dyes made them unprofitable in the other states, and the famous cacao of Nicaragua, which was formerly an important export, is now grown in quantities little more than sufficient to supply the local demand. The only important products of the lake basin today are plantains, corn, beans, sugar, and cacao, which are planted for local consumption, and cattle, which are still raised in large numbers, notwithstanding the losses inflicted on ranch owners by foraging parties and bandits.

Outside of the hot plains of the interior, there have until recently been few settlements of importance. The climate of the mountains to the northwest and southeast of the lakes is much more suitable to European colonization than that of Granada and Leon, but the latter cities, situated as they are on what was formerly the transisthmian commercial route, have always been preferred as a place of residence by the creole families. The majority of the towns which were established in the sixteenth and seventeenth centuries in the regions of Matagalpa, Jinotega, and Segovia were soon destroyed by the fierce mountain Indians or by pirates who came up the rivers from their bases of operations on the East Coast; and those which survived, with few exceptions, are today but little more than straggling villages. In the *sierras* between the lakes and the Pacific, there were at the time of the conquest a number of Indian villages, but their growth was discouraged by the fact that the lack of rivers and springs made it difficult to secure even drinking water in the dry season. Neither district received much attention from the government until the latter part of the nineteenth century.

During the last twenty-five years, however, a number of coffee plantations have been established both in the departments of Matagalpa and Jinotega, and in the mountains near Managua and Granada. These are not so large nor so well equipped as those in other countries of the Isthmus, and their product is much less than that of Guatemala or Salvador, but their development has nevertheless greatly increased the commerce of the country. It has not, however, affected general economic and political conditions so much as it would have if the majority of the plantations were not owned and managed by foreigners. Nicaraguan citizens hold only a part of the properties in the southwestern *sierras,* and those in the North are almost entirely in the hands of Germans, Englishmen, and Americans. The natives have participated less in the prosperity due to the new conditions than in any of the other countries where coffee has become the principal national product.

The Matagalpa and Jinotega districts have a large Indian population, living in little settlements scattered through the mountains. These tribes were not subjugated by the colonial authorities until nearly two centuries after the establishment of Leon and Granada, and even at the present time, when most of them have adopted the Spanish language and religion, they show little admixture of white blood. At the time of their pacification they received large tracts of land from the crown, which they still hold in common and apportion at regular intervals among their members. As the extent and the exact boundaries of these grants have never been definitely settled, they have been a cause of constant friction between the native communities and the white planters. The officials of the central government have often carelessly sold land belonging to the Indians to the coffee growers as a part of the public domain, and the planters themselves have in some instances taken possession of the property of the aboriginal communities without any right to do so. Projects for the surveying of the Indian lands and for the sale of those which their owners do not need to the coffee planters have for some time occupied the attention of the authorities at Managua.

The labor situation in the northern coffee belt presents considerable difficulties. The Indians, who see little advantage in exchanging their free life in their own villages for one of toil on the plantations, do not furnish the regular and dependable supply of workmen which are indispensable for the proper cultivation of the plantations, although they do not refuse to work for a few days when they have need for a small sum of ready money. Under Zelaya, an attempt was made to solve the problem by the passage of a peonage law similar to the *Ley de Trabajadores* in Guatemala. This system seems never to have borne so heavily upon the Indians as in the latter republic, but it at least gave the planters a means for securing a regular force with which to work their properties. Further aid was furnished by the recruiting of laborers by force during the harvest time, when many Indians from Matagalpa were even forced to travel for many days on foot across the hot plains of the interior to work for friends of the administration in the *sierras* south of the lakes. The labor laws were abolished by the Conservative administration, however, and since 1910 the planters, unable to enforce contracts which they make with the Indians, have often had difficulties in harvesting their crops. Their position has been alleviated somewhat by the fact that the local authorities have in many cases illegally enforced the old law; but the uncertainty of the labor situation has greatly discouraged the extension of the plantations and the introduction of new capital.[1]

The East Coast, which is for all practical purposes farther from the cities of the interior than it is from New Orleans, has only within the last quarter century become an integral part of Nicaragua, for until 1894 it enjoyed a sort of independent existence under British protection as the "Mosquito Kingdom." This was a fictitious state of half-breed Indians and negroes, who had from early times maintained commercial and to some extent political relations with the nearby settlements of English pirates and woodcutters, and through them with the governor of Jamaica. In the middle of the nineteenth century, when the attention of the world was first called to the possibility of constructing an interoceanic canal by way of the San Juan River, these relations were made the pretext for the establishment of a protectorate over the entire eastern portion of Nicaragua and for the seizure of Greytown, at the mouth of the San Juan, which had never even been in the domain claimed by the Indians. The territory which was thus brought under British control was in reality governed, not by the savage and degenerate native chiefs, but by the British and other foreigners who had settled along the Coast. The United States from the first refused to recognize the protectorate, and protested vigorously and in the end successfully against

[1] In a previous chapter, the author has stated it to be his opinion that the plantations of Guatemala could be operated successfully without a peonage system. The effect of the repeal of the labor laws in Nicaragua would seem to prove the contrary, were it not for the great difference between the Indians of the two countries. In Guatemala, the Indians depend upon the planters for a living, as they have little land of their own. They were, moreover, almost wholly an agricultural people before the Spanish conquest, whereas the Indians of Matagalpa have always secured at least a portion of their food by hunting, and have never been accustomed to any but spasmodic and irregular agricultural labor. They have also great tracts of land of their own, of which, unlike the tribes in Guatemala, they have never been dispossessed.

the violation of Nicaragua's sovereignty. The Clayton-Bulwer Treaty, signed in 1850, bound both powers not to colonize, occupy, or exercise dominion over any part of Nicaragua or Central America, but the British government refused to admit that this obliged it to withdraw its protection from the Mosquitos, and the continued occupation of Greytown, as we have seen, was one of the causes which led the people of the United States to support the filibustering expeditions of Walker. In 1860, Great Britain agreed to abandon the protectorate on condition that Greytown should be made a free port, and that the Indians should be given a reservation in which they were to be free to govern themselves in accordance with their own usages. This meant that the foreigners on the Coast were practically to be at liberty to manage their own affairs without interference by the native authorities. The arrangement was unsatisfactory from the first, for the residents of Greytown and Bluefields objected to every exercise of Nicaraguan sovereignty, and Great Britain upheld them in their attitude, and thus in fact continued to exercise a protectorate over them.

Matters came to a crisis in 1893, when Zelaya made a war with Honduras the pretext for sending an army into the reservation and seizing the control of the government. The Indians and the foreigners on the Coast protested strongly against this action, but Great Britain, wearied of the difficult and equivocal position in which her relations with the Mosquitos had placed her, refused to uphold them. They had, therefore, no choice but to submit. In 1894 a convention called by the Nicaraguan commander and dominated by him voted for the complete incorporation of the reservation into the Republic as the Department of "Zelaya," and the Republic has ever since exercised complete jurisdiction over the former "sambo" kingdom.

Like other sections of the Caribbean litoral, the East

Coast of Nicaragua is inhabited chiefly by Americans and English-speaking negroes. Its principal product is the banana. Bluefields, which is the administrative center and the seaport, is connected with New Orleans by a regular line of small steamers, and has far more commercial and financial relations with the United States than with the interior. During the Liberal regime, many important concessions were granted for enterprises in the newly incorporated territory, which later became a source of no little embarrassment to the government. In some cases the higher officials made grants which were actually harmful to the community as a whole, for their own personal profit, while in others large tracts of land were ceded or special privileges were granted to unscrupulous promoters who had little intention of carrying out in good faith the obligations which they assumed, but who appealed to their own governments for aid whenever they became involved in disputes with the native authorities. Some of the monopolies established, and particularly the exclusive right which one company received to operate steamers on the Bluefields River, caused great discontent on the Coast itself, and led the foreign colony there to take a prominent part in organizing and supporting the revolution of 1909, by which Zelaya was overthrown.

The means of transportation between the various sections of Nicaragua are as yet very primitive. In the interior, they are by no means bad, for it was comparatively easy to build a railroad from Corinto, the chief port on the Pacific, to all of the important cities of the lake region and to the coffee district west of it; and the lakes themselves afford a cheap means of transportation to the regions around their shores. Matagalpa and the northern departments, however, depend upon the rudest kind of cart roads, and are almost inaccessible in the rainy season. Communication with the Atlantic Coast is still more difficult, especially at present, for the steamer service which formerly existed on the San Juan River has been allowed to deteriorate, and the overland route to Bluefields involves several days of traveling through a sparsely settled tropical forest on mule back. Preparations are now well advanced for the construction by American capital of a railway from Bluefields to Lake Nicaragua, which would make travel from the East to the West Coast comparatively easy. Another road is planned from the main line of the Pacific Railway to Matagalpa, and it seems not improbable that this and the Bluefields line may eventually be connected, so that it will be possible to cross the Republic from one ocean to the other.

The execution of these projects, and in fact Nicaragua's whole prospect for the immediate future, depend upon her relations with the United States. Since 1911, both the political affairs and the economic development of the country have not been entirely in the hands of her own citizens, for the government at Washington, in its efforts to promote peace in Nicaragua and in Central America, has entered upon a course which has forced it on several occasions to intervene decisively in the internal politics of the country, and two firms of American bankers, as a result of their financial assistance to the government, have gradually assumed control of the customs houses, of the railways, of the currency system, and even of the internal revenues of the Republic. The course of events which has brought this to pass will be described in Chapter XI.

CHAPTER V

SALVADOR

Geographical Description—History—Improvement of Political Conditions in Recent Years—Activities of the Government—Agricultural Products—Social Conditions—Means of Transportation—Relations with the United States—Prospect for the Future.

SALVADOR is the most important of the Central American republics, after Guatemala, although she has a far smaller territory than any of her neighbors. Almost all of her total area of 7,225 square miles is suitable for cultivation, and there are few parts of it which are not inhabited by a dense population. Notwithstanding the fact that she has no coast line on the Atlantic and has thus been deprived of direct communication with Europe and the Eastern United States, her foreign trade is far greater than that of Honduras and Nicaragua, and but little behind that of Guatemala and Costa Rica, while her upper classes are more closely in touch with the outside world, and have shown a greater tendency to adopt foreign customs and practices than those of the majority of the other countries. Her capital, San Salvador, is a busy, up-to-date commercial center, which impresses the traveler as one of the most progressive cities of the Isthmus.

Extending from Guatemala on the west to the Gulf of Fonseca on the east,[1] the Republic occupies a section of the broad plain along the Pacific Coast of the Isthmus, and like the similarly situated section of Guatemala, is traversed by a chain of volcanic peaks,

[1] It should be noted that the Isthmus is bounded by the Atlantic on the north and the Pacific on the south in Guatemala, Salvador, and Honduras, whereas the former ocean lies east and the latter west of Nicaragua and Costa Rica.

many of which are still active or have been active within very recent times. The soil, consisting mainly of decomposed lava, is extremely fertile. The slopes of the mountains are excellently adapted for the cultivation of coffee, and in the lower altitudes, although much of the country is rough and broken, nearly all of the other characteristic Central American products can be grown. There is a plentiful rainfall from May to October, and an abundant water supply for the dense population is provided by several lakes and by a number of streams which do not dry up during the rainless season. The Lempa, which divides the eastern from the western half of the country, after flowing through the northern departments from its source near the Guatemalan frontier, is by far the largest river on the Pacific side of the Isthmus. As the more important cities are situated in the valleys at the foot of the volcanoes, or in the low plains along the coast and on the banks of the Lempa, few of them are more than two thousand feet above sea level, and their climate is consequently less agreeable than that of the most densely populated parts of Guatemala and Costa Rica. Except in the lower Lempa Valley, however, the people are fairly healthy, probably because the porousness of the soil discourages the breeding of mosquitoes and thus holds in check some of the diseases most prevalent in other parts of the tropics.

The people are of much the same racial character as those of Nicaragua and Honduras, although there seems to be rather more Spanish blood in their veins, and less admixture of negro, than in those countries. The majority are in part at least of Indian ancestry, but all speak Spanish, and there are only a few communities where the aborigines have maintained their individuality and their primitive customs. Among the upper classes, the greater number are of pure or nearly pure European descent, but Indian blood is no bar to social or political prominence. The people as a whole are fairly industrious, considering the climate and the prevalence of hookworm and other intestinal parasites, and the standard of living among the laboring classes is considerably higher than in Guatemala or Nicaragua. The landowning class is perhaps the wealthiest and the most enterprising in the Isthmus.

The early history of Salvador was as turbulent as that of her neighbors. For many years after the declaration of independence she was almost continuously in a state of civil war, partly because of the rivalry between the political leaders and the jealousy between the cities within the state itself, and partly because of the incessant quarrels between the state authorities and those of Guatemala. As we have seen, her people played a prominent part in the struggles which accompanied the first attempt to establish a Central American federation. The prolonged war in which the citizens of Salvador and of one section of Honduras overthrew the Conservative government in Guatemala in 1829 was followed within three years by new difficulties which led President Morazán in his turn to remove the state authorities in San Salvador and to transfer to that city the seat of the federal administration. From then until the final fall of the great unionist leader, Salvador was frequently involved with one or another and at times with all of her neighbors, because of the opposition of the latter to the federal authorities. She was the last of the five states to admit the dissolution of the union, and at the present time she is the chief center of the party which favors its restoration.

The Liberal party, which had supported Morazán, was driven from power by the intervention of President Carrera of Guatemala in 1840, and for five years the government was under the control of Francisco Malespín, one of Carrera's friends, who used his position as *comandante de armas* to make and unmake presidents and to dominate the policy of the civil authorities. The Liberals were able to return to power in 1845, after a bloody struggle in which Malespín, although now estranged from Carrera, was assisted by the government of Honduras. They were again driven out in 1852 by Carrera, and four Conservative leaders occupied the presidency for short terms. The Liberals, under the leadership of Gerardo Barrios, regained power in 1860, but were forced to relinquish it two years later as the result of another war with Carrera. In 1863, the Conservative leader, Francisco Dueñas, became president, and conducted the government efficiently and successfully until 1871, when the Liberal party, which was at the same time carrying on successful revolutions in Guatemala and Honduras, defeated him and placed at the head of the state Santiago González, who remained in office until 1876. His successor, Andrés Valle, became involved in another war with Guatemala, arising from an intervention by both states in the internal affairs of Honduras, and was replaced by Rafael Zaldívar, one of the leading followers of the former president Dueñas. This able ruler remained in office until 1885, maintaining the friendliest relations with President Barrios of Guatemala, despite the fact that one belonged to the Conservative and the other to the Liberal party. When Barrios attempted to renew the Central American Union by force, and entered upon the campaign which ended so disastrously for him at Chalchuapa, however, Zaldívar took the field against him. A short time after this war, Zaldívar was forced to resign by a revolution headed by Francisco Menéndez, and the latter was president until his death in 1890. After him, the Republic was ruled by the Ezeta brothers, two military leaders who seized the presidency by a *coup d'état* and maintained themselves in office by despotic and rather barbarous methods until they were overthrown by an uprising in the city of Santa Ana in 1894. Rafael Gutiérrez, who became president in that year, was an able and patriotic executive, but some features of his administration caused considerable discontent, and his participation in the Treaty of Amapala, by which Salvador entered into a loose union with Honduras and Nicaragua, caused his fall in 1898.

The new president, General Tomás Regalado, served his full term and passed on the chief magistracy in an orderly manner to Pedro José Escalón in 1903. From that time there has not been a successful revolution in Salvador, although discontented political leaders have occasionally made ineffectual attempts to overthrow the government. In 1906, General Regalado, who was very influential in the administration of President Escalón, brought about a short and purposeless war with Guatemala, which ended with the death of its author on the battlefield. In 1907 there was another war, between Salvador and Nicaragua, about the presidency of Honduras, and in that and the following year President Zelaya of Nicaragua attempted several times, without success, to promote revolutions against the governments of Escalón and of Fernando Figueroa, who succeeded him. The Government of the United States exerted its good offices to put an end to the hostilities between the two countries, and finally threatened to use force if necessary to put an end to Zelaya's attacks on his neighbor, but peace was not entirely reestablished until the Nicaraguan president was overthrown in 1909. Figueroa was succeeded by Manuel Enrique Araujo in 1911. This president was assassinated in 1913, and the vice-president, Don Carlos Meléndez, completed the unexpired term and was reelected to the chief magistracy in 1915.

In the confused political history of Salvador, two important facts stand out: first, that the revolutions which occurred so frequently during the seventy-five years following the declaration of independence were due more to the interference of the other countries, and especially of Guatemala, than to the strife of factions at home; and second, that in recent times, when this kind of interference is no longer so frequent, there has been a remarkably rapid progress towards the establishment of a more stable form of government. For three-quarters of a century after 1821, the internal tranquillity of the country may be said to have been almost entirely dependent upon its relations with its neighbors. The parties which were formed during the turbulent years of the Central American Union continued to act together long after the states which made up the Union had become independent nations, and Conservative governments in Guatemala continued to regard themselves as the natural enemies of Liberal administrations in Nicaragua and Salvador, largely because of the bitter animosity between the leaders, which had been engendered by the events of the years 1821-40. Discontented factions in Salvador never hesitated to call in assistance from other countries to overthrow a hostile government at home, and the presidents of the other countries on their side were always ready to intervene to secure the establishment of a friendly administration in Salvador, in order to increase their own influence and to make more secure their own position. As the leaders who had participated in the wars under the Federation died, however, and the parties lost their fundamental economic and social characteristics, so that there was little real difference in principles or point of view between the Liberals of one country and the Conservatives of another, factional politics ceased to a great extent to be international. Intervention to overthrow a government of opposite political complexion was then no longer so necessary as a measure of self-preservation, as it had been when every Liberal or Conservative who came into power in one of the states felt it his duty to use all of the resources at his command to secure the domination of his own party in the others. Guatemala has not played a decisive part in overthrowing a president of Salvador since the battle of Chalchuapa in 1885, and Honduras and Nicaragua have now fallen so far behind their neighbor in population and resources that their intervention is no longer seriously to be feared. The attempts of the president of the latter country to encourage revolutions in Salvador in 1907 and 1908 were failures, although they caused the government considerable uneasiness and expense.

Since 1908, moreover, international wars between the Central American states have been made practically impossible by the fact that the United States has employed diplomatic pressure and sometimes actual force to secure the observance of the Washington Conventions of 1907, by which the five countries pledged themselves to abstain from interfering in each other's internal affairs. At the present time it is not probable that an army from one state would be allowed to invade one of the others for the purpose of bringing about a change of government. The prevention of this kind of aggression, of which there were instances almost every year before 1907, has done much to discourage revolutions in Central America, because there is little chance, except in cases where there is a very general and very violent popular discontent with the government in power, for a revolt to succeed without active assistance from outside.

Since the character of her international relations has changed so that external influences no longer make the establishment of internal peace impossible, Salvador has become one of the most orderly and best governed of the Central American republics. Her political affairs are almost entirely in the hands of a small educated class, among whom landed proprietors are more powerful and professional politicians and revolutionists on the whole less numerous and less influential than elsewhere in the Isthmus. This class was for many years divided within itself into hostile factions, which were kept alive, long after the disappearance of their original sources of difference, by the intrigues and interventions of the neighboring governments. After the violent animosities created by the wars during the first Central American Union died out, however, and after the cultivation of coffee and the development of commerce had opened up greater opportunities for the acquisition of wealth and power than were offered by the contest for public offices, the ruling class as a whole turned its attention from politics to agriculture. The damage inflicted by the frequent civil wars was severely felt by the proprietors of the plantations, who were realizing for the first time the possibilities of the new life which the importation of foreign luxuries and the ability to travel abroad placed before them, and they consequently became almost a unit in their desire for peace and a stable government. An attempt to start an old-fashioned revolution at the present time, unless there were some strong reason for desiring to overthrow the government, would probably meet with determined hostility among the greater part of the wealthier and more intelligent classes.

It cannot be said, however, that Salvador is inherently a peaceful country in the same sense in which this is true of Costa Rica. The lower classes have no more inborn respect for authority and love of peace than have those of Nicaragua and Honduras, whom they strongly resemble in their racial characteristics and customs, and a large element among them have always taken part in wars and revolutions with the same gusto that is shown by the *mestizos* of the more turbulent countries. If they are on the whole less prone to revolt, this is due to the fact that they are fairly contented under present conditions, and that they are held under control by a much stronger and better organized military power than in those countries. The government is maintained in office, not by popular respect for authority or by the will of the people, but by force, for there are always elements, even among the upper classes, which are awaiting an opportunity to overthrow it.

There is at present, however, no organized opposition, as the old historical parties have nearly died out and the formation of new ones has been discouraged by the policy of the government, which generally either wins over discontented political leaders by the gift of offices or money, or forcibly prevents them from carrying on propaganda hostile to it. In former times, opponents of the group in power were exiled or even murdered, but recent administrations have attempted rather to conciliate their opponents and to maintain the good will of the common people, and there has been little of the severity towards defeated rivals which has helped to keep alive factional hatred in Guatemala and Nicaragua. Nevertheless, opposition to the government is still suppressed with a firm hand, and murders for political purposes are by no means unknown.

The political institutions are no more democratic than those of the neighboring countries. Except where a successful revolution intervenes, the presidency is passed on by each incumbent to a successor of his own choosing, and all of the other nominally elective offices are filled in accordance with the wishes of the administration, since the authorities control the elections by preventing the nomination of opposition candidates and by exerting pressure on the voters. Every department is under the absolute personal control of the president, so far as he wishes to exercise his authority, and the responsibility for everything which occurs during the administration rests upon his shoulders. The Congress has at the present time some degree of independence, and the judiciary is not subjected to the same dictation by the executive as in some of the other countries, but neither is in any real sense co-ordinate with the latter, nor would be able to resist it if a serious difference of opinion arose.

Of late years, however, the presidents of Salvador have made little attempt to exercise the absolute and arbitrary authority which some of the recent rulers of Guatemala and Nicaragua have enjoyed, for they have generally been content to abide so far as possible by the provisions of the constitution and to relinquish their office to one of their supporters at the end of their legal term. Since 1898, with a single exception, changes of administration have taken place without the intervention of force, and the one president who was assassinated was followed by the constitutionally elected vice-president, without disorder or further bloodshed.

The chief support of the government is the army, which is better trained and better equipped than that of any other Central American country. A large proportion of the soldiers, apparently, serve voluntarily. Moreover, many remain with the colors for long periods, and learn to take a certain amount of pride in their calling. The officers are of an unusually high type, because the comparatively good salaries and the education offered by the Polytechnic School have induced many young men of the better classes to adopt the military profession as a career. Both officers and men seem on the whole to be loyal to the government and show little tendency to political intrigue,—a statement which cannot be made with regard to the forces of some of the other republics. The army is far larger than the wealth or the actual necessities of the country would seem to justify, and heavy expenditures upon it have been a source of some discontent; but the existence of a well-organized and well-trained body of troops has undoubtedly been a strong factor in favor of stable government and a valuable protection against attack from without.

The civil police is also efficient and well equipped

compared with that of the neighboring countries. Besides the usual city forces, there is an organization called the *Guardia Civil* in the rural districts near the capital which patrols the roads and does much to protect life and property. Crimes of violence, however, are by no means uncommon, and are very frequently allowed to go unpunished, for the activity of the army and the police, as in the other Central American countries, is directed more towards the maintenance of the authority of the government than towards the prevention of wrongdoing. The suppression of revolts and the control of all parts of the Republic by military force is easier than in any of the neighboring countries, because of the small area to be policed and the denseness and compactness of the population.

The chief functions performed by the government are the preservation of order, the management of the customs houses and the other sources of income, and the operation of such fundamentally necessary public services as the postal and telegraph systems. A comparatively small amount of money, considering the wealth of the country, is available for other purposes, because of the heavy cost of the military establishment and the losses due to inefficiency and peculation in the collection and expenditure of the revenues. Sanitary measures and public instruction have not received the attention which might be expected among so progressive a people and little has been done, except by private initiative, to develop the resources of the country or to stimulate foreign commerce. Although abortive attempts have been made from time to time to establish agricultural and industrial schools, the government has little interest in such institutions, and has never given them sufficient funds to accomplish anything of great value. The system of highways, which is of especial importance because of the lively internal commerce, leaves much to be desired, but its defects are due more to almost insurmountable difficulties arising from heavy rainfall and from the physical formation of the country than to lack of interest. There are, however, cart roads, which are fairly good in the dry season, in all parts of the Republic, and near the capital there are several roads suitable for automobiles, which are owned by many of the wealthy people of the city.

The public schools have received less attention than in some of the other countries. The Department of Public Instruction, which possesses many well-informed and able officials, has done what it could with the scanty resources at its command, but the government has not supported it with adequate appropriations, and has not always shown care or impartiality in the appointment of teachers. Only about one-fourth of the children between six and fourteen years of age are receiving instruction.[1] The schools in the capital and in the larger cities, although badly equipped and very badly housed, do excellent work, and the visitor cannot fail to be impressed by the enthusiasm shown by the children and by the teachers. The latter are generally inadequately trained, but they appear to have a natural gift for arousing the interest and holding the attention of their pupils. In the country, educational opportunities are much more limited, for the rural schools have but three regular grades, with a complementary year in which instruction in some trade is given, and there is little opportunity for the children to receive a secondary education unless they can afford to spend five years completing their primary course in one of the cities. The education of the lower classes has been purposely restricted to a few fundamentals, because the authorities have desired to discourage the tendency, so harmful in all parts of Central America, towards the

[1] According to figures furnished to me by Sr. Juan Lainez, Director of Primary Instruction, there are 245,251 children between the ages of six and fourteen in Salvador, of whom 60,860 are enrolled in public and private schools. The average attendance is considerably less than the number enrolled. The budget for Public Instruction for the year 1916 was $1,205,074.44, or approximately $408,000 in U. S. currency.

adoption of the learned professions at the expense of agricultural pursuits. No government aid is now granted to poor children for advanced study either at home or in foreign countries, and every effort is made rather to encourage those who have completed their primary course to fit themselves for the cultivation of the soil or for some trade. In the capital, schools have just been inaugurated where practical instruction for this purpose is given. There are a number of secondary institutions in the larger cities which compare favorably with those in other parts of Central America, although they also suffer from lack of funds and from the absence of well-trained teachers. The same is true of the University, where law, engineering, pharmacy, and other professions are taught. The wealthier families educate their children in private institutions rather than in the public schools, and more and more young people at the present time are being sent to complete their studies in foreign countries, and especially in the United States.

The administration of public affairs is considerably less corrupt and somewhat more efficient than in Guatemala, Nicaragua, or Honduras. The integrity of many of the higher officials is above suspicion, and theft is apparently not practiced on a large scale in any department of the government. The judiciary is neither so hopelessly venal nor so inefficient as in some of the other countries, and the Supreme Court is a body which commands general respect. The administration of the postal and telegraph systems is fairly reliable, although it is typically Central American in its methods and in its spirit. Conditions are nevertheless very far from what they should be. Even at the present time, under a president whose honesty and whose progressive ideals are doubted by no one, public officials are too often appointed for purely personal reasons rather than with any regard to their fitness, and graft is practiced more or less openly in all of the departments, with the knowledge, if not with the consent, of the higher authorities. Large amounts of money are paid from the public treasury on different pretexts to political leaders whom the administration desires to conciliate, and men of little ability or patriotism are given positions of responsibility and authority for which they are not at all fitted, and in which their conduct is not infrequently scandalous. These conditions are to a great extent beyond the control of the government, for an administration which failed to consolidate its power by such methods probably could not maintain itself very long in office. The old-style professional revolutionists, many of whom have a considerable following among the lower and middle classes, are still too powerful to be disregarded, and the idea that offices and graft are the legitimate rewards of political activity is no less paramount than formerly. There is every prospect, however, that political conditions will improve as the government becomes more stable, and as public opinion, already a powerful influence for good, becomes more enlightened and exerts more control over the factional leaders.

Economically, Salvador is one of the most prosperous countries of the Isthmus. Her principal product is coffee, grown on the slopes of all the higher volcanoes and hills, which is exported to the amount of from sixty to seventy million pounds annually to France, the United States, and other countries. In the lower parts of the country, there are many large cattle ranches and cane plantations, which produce meat and sugar for local consumption. Corn is raised everywhere, even more than in other parts of Central America, because of the denseness of the population and because of the large *per capita* consumption. One small section of the Pacific Coast, called *La Costa del Bálsamo,* is notable for its exports of balsam of Peru, a forest product which is found in its wild state only in this one spot.[1] The trees from

---

[1] It has been introduced into Ceylon. *Encyclopædia Brittanica,* article on "Balsam."

which this medicinal gum is extracted have within recent years been brought under systematic care in large plantations, and have proved a source of considerable wealth to the native capitalists, as well as to the Indians who collect the balsam in the forest by primitive methods.

The upper classes are as enterprising and progressive as any social group in Central America. A large proportion of them have traveled abroad and have adopted foreign ways of living at home, and as a whole they have shown a responsiveness to new ideas and an energy and patriotism which promises much for the future of their country. The owners of the large plantations live in the cities, but they take a deep interest in the management and development of their properties, and usually spend a portion of the year upon them. Few are free from the Central American tendency to extravagance and improvidence, but they have nevertheless been sufficiently enterprising and progressive to maintain their dominant position in the economic life of the country while the resources of the other republics have been falling more and more into the hands of Europeans and North Americans. There are some rich agriculturalists who are foreigners, but they are relatively few as compared with those in Guatemala and Nicaragua. The great majority of the more valuable plantations still belong to citizens of Salvador, and much of the stock in the banks and in the more important industrial enterprises is controlled by native capital. This fact is of great significance, because it indicates that the people of the Republic have adapted themselves to modern conditions more readily than have their neighbors. The preservation of the class which furnishes the natural leaders and rulers of the community cannot but have a beneficial social and political effect.

The lower classes, housed in dirt-floored thatched huts, and subsisting on a diet in which the corn *tortilla* is the chief feature, offer a striking contrast to their wealthy and Europeanized superiors, but they are nevertheless somewhat better off than in any of the neighboring republics except Costa Rica. The majority of them have regular work on the plantations, where they are supplied with homes and food and receive wages which compare favorably with those paid in Honduras and Nicaragua. Their standard of living is somewhat higher than in those countries, and they are in general better treated both by their employers and by the authorities. A large proportion of the laborers on the bigger plantations are given patches of land to cultivate for themselves. In the central part of the country there are many small landholders, who find a ready market for their products in the cities, and are enabled by the possession of a regular money income to enjoy many little luxuries which are unknown in the more backward parts of the Isthmus.

In the cities, and especially in the capital, small-scale commerce and manufacturing are very active. Great quantities of vegetables, milk, firewood, and other country products are daily brought into town in ox-carts by the peasants, who exchange them for the manufactured articles which they need, and the market and the countless small stores in the vicinity are always a scene of great animation. There are a number of little manufacturing establishments, where candles, shoes, soap, and cigarettes are made, chiefly by hand labor, and the products of these are bought by the lower classes in surprisingly large amounts. Only a few of the smaller commercial establishments, however, belong to natives of the country, for the greater part of the retail trade is in the hands of foreigners.

External commerce has attained large proportions, despite the fact that the Republic has no access to the Atlantic. As in the other countries of the Isthmus, there are few North American merchants; and English, German, and Dutch houses control the import and wholesale trade. Until the outbreak of the European war, Salvador purchased a smaller proportion of her imports from the United States than did any of the other republics of the Isthmus, but this condition has necessarily changed within the last two years. Of the exports, the coffee, which is the only item of first importance, is shipped to some extent to San Francisco, but more to France and Germany.

Both external and internal commerce have been greatly aided by the fact that the territory of the Republic is so small, and that all parts of it are so close to the Pacific Coast. The problem of transportation has not been nearly so difficult as in some of the other countries. There are now few important towns which have no railway connection. The most important line is that of the Salvador Railway Company, an English corporation which provides a cheap, rapid, and in every way excellent service from the capital and Santa Ana to Sonsonate and Acajutla. Over this passes the greater part of the freight and passenger traffic, for Acajutla, although merely an open roadstead, where loading and unloading is difficult and expensive, is the principal port of the Republic. Another line is being built by the International Railways of Central America, the American concern which operates the Guatemala system, from La Union on the Gulf of Fonseca to San Salvador. This passes through many important cities in the eastern departments, and has now reached San Vicente, about forty miles from the capital. The service is not so good, and the rates are higher than on the Salvador Railway Company's line, and the usefulness of the road is greatly diminished by the fact that its builders have as yet failed to construct a permanent bridge over the Lempa River, to cross which freight and passengers must submit to a disagreeable and hazardous transfer in scows during the rainy season. It is, however, of immense importance to the rich sections through which it passes, and when it is completed, connecting the capital with the land-locked harbor of La Union, it will not only provide a new outlet for the commerce of Salvador, but will also open a much more rapid and convenient route to Honduras and Nicaragua, which are reached in a few hours by water from La Union. The same company plans to build a line from Santa Ana to Zacapa, on the Guatemala Railway, which will make both San Salvador and La Union accessible directly by railway from Puerto Barrios on the Atlantic. When this is done, the journey from the United States to each of the three central republics of the Isthmus will be shortened by several days.

Besides the ports mentioned, Salvador possesses two others. La Libertad, immediately south of the capital but separated from it by a steep range of hills, is an open roadstead from which a large amount of coffee produced in the neighborhood is shipped. El Triunfo, on a rather shallow bay east of the Lempa River, is close to another coffee-growing district, but it will have to be greatly improved before it can be made a regular port of call for large steamers. Both of these are connected with their tributary country by cart roads, which are good in the dry season, but become very bad when it rains.

As elsewhere on the Pacific Coast of Central America, there has been hardly any steamship service at these ports since the beginning of the European war except that of the Pacific Mail, whose ships touch there at irregular intervals and afford expensive and rather unsatisfactory accommodations for freight and passengers. The Pacific Steam Navigation Company also operates one small steamer, formerly the property of the Salvador Railway Company, between Panama and Salina Cruz, stopping at most of the ports on the way, and the government of Salvador owns a still smaller vessel which plies between the ports of the Republic and San José, Guatemala. Salvador suffers far more from the inadequacy of the West Coast steamship service than do any of the other countries, for Guatemala and Costa Rica have excellent connections with the United States and Europe by way of their Atlantic ports, and Nicaragua and Honduras have comparatively a small amount of foreign commerce. The Republic will not be able to develop as it should until its connections with the outside world are greatly improved.

The relations between Salvador and the United States have never been so close as in the case of those republics where more American capital has been invested and where regular and direct steamer communications have encouraged commerce and travel; and in recent years the friendship between the two countries has been endangered, although it has by no means been destroyed, by political questions. The influence exerted by the United States in the internal politics of some of the nearby countries, especially in the case of Nicaragua, and the proposal to establish an American naval base in the Gulf of Fonseca, close to the port of La Union, have greatly alarmed public sentiment in Salvador, and have called forth strong but ineffectual protests from her government. This fear of what the people of the Republic regard as American tendencies towards expansion has caused a rather marked distrust and dislike of the United States among certain classes,—a feeling which can be dispelled only by the most careful regard for Central American rights and susceptibilities in the future. With frankness and fair treatment on both sides, however, the relations between the two republics are bound to grow more friendly as they grow closer; for the influence of the increasingly large number of natives of Salvador who travel and study in North America, and of the Americans who are now in Salvador, should do much to bring about a better understanding.

The prospect for the future of Salvador seems very bright. Political and social conditions are improving steadily, and the prosperity of the Republic, with its fertile soil and industrious population, seems secure. The progressive spirit of the ruling classes and their rapid absorption of foreign ideas afford reason to believe that the control of the economic life of the country by foreign interests, which is becoming more and more marked elsewhere in the Isthmus, may here be avoided. The introduction of foreign capital is of course very necessary for the development of the country, as is the immigration of foreigners of the better class, but it is to be hoped that this may take place without resulting in the impoverishment and the decay of the leading native families. If the best people of the Republic can continue in the future to play the part which they play at present in politics and agriculture, the little country promises to remain one of the most prosperous and most civilized states in tropical America.

CHAPTER VI

HONDURAS

General Description—History—Effects of Continual Civil War—Lack of Means of Communication—Backwardness of the People—The North Coast.

THE territory of Honduras may be roughly described as a triangle, the base of which is formed by the shore of the Caribbean Sea, and the other sides by the Guatemala-Salvador boundary on the southwest and by that of Nicaragua on the southeast. At the apex, on the south, there are a few miles of coast on the Gulf of Fonseca which give the Republic its only outlet on the Pacific. The country is very mountainous, but, unlike its neighbors, is in no part of volcanic origin, for the chain of craters which elsewhere traverses the Isthmus several miles inland from the coast passes by Honduras through the conical islands of the Gulf of Fonseca, leaving the mainland entirely outside of the belt of decomposed tufas which forms the most fertile agricultural districts of other parts of Central America. There are thus none of the rich eruptive plains and gently sloping mountainsides which have encouraged the establishment of the great coffee and sugar plantations of Guatemala and Salvador and have made it possible for the regions near the Pacific Coast in all of the other countries to support dense populations. The southern portion of Honduras is occupied by a series of rugged mountain chains, where only small amounts of land in the valleys are suitable for cultivation and the rainfall is scanty and irregular. The first Spanish settlements were established in this district, notwithstanding the difficulties of raising food and transporting supplies from the outside world, because of the gold and silver mines, which in colonial times made Honduras one of the most important provinces of the Isthmus; and when the mines were abandoned, during the years of anarchy which followed the declaration of independence, the inhabitants still clung to their decayed villages and supported themselves as well as they could by agriculture. North of the continental divide, the mountains are lower and less precipitous, and there are great stretches of open savannahs and pine-covered hills, where the rainfall is plentiful and the grass is green at all seasons of the year. The soil is not very fertile, except in the river bottoms, but the region is admirably adapted for the raising of cattle. The cities of the south and of the interior are still the center of the political life of the country, but since the development of the banana trade they have been rapidly outstripped in economic importance by the newer towns created by foreign enterprise on the North Coast. The region near the Caribbean Sea is a low plain, extending for many miles into the interior, traversed by scattered mountain ranges and by several large, slow-flowing rivers. Here there are many settlements of North Americans, West Indian negroes, and natives, who are occupied chiefly with the cultivation of bananas.

The people are a mixed race. Spanish is the only language, and Catholicism the only religion, but even in the cities there are few persons who are entirely white, and in the country districts, although there are almost no pure-blooded Indians except on the uncivilized Mosquito Coast, the majority of the inhabitants have far more American and African than European blood. The aborigines of Honduras were never so numerous or so civilized as those of Guatemala, Salvador, and Nicaragua, and they were exterminated after the conquest to a somewhat greater extent than in those countries because of the hard labor in the mines; but their characteristics are nevertheless those which are most marked in the half-breed population of today. Negro blood also is very evident in the people in the regions north of the continental divide, and in many places, especially near the coast, seems to predominate over the other racial constituents. It was far easier for runaway West Indian slaves and other immigrants of the same color to reach the interior from the Caribbean Coast of Honduras than elsewhere in the Isthmus, because the country back of the coast line was more open and more attractive, to them, on account of its warm climate. What effect this element has had on the development of the Republic it is difficult to say, but it is possible that it may account in some measure for the backwardness of most of the regions in which it is found.

The central position of Honduras has forced her, whether she wished to or not, to take part in nearly every international conflict which has occurred in the Isthmus; and the continual intervention of her stronger neighbors in her internal affairs, combined with factional hatred and greed for the spoils of office on the part of her own citizens, have kept the Republic in a state of chronic disorder down to the present time. Because of the economic backwardness and the isolation of her people, she has been affected comparatively little by the factors which have in recent years tended to discourage internal disorder and civil strife in Salvador. Her government has never become so strong that it was able to repel aggression from without or to hold in check its enemies at home, and no part of her territory, with the possible exception of the North Coast, has reached a stage of agricultural or industrial development sufficiently high to give rise to a class of plantation owners or capitalists more interested in the maintenance of peace than in the dominance of one or the other political faction. She does not enjoy the favorable climate and the fertile soil which have encouraged the development of the great agricultural enterprises of the neighboring states, and she has been prevented from using the very valuable natural resources which she does possess by constant disturbances promoted both by external and by domestic enemies.

Dissensions within the country broke out soon after the authority of Spain was thrown off in 1821. The Spanish governor at Comayagua, who had already repudiated the authority of the Captain General in Guatemala, was opposed by the people of Tegucigalpa and several other towns, and his attempts to establish his supremacy were the beginning of a desultory conflict which lasted with few intermissions for a number of years. After the establishment of the Federal Union, Comayagua sided with the Conservatives and Tegucigalpa with the Liberals, and an army from the latter city, led by Morazán, played a large part in defending Salvador and in overthrowing the federal authorities in 1829. The triumph of the revolution in Guatemala led to the establishment of a Liberal state government in Honduras, but this fell after the disruption of the Union, when President Carrera of Guatemala aided the Conservatives to return to power (1840). From that time until 1911, the Republic was kept in a state of turmoil by a series of revolutions and civil wars, instigated and often actively participated in by Guatemala, Salvador, or Nicaragua, and sometimes by all three. Francisco Ferrer, supported by Carrera, held the supreme power from 1840 to 1852, first as president and then as commander-in-chief of the army. His successor was Trinidad Cabañas, a Liberal, who had been in office only three years when Carrera sent an army into the country to supplant him by Santos Guardiola. This ruler was assassinated in 1862. His successor, allying himself to Salvador, became involved in a war against Guatemala and Nicaragua, and the victory of the two latter states resulted in the "election" of José María Medina as president of Honduras. He was overthrown in 1872 by the intervention of the Liberals who had just returned to power in Guatemala and Salvador. Ponciano Leíva assumed the chief magistracy in the following year, but was forced to relinquish it in 1876 by the intrigues of President Barrios of Guatemala. Marco Aurelio Soto, a man of ability and great influence, succeeded him, but he was also forced to resign in 1883 because of the hostile attitude of Barrios, and was succeeded by Luís Bográn, who held office until 1891. Ponciano Leíva, who followed Bográn, was again forced to resign in 1893 by a threatened revolution. His successor, Domingo Vásquez, was overthrown a year later as the result of a disastrous war with Nicaragua, and Policarpo Bonilla, an ally of President Zelaya and an ardent Liberal, became president. After one constitutional term, he turned over his office to General Terencio Sierra. Sierra was overthrown in 1903 by Manuel Bonilla, who had started a revolution when the president made an attempt to impose on the country a successor of his own choosing.

In 1907, as the result of a quarrel between Bonilla and President Zelaya of Nicaragua, the latter sent an army into Honduras to aid a revolutionary movement headed by Miguel Dávila. Salvador, fearing the increase of Zelaya's influence, came to the aid of Bonilla, but was unable to prevent the complete victory of the revolution. Zelaya now threatened to attack Salvador, and the president of that country, in league with Guatemala, prepared to support a counter revolution in Honduras. A general Central American war would undoubtedly have followed, had not the United States and Mexico jointly interposed their mediation and suggested that all of the republics of the Isthmus send representatives to Washington to discuss the questions at issue between them. This was the origin of the celebrated Washington Conference. One of the most important conventions adopted by the delegates of the five countries provided for the complete neutralization of Honduras and the abstention of her government from all participation in the conflicts between the other governments of the Isthmus.[1]

This treaty had little effect for the time being on the situation of Honduras, for nearby countries encouraged and materially assisted a number of uprisings against the government of Dávila during the four years following 1907. Zelaya helped his ally to suppress these, but when the Nicaraguan dictator himself fell the fate of the administration which he had protected in Honduras was sealed. Manuel Bonilla invaded the Republic from the North Coast in the latter part of 1910, and decisively defeated Dávila's troops after a few weeks of fighting. When it was evident that the revolutionists were gaining the upper hand, a peace conference was arranged through the mediation of the United States, and both factions agreed to place the control of affairs provisionally in the hands of Dr. Francisco Bertrand. In the election which followed, Bonilla was made president by an almost unanimous vote. He held office until his death in 1913, when Dr. Bertrand, the vice-president, succeeded him. The latter is still at the head of affairs, having been reëlected in 1915.

Today, more than ever before, there seems to be good reason to hope that Honduras may enjoy a long period of peace. A large part of the people are wearied of the continual disturbance in which they have lived, and are beginning to distrust the factional leaders who have hitherto been able to incite them to revolt at every unpopular or aggressive action of the authorities. The government of Dr. Bertrand has pursued a conciliatory policy towards all political elements, and by treating its enemies with far less severity than has been customary in the past has given them little excuse for rebellion. The so-called parties of today have become little more than groups of professional office-seekers, without pro-

[1] For a more complete discussion of the Washington Conference, see Chapter X.

grams or permanent organizations. While many of the causes of discord at home have thus been removed, the external influences which have hitherto made stable government impossible have lost much of their importance in the last four years. The other governments have been prevented from encouraging or allowing the preparation in their territory of revolutionary expeditions against Honduras, or from intervening themselves in the internal affairs of their neighbor, by the attitude of the United States. The decisive intervention of that Republic in the last revolution in Nicaragua and the intimation, by a timely show of force, when outbreaks were threatened elsewhere, that similar action might be taken if it proved necessary, have had a salutary effect on potential revolutionists in all of the states of the Isthmus, for there are few Central American political leaders who desire to see the events of 1912 repeated in their own countries.

The government of Honduras has always been and is today a military despotism where all branches of the administration are under the absolute control of the president. Graft and favoritism are as much in evidence as in the neighboring countries, and the public offices, occupied exclusively by the friends of those in power, are swept clean and refilled after each successful revolution. Nevertheless, the country has had a series of able and patriotic presidents, who have done what they could, with the scanty resources at their command and in the face of very great difficulties, to encourage agriculture and commerce. Very real progress has been made in the field of education, and recently in the building of roads, and that more has not been accomplished has been due to the poverty of the national treasury, the waste of revenues by civil wars, and the deep-ingrained practice of graft in the public offices, rather than to any lack of progressive spirit. The idea of enriching themselves at the expense of the public is so much a part of the creed of the professional politicians who form the bulk of each party and the backbone of the revolutions to which each successive government owes its existence that it is impossible even for a president of the highest civic ideals to devote the entire resources of the government to internal improvements.

The effects of the disorder and misrule from which the Republic has suffered for nearly a century are most clearly evident in the southern departments and the interior, which are the home of the majority of the people. The mines, in which many of the inhabitants of the province had been employed in colonial times, were abandoned soon after the declaration of independence, and those who were dependent upon them were left to make a living as best they could. A large number joined the factional armies, which were hardly disbanded during the lifetime of the Central American Federation. Others turned their attention to agriculture or cattle raising, but did little more than secure a bare subsistence, working under a great disadvantage because of the impossibility of transporting their products to a market, and constantly facing ruin from the visits of revolutionary armies. Those who tilled the soil confined themselves to producing small amounts of corn, beans, and sugar from year to year for their own consumption. Conditions were more unfavorable for the establishment of large plantations than they had been in the other countries, because revolutions were more continuous and more destructive, and because there was in Honduras comparatively little land suitable for the cultivation of coffee, indigo, or sugar for export. The raising of cattle, which might otherwise have been carried on under very favorable conditions, especially in the open, grassy valleys of the Olancho, was made all but impossible by the civil wars, for no one suffers more from the passing of a Central American army than the herdsman. There are indeed many ranches in the interior and on the South

Coast at present, but they are run carelessly and with primitive methods. The owners, who have lost a large part of their stock time after time by military requisitions or by confiscation, make no effort to introduce animals of a better breed from abroad or to give their cattle more than the most elementary care, leaving the herds to wander in an almost wild state over great stretches of land, and only interesting themselves in them when they have occasion to drive a few hundred head to market. A slight change in this respect is even now noticeable, however, for some of the land-owners are beginning to pay more attention to the welfare of their stock and to fence in and otherwise improve their properties. If the Republic enjoys a few more years of peace, and if a better market can be provided abroad for live animals or beef, Honduras might easily become the most important cattle-raising country of the Isthmus.

Many of the mines were reopened by promoters from the United States in the last quarter of the nineteenth century, but the majority were abandoned a few years later because of the decline of the price of silver, which was the chief product. At the present time there are a number of companies and individuals extracting the precious metals on a small scale, but the only plant of real importance is that of the New York and Honduras Rosario Mining Company at San Juancito, near Tegucigalpa. The silver shipped by this one firm comprises almost the only important export of the southern departments, and nearly twenty-five per cent of the total exports of the Republic. There are very great undeveloped mineral resources, and many new mines would doubtless be opened if the difficulty of transporting machinery into the interior could be overcome, and if the political conditions of the Republic should be made sufficiently stable to encourage the investment of foreign capital.

One of the factors which has done most to retard the economic development of the country is the lack of means of communication. Tegucigalpa is now the only Central American capital which is not connected with at least one seaport by railway. Even ox-carts can be used only in a very few places in the interior, for the construction of roads between the principal centers of population has been more difficult than elsewhere in the Isthmus because of the greater distances to be traversed and the broken character of the country. The chief towns of the Republic are scattered from the Guatemalan to the Nicaraguan frontier and from the North Coast to the South, and the mountain ranges between them, although not so high as in the neighboring countries, are often so sharp and rugged that they are difficult to cross even on mule back. As has already been said, moreover, the expenditure of the energies of the people and the financial resources of the government on civil war has made it impossible to devote much attention to internal improvements. Transportation between the different sections, therefore, is principally by rough mule trails, but there is nevertheless one splendid highway, from Tegucigalpa to San Lorenzo on the Gulf of Fonseca, which has no equal in Central America. The regular services of motor cars and trucks on this route have greatly reduced the difficulty of transporting freight and passengers between the capital and its port of entry at Amapala, although the rates charged are exceedingly high, even as compared with those charged on Central American railways.[1] Similar roads are now being constructed, very slowly, from Tegucigalpa to Comayagua and to the Olancho, but they are so expensive to build and to maintain that it seems likely to be many years before those sections of the country

---

[1] The rates charged are equivalent to $10 in gold for each passenger, and $1.20 to $1.60 per hundred pounds for freight. The distance is eighty-one miles.

will enjoy communication by automobile with the capital.

Tegucigalpa, with the nearby municipality of Comayagüela, is a prosperous little town, with a thriving commerce and many families of wealth and culture, but outside of the capital, if we except half a dozen foreign settlements on the North Coast, there are few places which show any signs of contact with modern civilization. The majority of the people reside in the provincial cities, which are decayed villages of from three to five thousand inhabitants, or in still more desolate smaller settlements. There are also thousands of families scattered through the mountains, living in thatched *ranchos,* and subsisting almost entirely on the produce from their cornfields and plantain patches. Even the more important towns are almost entirely isolated economically and socially. A small amount of internal commerce is carried on by means of mule trains, and the mails are carried to almost all of the towns and villages with tolerable frequency and regularity, but the great mass of the people have little interest in anything outside of the community in which they live, and little conception of a world beyond the boundaries of their own country.

It is not surprising that people living under such conditions should have advanced little in civilization beyond their savage ancestors. Even those who might have risen above their environment, had they had the opportunity, have been kept down by almost insuperable obstacles. There is no incentive to improve agricultural properties, or to lay up a store of products for possible future needs, when all that a man has is likely to be taken from him at any time, and there is no object in raising more produce than is required for the support of the farmer's family when there is no market in which it can be sold or exchanged for other goods. It is dangerous and expensive to transport products from one part of the country to another where they may be needed, and there are few articles which the peasant can purchase when he does secure ready money. Little is manufactured in the country, and imports from abroad, by the time they have borne the heavy freights from North America and Europe via Panama to Amapala, the exorbitant charges of boatmen, brokers, and customs officials at that port, and the expense of transporting them into the interior, are beyond the reach of any but the rich. In the interior, one may ride in some places for days without passing a place where articles manufactured abroad can be bought, and those commercial establishments which do exist, outside of Tegucigalpa, carry only the most inferior textiles, machetes, and other necessities, together with a few very cheap articles of personal adornment, at prices from three to five times those which would be demanded for the same things in the United States.

Such conditions have inevitably condemned the people to a hand-to-mouth existence, which has eradicated all tendency to thrift. Improvidence, which seems to be an inborn characteristic of the Spanish-Negro-Indian population, has been encouraged by the ease with which the corn and beans necessary to support even a large family can be produced, for there is an abundance of unoccupied land in most parts of the country which can be cultivated with little labor by the primitive methods in vogue, and which will usually produce at least two crops each year. It would seem, therefore, that the people should lead an easy, if not an interesting existence, but the very conditions which have made it possible for them to secure a living with little difficulty have contributed to make them in some ways the poorest and most miserable of the *ladino* populations of the Isthmus. Unaccustomed to hard work or to taking thought for the future, they rarely plant more corn during the rainy season than is barely necessary to last them through the dry months, so that a drought or other mishap to their crops causes widespread want and suffering, aggravated by the difficulty of bringing food from other parts of the country where it may be abundant. There is no other inhabited part of Central America where the traveler finds it so hard to secure provender for himself and his mule as he does in most parts of Honduras during April and May.

As might be supposed, the people are densely ignorant and unprogressive. Schools have been established in many of the towns and villages, but the percentage of illiteracy in the community as a whole seems to be very high. Religion is at a low ebb, although one section of the Republic, around Comayagua, seems to be the most fanatically Catholic portion of Central America. Outside of the larger towns, there are almost no priests, and the people, although superstitious, pay little attention to the precepts of the Church. It must not be supposed, however, that the Honduraneans are necessarily inferior, intellectually or physically, to the inhabitants of the other republics. They are naturally quick and intelligent, and they are said to be as efficient laborers as any of the other Central Americans. Foreign mining corporations in all parts of the Isthmus prefer them to the inhabitants of any of the other countries as workmen, not only because of their greater skill, but because of their comparative trustworthiness. There is every prospect that they will advance rapidly in civilization when their country is brought into closer contact with the outside world.

The economic backwardness of the country, which is in itself an effect of the civil wars, is at the same time one of their causes. The great majority of the people have little to lose by internal disorders, for there are few who own more than a cheaply constructed adobe house and a small corn patch. They welcome a revolution, with its opportunity for plunder and for living at someone else's expense, as an agreeable change from the monotony of their lives and an opportunity temporarily to improve their condition. Among the upper classes in the cities, many of whom devote themselves to politics rather than to more useful occupations because neither large scale agricultural or commercial enterprises nor the learned professions afford a secure income, there is always a large number of discontented office-seekers, ready to engage in any kind of intrigue which offers an opportunity to make a living at the public's expense. The organization of a revolutionary conspiracy is thus an easy matter, and the raising of an army among the common people is hardly more difficult. Money and arms are secured from foreign corporations which desire special favors, and material and moral support can almost always be obtained from one of the other Central American governments. With so many circumstances in their favor, it is not remarkable that the party leaders have been able time after time to plunge the country into civil war, sacrificing its welfare to their own ambitions and rivalries, and frustrating the efforts made by their more patriotic and far-sighted fellow-citizens to improve their country's economic and social conditions.

Although at least eighty per cent of her people live in the central and southern departments, the most important portion of Honduras, from the point of view of the outside world, is the long coast line on the Caribbean Sea. This region is not only more productive than other parts of the Republic, because of its fertile soil and heavy rainfall, but it also has the immense advantage of being close to the Gulf ports of the United States, with which it is in regular communication by means of several lines of fast steamers. In recent years, its agricultural possibilities have been developed on a large scale by immigrants and capital from that country. Its ports, where English is the language most generally used and American influence is predominant, have become prosperous commercial towns, and one of them, La Ceiba, is the most important city in the Republic, after Tegucigalpa, and has more foreign commerce than all of the interior districts together.

The native element on the Coast is somewhat larger than in the similar sections of Guatemala and Costa Rica, because the government has opposed certain legal obstacles to the free immigration of West Indian negroes. This policy has enabled other sections to profit to some degree from the prosperity of the banana farms, because many laborers from the interior spend longer or shorter periods working there, earning wages far greater than they could secure at home. There is little commercial intercourse between the two sections of the country, however, as the roads which unite them are not suitable to any traffic other than pack and saddle mules. Travelers frequently make the journey from the United States to Tegucigalpa by the overland route, and the mails are brought over regularly from the weekly steamers which touch at Puerto Cortez, but almost none of the exportations or importations of the interior are shipped through the Caribbean ports. The North Coast had until lately little political connection with the other departments of the Republic, but within the last few years the government has established civilian officials and military forces there, and has endeavored to strengthen the feeling of allegiance among its inhabitants. The people of the banana district, and especially the foreign residents, have played an important part in recent revolutions, most of which have had one of the Caribbean ports as a base.

The bananas which are the principal product of the coast are raised and exported by numerous small growers and by a few great fruit companies, each of which possesses its own line of steamers and controls the agriculture and commerce of the district in which it operates. These concerns, nominally independent and competing, are generally supposed to be closely connected with, if not under the control of, the United Fruit Company, which itself has plantations and buys fruit at one or two places. The "United" has for some years been on unfriendly terms with the Honduranean government, and it is said that it prefers for this reason to operate through supposedly unrelated subsidiaries, which are in a better position than it could be to obtain concessions and privileges at Tegucigalpa. Most of these fruit companies have obtained concessions from the government under the terms of which they agree to build a railroad from the North Coast to some point in the interior, and receive in return the right to appropriate for their own use amounts of land varying from 250 to 500 hectares (that is, from 617.5 to 1,235 acres) for every kilometer constructed along the main line and its branches. They are allowed to improve the ports to which their steamers sail and to build wharves for the use of which they charge a fee to other exporters. The object of the government in making these contracts has been to provide means of communication between the Atlantic ports and the interior towns, with the idea of extending the railroads eventually to the capital, but the fruit companies, interested merely in securing land suitable for the planting of bananas, have usually built only those sections of their lines which are in low, flat country, and when this has been accomplished have turned their attention to the construction of branches through districts of the same kind. Most of them are under obligations to extend the railways to the interior towns within a certain term of years, but the government seems so far to have been unable to find means to give effect to this part of the contracts. The desire to secure railway communication between the capital and the North Coast has been so strong that valuable and far-reaching privileges have often been granted, with little consideration and with no effective safeguards, to companies which have promised more than they had any intention of carrying out; and other concessions, often actually prejudicial to the interests of the Republic, have been secured occasionally by foreigners who have aided revolutionary leaders in securing control of the government. Because of the lessons learned through many hard experiences with unscrupulous promoters, however, the native authorities are much more cautious of late about investigating the character and financial standing of persons applying to them for favors, and the majority of the contracts recently entered into have been more equitable in their terms and more explicit in their provisions than those of former years.

The North Coast not only exports bananas, but also small quantities of lumber, cattle, rubber, and other products. Special concessions have been granted from time to time for cutting mahogany and cedar, providing usually that the government shall receive five dollars, United States currency, for every tree; and contracts have been made occasionally with foreigners for the development of other natural resources. Since the beginning of the European war many of the planters, who have been unable to export their bananas because of the withdrawal of the steamers which had hitherto carried them to the United States, have turned their attention to the breeding of cattle and hogs, which thrive on the otherwise useless fruit, and which are readily sold either in Honduras itself or in the neighboring countries. This new industry has saved many of the foreigners along the Coast from the ruin which in 1914 seemed inevitable, and there is every reason to suppose that it will become more and more important in the future.

The commercial relations of Honduras with the outside world are small as compared with some of the neighboring countries. The chief exports, and almost the only ones which reach large amounts, are the bananas from the foreign-owned plantations on the North Coast and the silver from the one large mine already mentioned. The coffee crop, cultivated by primitive methods on small patches of ground, little more than suffices to supply the local demand. Other products,—hides, lumber, cocoanuts, etc.,—are shipped abroad in comparatively small amounts. The imports differ little in character from those of the other Central American countries. Their amount is small because the people have no crop which provides them with money for the purchase of foreign goods. The imports somewhat exceed the exports at the present time because of the railway material and mining machinery which is being brought in by foreign investors, and because a certain amount of goods is undoubtedly being paid for every year under present conditions by the shipment abroad of silver coin. By far the largest part of the Republic's trade is with the United States, and more than half of it is carried on through the North Coast ports, which have regular steamer connection with New Orleans and Mobile. The interior and the South Coast, which have no outlet at the present time except through Amapala, have few exports, and can buy little from foreign countries because of their poverty and because the expense of transporting goods from Amapala to the capital and from there to the interior towns is so great that most imported articles are far beyond the reach of the mass of the people.

In spite of the poverty which characterizes Honduras today, her future is not necessarily less promising than that of other parts of Central America. Her people are not backward because they are degenerate, but because they have been prevented from developing the natural resources of their country by the lack of means of transportation and by continual civil war. As has already been stated, they are by no means lacking in intelligence or ability. The country itself, perhaps, does not enjoy the natural advantages which have brought about the prosperity of some of its coffee-growing neighbors, but it nevertheless possesses great fertile tracts which are as yet hardly explored, and great undeveloped mineral resources, which will be opened to the world by the building of railways and the investment of foreign capital, if the present era of peace continues. There is no section of the Isthmus more favorably situated for banana growing, for cattle raising, or for mining than are the northern departments of Honduras. The Caribbean Coast, and the great plains and open valleys tributary to its ports, which are already more important commercially than the older settlements of the interior and the southern departments, seem likely in the near future to become the home of the larger portion of the Republic's inhabitants. If this occurs, and if the railways already under construction are extended through this region into the interior, there will be no other country of Central America so easily accessible from the United States and Europe, and none which should enjoy closer commercial and cultural relations with the outside world.

CHAPTER VII

COSTA RICA

Concentration of the Population in One Small District—Predominance of Spanish Blood—Social Conditions Resulting from Absence of Indian Laborers—Political Tranquillity—History—Character of the Government To-day—Foreign Commerce and Means of Transportation.

ALTHOUGH the territory of Costa Rica is approximately 23,000 square miles in area, nearly all of her four hundred thousand inhabitants, with the exception of some small groups of Indians and negroes who take no part in the political life of the country, live on one small plateau, from three to four thousand feet above sea level, surrounded by the volcanoes and ranges of the Central American *cordillera*. The population is so dense in this *meseta central,* as it is called, that it is seldom possible to walk more than a few minutes without passing a house. San José, Cartago, Heredia, and Alajuela, the four principal cities, are connected with one another by a single cart road less than thirty miles in length, and few of the smaller towns and villages are more than a day's walk from the capital. Almost every acre, in the valley and on the sides of the mountains, is used for agricultural purposes. The people have never shown any inclination to expand into the mountainous country to the southward, where communication with the towns would be rather difficult, or into the hot and insalubrious regions on the coasts. The Atlantic seaboard, as in the other Central American countries, is given over to banana plantations, owned and worked by foreigners; and the provinces bordering on the Pacific are sparsely inhabited by an unprogressive race who are largely of Indian descent. Both of these districts, because of their products, are of importance economically, but the social and political life of the country has its center in the cool and fertile *meseta central*.

Here there has grown up a nation which is entirely different from any of the other Central American republics. The Spanish pioneers who founded the city of Cartago in the latter part of the sixteenth century were unable from the outset to establish a colony similar to those in other parts of the Isthmus, because there was no dense agricultural population to be divided up as laborers among the settlers. Elsewhere the Indians, already living in large towns and devoting themselves to agriculture, had been forced with surprisingly little difficulty to work for their new masters; but in Costa Rica there were only a few scattered tribes, in a low stage of civilization, who cultivated the soil in a rude way simply to supplement their natural food supply obtained by hunting. Unaccustomed to steady labor, they were not promising material for a serf class like that existing at the time in Guatemala and Nicaragua. The settlers nevertheless introduced the *repartimiento* system immediately after their arrival in their new home, notwithstanding the royal order forbidding further enslavement of the Indians, and they are said to have treated those natives who were within reach with even greater cruelty than had been practiced in the other colonies.[1] In consequence of this oppression, the numbers of the aborigines decreased very rapidly, and the settlers found themselves forced more and more to do their own work, in spite of their efforts to replenish the supply of slaves with war captives from Talamanca and other unsubjugated districts. Indian labor seems never to have been a considerable factor in the economic life of the country.

At the present time there are few remnants of the

[1] See L. Fernández, *Historia de Costa Rica durante la Dominación Española*.

aboriginal tribes in the interior, although Indian blood is still very evident in the people of Guanacaste and other outlying districts. The inhabitants of the central plateau are distinctly Spanish in race and civilization. The white families, moreover, do not seem to be of the same type as those of Guatemala and the other countries. The majority of the people of Costa Rica, it is commonly said, are descended from *Gallegos,* one of the most law-abiding and hard-working of the numerous races that occupy the Iberian Peninsula, while those of the other countries are predominantly Andalusian. However this may be, the traveler cannot avoid noticing a certain dissimilarity in appearance and in customs and personal traits, between the prominent families of San José and those of other Central American capitals.

The absence of a large Indian population had an economic and social effect which can hardly be exaggerated. The unfortunate settlers of Costa Rica, throughout the colonial period, were in a condition which caused them to be pitied by all of their neighbors. Instead of living in large towns, supported by tributes brought in by the Indians of their *encomiendas,* the majority of the creoles found themselves forced to settle in the country, where each family raised by its own labor everything that it consumed. The harvests, as Governor Diego de la Haya reported in 1719, were gathered "with the personal labor of the poor Spanish settlers, because of there being very few slaves in all the province."[1] The colony was so poor that the name Costa Rica became a standing joke. Although there was plenty of food, clothes and other articles of European manufacture could be secured only with the greatest difficulty, because there were no exports with which they could be purchased. The people were almost completely shut off from the outside world. As those who could do so left the country, and there was no immigration, the

[1] Quoted by Fernández, *op. cit.* p. 316.

population grew very slowly. The little community was, however, spared the problems arising from the presence of a large class of laborers of another race, and the Spaniards, although they sank into a state of dense ignorance and were forced to adopt most primitive ways of living, acquired industrious habits which still distinguish them from their neighbors. Each settler cultivated a small amount of land, sufficient for the support of himself and his family, and was prevented from extending his holdings by his inability to employ laborers and by the fact that he had no market for his products. With the growth of the population, the entire *meseta central* eventually became occupied by little farms. There were a few wealthy and influential families, who had been given special privileges by the Spanish government, but they never occupied the dominant position which the aristocracy of Guatemala and Nicaragua had been able to assume, and the land which they held never amounted to more than a small portion of the cultivated area of the colony.

In colonial times, a large part of the land belonged to municipalities rather than to individuals. As the population expanded, it became customary to give to the founders of each new village a tract of land to be held for the common use, part of it to be divided among the inhabitants from time to time according to their ability to cultivate it, and part to be held as pasture or forest. In 1841 President Braulio Carillo ordered that a large portion of these *tierras ejidales* should become the property of those who were at the time cultivating them. This decree was later annulled, but a similar law was passed in 1848, permitting the cultivators to buy for a small price such parts of the common lands as they had fenced in and were using.[1] These measures resulted in a great increase in the number of small holdings.

[1] Costa Rica, *Colección de Leyes*, VI, 133; IX, 453.

The large uncultivated tracts owned by the central government have been sold at low prices to anyone who wished to buy them, or have been given away as premiums to encourage the planting of coffee or cacao. Many persons acquired large estates in this manner, especially during the last years of the nineteenth century, and a class of large landholders has thus gradually grown up. These have in most cases converted their properties into coffee plantations or cattle ranches, but many large tracts have never been brought under cultivation, because their owners have lacked the enterprise and the capital to do so. When the quantity of public lands in the more accessible parts of the country began to grow small, attempts were made to check the reckless sale of them to persons who did not intend to turn them to account agriculturally, and to encourage their division into small holdings. The amount sold to any one purchaser was gradually reduced, and in 1909 a law was passed giving each head of a family the right to claim fifty hectares of government land, free of cost, provided that he actually settle upon it and cultivate it. The greater part of the more favorably situated districts, however, have now passed into private hands, and the people show little desire to undertake the conquest of the inaccessible country outside of the *meseta central*. The establishment of new plantations and the opening of means of communication require more money and a larger labor supply than the natives of the country can provide. For these reasons, the legislation intended to increase the amount of the Republic's territory used for agricultural purposes has not been very successful.

Although there are now many large plantations scattered here and there through the country, the greater part of the *meseta central* is still divided into small farms. In the year 1906, there had been inscribed in the public land register 110,201 different properties, of which the average value was less than five hundred dollars American gold.[1] Even when allowance is made for the fact that there are many foreigners and rich natives, each of whom possesses a large number of separate properties, it is evident that an overwhelming proportion of Costa Rican families own their own homes. There is in fact practically no landless class, with the exception of a few thousands of laborers in the cities.

The political development of this compact community of white peasants has necessarily been very different from that of the neighboring countries, where a small upper class of Spanish descent had ruled and exploited many times its number of ignorant Indians and half-breeds. In Costa Rica the fact that nearly all of the inhabitants were of the same stock and had inherited the same civilization has always made the country more democratic, and has forced the class which controlled the government to consider to some extent the wishes and interests of the masses. The development of the Republic, unlike that of its neighbors, has for this reason been toward rather than away from the realization of the republican ideals held by the framers of the first Central American constitutions. The small landholders have always exerted a strong influence on the side of peace and stable government, for they have rarely joined in attempted revolutions, and have shown themselves inclined rather to take the part of the constituted authorities when disaffected politicians endeavored to plunge the country into civil war. Costa Rica has seen none of the protracted and bloody struggles which have darkened the history of the other republics, for the violent changes of government which have occurred from time to time have been effected rather by military conspiracies in the capital than by campaigns in the field.

The geographical situation of the Republic, moreover,

[1] For these figures, I am indebted to the kindness of Mr. Manuel Aragón, formerly director of the Costa Rican statistical office.

has enabled it to escape from the outside influences which until very recent years made the establishment of stable government almost impossible in other parts of Central America. At the southern extremity of the Isthmus, separated from its nearest neighbors by several days' travel through practically uninhabited territory, it has been able to hold aloof from the quarrels between the other republics, and has never been forced to submit to their intervention in its internal affairs. Costa Rica separated herself at an early date from the Central American Union, and has taken little part in the attempts for its restoration, for her statesmen have been unwilling to yoke their destinies with those of the turbulent communities north of them.

During the first years of Central American independence, the war between the imperialist and republican parties in other parts of the Isthmus had its counterpart in Costa Rica in a short struggle between Cartago and Heredia, which favored annexation to the Mexican Empire, and San José and Alajuela, which opposed it. The victory of the republicans led to the removal of the capital from Cartago to San José, where it has since remained. For nearly half a century the government was controlled by a few powerful families, among whom the most prominent were the Montealegres and the Moras, and the number of persons who participated in public affairs was very limited. The first president, Juan Mora, was successful in organizing a fairly efficient administration and in promoting the almost nonexistent commerce of the country, and Braulio Carillo, who took charge of the government in 1835, after two years of agitation and disorder, carried on the policy of his predecessor and laid the basis for the present prosperity of the country by encouraging the production and exportation of coffee, which rapidly became the Republic's chief crop. He also definitely established the capital at San José, although to do so it was necessary to put down an armed uprising by the other towns, which desired that the seat of the government should move from one place to another. Carillo was defeated for re-election in 1837, but he regained his position by a *coup d'état* in 1838 and for four years exercised dictatorial powers. During this period, the administration was reformed and made more centralized, the courts were reorganized and a penal code was drawn up, and Costa Rica's share of the debt incurred by the federal government was paid in full. Carillo was overthrown by a bloodless revolution in 1842, when Francisco Morazán, landing on the Pacific Coast, won over the chiefs of the army which the president sent against him, and occupied the capital. The victor had hardly reached San José when he began to raise troops and money for an attempt to re-establish the federal union, from the presidency of which he had recently been ejected by his enemies. Angered by this attempt to force them into a war of aggression on their neighbors, the people deposed Morazán and put him to death.

During the seven years which followed this revolution, continual quarrels between political factions and constant interference by the military leaders made it impossible for any administration long to maintain itself in office. In 1849, however, with the election of Juan Rafael Mora, another era of stable government commenced. The army was reduced to obedience, and order was restored throughout the Republic. During this administration, Costa Rica took the leading part in the war against Walker in Nicaragua. Mora was overthrown in 1859 by a conspiracy in San José, and two military chiefs named Blanco and Salazar, who were allied to the Montealegre and Tinoco families, came into power. Through their influence, José María Montealegre was made president. Mora, who had attempted an unsuccessful counter revolution, was put to death, and the members of his family were exiled.

The severity of the government's action aroused much bitter feeling, but civil war was avoided by a compromise, as the result of which Jesús Jiménez was elected president in 1863 and José María Castro in 1866. The latter was deposed by a pronunciamento of Blanco and Salazar in 1868, and Jiménez, as first designate, or vice-president, again took charge of the government. The new president made a determined effort to destroy the control which the army had been exercising over the administration, by removing Blanco and Salazar from their commands and forcing the other officers to obey the civil authorities. In doing this, however, he deprived the small group which had controlled the government for so many years of its chief support.

Jiménez was deposed in 1870. A handful of men boldly entered the artillery barracks, concealed in an ox-cart under a load of fodder, and seized them, and with them the control of the city, almost without bloodshed. The leader of the revolution was Tomás Guardia, an army officer, who, unlike Blanco and Salazar, had little political connection with the great families. This man was the real ruler of Costa Rica from 1870 until his death in 1882, although he did not at once assume the presidency. His government was a repressive military dictatorship, in which his own personal followers held all of the principal offices. The great families, whose leaders were exiled and deprived of their property, were reduced almost to insignificance as a political factor, and have never entirely regained their former influence. Guardia was succeeded after his death by his close associate, Próspero Fernández, who was at the time in command of the army. When the latter died in 1885, his son-in-law, Bernardo Soto, took charge of the administration as first designate, and caused himself to be elected president for the term beginning in 1886. These two rulers did much to improve the administration and the government finances, both of which Guardia had left badly disorganized. The administration of Soto was especially notable because of the work of Mauro Fernández, his Minister of Public Instruction, who for the first time established free and compulsory education throughout the Republic. The small group which had been in power, however, had made many enemies, among whom the most powerful were the clergy. The opposition grew so strong, as the election of 1889 approached, that Soto found himself unable to impose his own candidate on the nation without incurring serious danger of revolution. He consequently allowed the first comparatively free and popular election which the Republic had ever known, in which José Joaquín Rodríguez, the candidate of the clerical party, was victorious. Many of the partisans of the government desired to retain control of the administration by the use of force, but they were prevented from doing so by the firmness of the president and by the attitude of the country people, who rose in arms and prepared to march on the capital to enforce the verdict which they had given at the polls.

Rodríguez severely repressed all opposition, and governed during the greater part of his term without the aid of Congress. In 1894 he forced the legislature to elect his friend Rafael Yglesias to succeed him. During the latter's administration, the currency was reformed and placed on a gold basis, and the commercial and agricultural development of the country was promoted in many other ways. Yglesias was reelected in 1898, but in 1902 he turned over the chief magistracy to Ascensión Esquivel, who had been selected by a compromise between the government and its opponents.

With the election of Esquivel began an era of republican and constitutional government which was unprecedented in the history of Central America. Since

1902, the Republic has enjoyed an almost complete freedom from internal disorder, with perfect liberty of the press, and genuine, if somewhat corrupt, elections. Cleto González Víquez, who followed Esquivel in 1906, and Ricardo Jiménez, president from 1910 to 1914, were chosen by a majority of the voters in contests in which practically all of the adult male population of the Republic took part. Alfredo González, Jiménez's successor, was placed in office by Congress in 1914, after no candidate had received a majority of the popular vote. The legality of his election was considered doubtful, but he remained at the head of the government until January, 1917. His advocacy of radical financial reforms, including a direct property tax and a heavy progressive income tax, aroused much hostility among the wealthy classes and alienated several of the more influential political leaders, with the result that he was overthrown by an almost bloodless *golpe de cuartel* engineered by Federico Tinoco, the Minister of War. The latter was formally elected president of the Republic on April 1, 1917. Each of the recent rulers of Costa Rica has devoted himself with enlightened patriotism to promoting the welfare of the country, and great advances have been made in reorganizing the finances, in safeguarding the public health, and in providing for the education of the masses of the people.

The inhabitants of Costa Rica now enjoy more stable and more nearly democratic political institutions than any of their Central American neighbors. Constitutional government works in practice, and the letter of the law is generally respected, even though its spirit is often ingeniously circumvented. The president walks through the streets much like a private citizen, without fear of assassination or of being captured by his enemies, and the leaders of the opposition carry on their propaganda in San José without hindrance or persecution, and at times are even called in to consult with the president on matters of great importance. The press criticises the administration fearlessly and at times scurrilously, and animated political discussions may be heard every day on the principal corner of the main street of the capital. The elections are participated in by about as large a proportion of the entire population as in the United States.[1] If one candidate receives a majority of the votes cast, he becomes president, and if no absolute choice is made by the people, the question goes to the Congress, where it is decided by intrigues and deals between the political leaders. The administration is able to exert a decided influence in the selection of its successor through its control of the patronage and the army; but the final decision rests with the people or the popularly elected deputies, and it is not probable that any president would resort now to the forceful methods by which official candidates were placed in office a few decades ago. The only break in the peaceful development of constitutional government since 1902 was the *coup d'état* of 1917. That the dissatisfied party should have chosen violent means for obtaining control of the government, instead of waiting for the election which would have been held within a year, must be regretted by every friend of Costa Rica, but this very event nevertheless gave the people of the Republic an opportunity to show their capacity for self-government. Nothing could be more characteristic of Costa Rica than the whole-hearted co-operation of all political elements in the organization of the new administration, without either bloodshed or persecution.

Government by the people, however, has not really advanced so far as the number of votes cast at the elections would seem to indicate, for the great majority of the Republic's inhabitants still take little interest in political affairs. So long as order is maintained and

[1] In the election of 1913, 64,056 votes were cast. The total population in that year was estimated at 410,981.

their property rights are secure, they do not care particularly which group of politicians is in control and they are guided in voting more by the inducements held out by the rival candidates than by their judgments. Personalities rather than questions of national policy are the issue, for it is rarely that any candidate makes his campaign upon a definite political or economic platform. Between the elections, public opinion, although far more influential than in any of the other Central American countries, exercises little real control over the policy of the government. The newspapers are very widely read, and the people as a whole are remarkably well informed about current events, but the press nevertheless has comparatively little power, because no one believes in its impartiality or its incorruptibility.

The choice of candidates for public office and the conduct of the government are left almost entirely to a small number of landed proprietors, lawyers, physicians, and professional politicians residing in San José. These owe their influence partly to social position and wealth, but more especially to education; for although the members of the old principal families are still prominent, there are also many influential leaders who have risen from the lower classes by availing themselves of the educational advantages which the Republic offers to all its citizens. The ruling class is divided into a number of small political cliques, each of which professes allegiance to a party chief. As might be expected in an aristocracy composed chiefly of the leading people of a town of thirty thousand inhabitants, ties of blood and personal feeling play a very large part in the formation of these groups, especially as the prominent families are very large, and each is closely related with the others by intermarriage. A leader is often able to derive the major portion of his strength from his relatives alone, for the aid of ten or fifteen active and popular sons or sons-in-law, together with that of several score of brothers and cousins and nephews, is not to be despised in a country where there are at most only a few hundred active politicians. Besides his relatives and his intimate friends, however, each party chief has also a number of followers who are attached to him by the hope of obtaining employment in one of the government offices, for a very large number of persons among the upper class have little occupation aside from politics, and little income beyond that derived from official positions when their friends are in power.

The various leaders may have different political ideals and economic theories, which to some extent influence their relations to one another, but it can hardly be said that any of the present parties have definite principles or programs. Each desires primarily to win the elections in order to put its followers in office; and the platforms and the utterances of the leaders are shaped with this end in view, with the result that they receive little attention and less credence. When it is necessary in order to obtain control of the government, leaders of widely different points of view will join forces without any suspicion of inconsistency, and it is no very uncommon occurrence for a prominent member of one party to join another and very different group, because of a quarrel with his former associates or simply because the change improves his chances of advancement. Sectional jealousy is no longer a force in politics, since the capital has so far outstripped the other towns in population and wealth, and religious questions are rarely injected into the campaign. Attempts have been made to organize a popular party among the laborers and peasants, and this party has achieved some notable successes at the polls, but its policy when in power is very similar to that of the other factions. There is in reality little ground for political rivalry between the different classes of the population.

The so-called parties have so little permanent organization that they can hardly be said to be in existence during the greater part of the presidential term. About a year before an election, the heads of the stronger groups, who are often perennial candidates, begin to organize their own followers, and to bargain for the support of the less powerful leaders, with a view to inaugurating their campaigns. Committees and clubs are organized in each town and village, and desperate efforts are made to secure the support of influential citizens who are not permanently affiliated with any party, and to arouse the interest of the voters in general. Processions and serenades are organized to show the popularity of each candidate, and orators are sent to every town and village on Sunday afternoons to entertain the voters with abuse and denunciation of the rival aspirants. Party newspapers are established, but they confine themselves to printing long lists of local committees and adherents and to describing meetings and ovations. One may search their columns in vain for serious discussion of the issues of the campaign. Several of the regular newspapers take sides more or less openly, while others maintain an ostensible neutrality, but the press as a whole seems to have little influence over the voters. As the contest progresses, feeling runs higher and higher among the politicians, and the voters become first interested and then excited. The meetings and ovations, the continual political arguments on the streets, resulting in an occasional riot, and the wholesale treating by the party workers in the drink-shops, distract the attention of the people from their ordinary occupations, and temporarily disorganize the entire community. Elections are therefore looked forward to with a certain amount of dread by the more respectable classes.

Since the adoption of the law of 1913, the President, the members of Congress, and the municipal *regidores* have been chosen by direct popular vote instead of by electoral colleges. The balloting takes place on the same day in all parts of the country. Each citizen must inscribe his choice in a book where all may read it, and every party has representatives at the polls to secure fair play. This system prevents fraudulent counting, but it also encourages corruption and the exercise of improper influence on the individual elector. Bribery is practiced openly and on a large scale by all parties, and the voter is often prevented from exercising his own discretion in casting his ballot by the fear of offending the local authorities or other powerful personages in his village. The amount of intimidation and coercion, however, is insignificant as compared with that in the other republics, and attempts to influence voters by such means are generally condemned by public opinion. The president is prevented by the constitution from seeking his own re-election, but one of his associates is usually frankly supported by the administration as the official candidate, and thus has an immense advantage over his opponents, even though recent presidents have refrained from using the army and the police to interfere with their enemies' campaigns or to keep the adherents of the opposition party away from the polls on election day.

The large supplies of money which are perhaps the most important factor in the campaign are obtained by contributions from members of the party, who hope to obtain offices for themselves or their friends in the event of a victory, and from native and foreign business men who desire special concessions. The banks of San José usually assist one candidate actively though secretly, and considerable amounts are also obtained from certain rich speculators, in return for favors contingent on the election of the candidate whom they support. Consequently a new administration comes into office bound by numerous more or less improper pledges, and burdened by a considerable party debt. After the election of 1913-14, the victorious group liquidated a portion of its financial obligations by a levy on all office-holders, who were presumably the chief beneficiaries of the party triumph.

The choice of the voters does not always inspire the respect which it would in a democracy more conscious of its power and more jealous of its rights. The people of Costa Rica have more than once shown that they were ready to compel respect for their will when their interests were at stake, but as a rule they are disposed to recognize any administration which controls the capital, regarding civil war, with its attendant destruction of crops and livestock, as a greater evil than submission to an illegal government. It is not strange, therefore, that a defeated faction should occasionally attempt to seize the barracks in San José by force or by strategy, or that the president should exact conditions from an opponent victorious in an election before turning over to him the command of the military forces. No candidate opposed by the government has ever obtained the presidency without either making a compromise with his predecessor or else overcoming the latter's resistance by force, for even the freely elected presidents of the last decade have in every case had the approval, if not the active support, of the previous administration. The strength of the government, however, in reality rests far less upon the army than upon the disapproval of the people as a whole of any attempt to displace the constituted authorities in a disorderly manner, for the army itself is almost insignificant as a military force. There are a few troops in the barracks of the capital, but elsewhere order is maintained entirely by the civil police. It is a proud boast of the Costa Ricans that their government employs more school teachers than soldiers.

The President of the Republic has an almost absolute control over the machinery of the government. He not only appoints all administrative officers, but also in practice exercises a dominant influence over the deliberations of the Congress, where his ministers initiate the most important legislation. Even when his personal followers do not have a majority in the Chamber, he can usually command one by the use of patronage or of money from the treasury, which is often paid to the Deputies in the form of fees for professional services to the government. As party lines break down soon after an election, the minor political leaders who make up the legislative body are apt to be influenced less by hostility to the administration than by a desire to maintain their following in their own districts by securing public works for their towns and employment for their constituents. In times of emergency, moreover, the Congress itself frequently vests the President with practically absolute power, as it did when the country was passing through the economic crisis which followed the outbreak of the European war.

The Judicial Department, however, is far more nearly independent of the Executive. The Supreme Court, which is elected by the Congress every four years during the political slack season in the middle of the presidential term, appoints and removes all subordinate magistrates throughout the Republic. Politics enters very little into the composition of this body, partly because of the strong sentiment in favor of a non-partisan judiciary, and partly because party lines are almost non-existent at the time when the judges are chosen. The subordinate positions are also saved from the spoils system which rules in other departments of the government, although it is inevitable that purely personal considerations should enter to some extent into the appointments. The administration of justice is on the whole prompt and efficient, although the magistrates are not always distinguished for erudition or ability and those on the supreme bench sometimes show a human desire to make sure of their re-election as the time for this draws near, by keeping on good terms with the President and with the members of Congress. They are generally honest and impartial in their decisions, however, and their incorruptibility, with hardly any exceptions, is undoubted. That not only the people themselves but also the foreigners in the country have confidence in the courts is shown by the fact that there has been a conspicuous lack of the complaints of denial of justice which have complicated the relations of some other Latin American republics.

The local administration is highly centralized, but the people of each district enjoy a certain amount of local self-government through their municipalities. The representatives of the central government are the executive officers of these bodies,[1] and the Department of *Gobernación* has a final veto over all their acts, but the *regidores* are freely elected by the people of each town and village, and have very wide powers in matters of purely local interest. The lack of funds, however, arising from the fact that the municipalities have no source of revenue except certain license fees and fees for public services, forces them to leave to the central government many of the functions which are assigned to them by the constitution, and especially the support and direction of almost all the more costly public works, and at the same time makes them politically subservient to the President and the Congress, which can provide or withhold appropriations for local purposes. President Alfredo González attempted to make the local units truly autonomous, by authorizing them, in the fiscal legislation passed just before his fall, to levy direct taxes upon their inhabitants by adding a percentage to the national direct taxes.

The central government itself, thanks to a long period of internal peace and to the patriotism and ability of the men who have been at its head, has reached a high degree of efficiency and of usefulness to the community.

---

[1] In this Costa Rica differs from the other republics, where the *alcalde* and the local representative of the central government are two distinct persons, theoretically independent of one another.

Private rights are generally well protected, and the oppression of private citizens by the officials, while not unknown, is unusual. The security of persons and property is guaranteed by a well-organized police force, a fairly efficient judiciary, and an excellent land registry system. In spite of the difficulties presented by the mountainous character of the country and by six months of heavy rains every year, the Republic possesses a fair system of highways, although in this matter there is still room for improvement. The government-owned and operated railway from San José to the Pacific Coast compares favorably, at least in the service rendered, with those controlled by foreign corporations in other parts of Central America. There are sewers in the larger towns, and aqueducts supply healthful drinking water even in the small villages. The public health is also protected by a rigid quarantine service, by a veterinary service which inspects live cattle and meat, and by the regulation of contagious diseases and prostitution; and the government employs forty physicians in various parts of the country who treat the poor in their districts free of charge. Many of the public services, because of the lack of experience and training on the part of the officials, and because of the poverty of the government, are still in an unsatisfactory state, but they at least show an earnest desire on the part of the authorities to promote the welfare of the country.

During the last three years, remarkable progress has been made in improving sanitary conditions. The campaign against the hookworm, inaugurated in 1914 with the aid of the International Health Commission of the Rockefeller Foundation, already promises to effect an incalculable change in the condition of the country people, an immense number of whom suffer from this disease. The representative of the International Health Commission has been made the head of an official department under the Ministry of Police, and all local health officers

158   THE FIVE REPUBLICS

and police officials have been placed under his orders to assist him in the examination and treatment of patients and the execution of sanitary measures designed to check further spread of the disease. At the same time, he has been made Director of the School Medical Corps, in which capacity he has done much to secure proper care for the health of the children and to improve hygienic conditions in the schools. With the earnest co-operation of the government, notable results have been obtained even in the short time which has elapsed since the work was begun. It is impossible to estimate what the final effect of work such as this will be, for the extinction of the hookworm alone, to say nothing of the other results of the campaign of medical education and sanitary improvement which has been undertaken, cannot but have a lasting effect on the happiness of the people and on their capacity for labor.

The field of activity in which the rulers of Costa Rica have perhaps shown the most interest has been that of education. Its school system gives the Republic one of its strongest claims to be ranked among the progressive communities of the world. The nation which a century ago was so illiterate that it was difficult to find enough men who could read and write to fill the public offices, now provides free and obligatory instruction for all of its citizens, with a primary school in every settlement where there are thirty children to attend it. In 1915, there were 1,108 teachers and 34,703 children in the public schools.[1] New buildings and equipment are being secured as fast as possible, and new courses of technical and agricultural training are being introduced everywhere. There are five institutions for the secondary education of both sexes, two in San José, and one each in Cartago, Heredia, and Alajuela, offering instruction similar to that given in American schools. These have somewhat over eight hundred students in all. The latter

[1] Costa Rica, *Anuario Estadístico*, 1915.

are chiefly from the middle classes in the towns, but the brighter children from the country schools are also encouraged and financially aided in continuing their education after they complete the primary course. A national normal school has recently been established in Heredia to provide teachers for the entire system. Besides the government institutions, there are schools of law, pharmacy, music, fine arts, textiles, agriculture, and domestic science, most of them in San José, which receive some aid from the treasury. How high the percentage of literacy is, is attested by the large circulation of newspapers in the country districts.

An examination of the work of the government shows that the men who control the destinies of the Republic, however regrettable their political methods sometimes are, do not seek power solely for their own profit. If there is a large amount of favoritism and graft in official circles, there is also much progressive spirit and true patriotism. Most of the government employees are appointed for political reasons, but they ordinarily perform their duties with as much energy and zeal as can be expected in tropical America. Public money is often misused, and improper considerations sometimes govern the letting of contracts, but public works are nevertheless well executed. Wholesale theft from the treasury, which is too often regarded with cynical indifference in other parts of the Isthmus, would not be tolerated by public opinion in Costa Rica.

Costa Rica's freedom from internal disorder has enabled her to attain a prosperity which has entirely transformed the backward and poverty-stricken community of colonial days. In 1821, her people had almost no means of communication with the outside world. They produced nothing which they could export, and they were separated from either coast by several days of difficult and dangerous traveling. Commerce with the outside world, however, began soon after the declaration of independence with the development of the growing of coffee, which was exported for the first time in 1835.[1] The importance of this crop increased rapidly, especially after the construction of a cart road, which was completed in 1846, to the Pacific port of Puntarenas. The Costa Rica berry soon acquired and still holds a high reputation in the European markets.

The exporters at first encountered great difficulty and expense in shipping their product, which they had to send around Cape Horn, or later by the expensive route of the Panama Railway. The government, therefore, early endeavored to provide more adequate means of transportation. In 1871, work on a line from Puerto Limón on the Caribbean Sea to the capital was begun by Mr. Minor C. Keith. After difficulties which seemed almost insuperable had been overcome and thousands of lives had been sacrificed in the deadly lowlands of the East Coast, through train service to San José was finally opened in 1890, and the Republic found itself for the first time in direct communication with the United States and Europe. The railway, which still carries the greater part of the imports and exports, was leased in 1905 for a period of ninety-five years to the Northern Railway of Costa Rica, a concern owned by the United Fruit Company.

It was while building this road that Mr. Keith began to plant the banana farms which later developed into the enormous Caribbean properties of the United Fruit Company. Costa Rica still leads the Central American republics in the production of this fruit. Almost the entire East Coast has now been brought under cultivation, and English-speaking communities of Americans and Jamaica negroes have grown up everywhere along the railroad and its numerous branches. In spite of the ravages of the disease which has attacked the older plantations, more than eleven million bunches of bananas were

[1] Bancroft, *History of Central America*, Vol. III, p. 653.

exported from Limón and its tributary ports in 1913,[1]—a quantity the immensity of which can only be grasped when we realize that it would provide approximately a dozen bananas for every man, woman, and child in the United States. The Fruit Company is of course very powerful in this region, where even the police duties of the central government are to a great extent exercised through its agents. In the interior, the "United" has less influence. It has many friends as well as enemies among the party leaders, and it has not encountered so intense a spirit of jealousy and hostility towards foreign enterprises as is found in certain of the other republics; but whatever efforts it has made to influence the outcome of presidential and congressional elections, in order to be in a more advantageous position to ask concessions from the government, have usually been conspicuously unsuccessful.

In addition to the Northern Railway, the Republic has another line, owned and operated by the government, from San José to Puntarenas on the Pacific Coast. This also was commenced during the administration of General Guardia, but it was not completed until 1910. Being shorter and on the whole less expensive to operate than the Atlantic road, it should eventually become a formidable competitor of the latter when adequate transportation is provided by way of the Panama Canal.

In the last decade of the nineteenth century, when the price of coffee in the world's markets was high, the Republic enjoyed an era of great prosperity. The wealthier families were able to travel and to study abroad as they had never done before, and both society and the government entered on a period of extravagance, of which the magnificent national theater in San José is an enduring memorial. When the coffee prices fell, there was a reaction which checked the development of the country's natural resources. The area under culti-

[1] Costa Rica, *Anuario Estadístico*, 1913, p. xxxvii.

vation in the interior has now remained practically the same for many years, and the exports of coffee, which have declined in value, have increased little or not at all in quantity.[1] During this time, many of the more prominent native families have become impoverished, and the upper classes as a whole have hardly shown either the energy or the adaptability necessary to maintain their political and economic leadership under modern conditions. They devote themselves to politics and to the learned professions, but there are now comparatively few of the wealthy landholders who form the most influential class in the other Central American republics.

Banking, commerce, and mining are almost entirely in the hands of foreigners, although the majority of the coffee plantations are still owned by citizens of the country. These immigrants have identified themselves more completely with the community than in any of the other republics, often intermarrying with the natives and taking a prominent part in local affairs. San José, although not so large or so wealthy as Guatemala or San Salvador, is more like a European city than any other capital in the Isthmus.

The industrious, sturdily independent peasant class in the country districts has been little affected by the changes which have taken place in the cities. Through-

[1] The annual exports of coffee averaged 13,478,941 kilos, valued at 8,835,726 colones for the ten years 1891-1900; and 14,478,605 kilos, valued at 6,709,767 colones for the ten years 1901-1910. (Costa Rica, *Resúmenes Estadísticos*, 1883-1910.)

The exportations in the years 1912-1915, according to the *Anuario Estadístico* for 1913 and for 1915, were as follows:

Year.	Kilos.	Value in colones.
1912	12,237,875	7,623,561
1913	13,019,059	7,752,750
1914	17,717,068	10,028,731
1915	12,206,357	8,022,166

It should be noted that the value of the colon in 1915, and during a part of 1914, was approximately 20 per cent less than under normal conditions.

out the *meseta central* there are countless small farms, which not only supply their owners with corn, beans, and sugar cane for food, but at the same time frequently produce a small amount of coffee, which is sold to the proprietors of the large cleaning mills to be prepared for export. The farmers not only cultivate their own properties, but also work for several days in each week on the larger plantations. As wages are fairly high, they thus have a money income which enables them to live far better than their brothers in the neighboring countries. Most of them can read and write, and they are able to give their children educational advantages little inferior to those enjoyed by country people in any other part of the world. During the last few years, as we have seen, they have even acquired a not inconsiderable political power, which will become more important as they become more experienced in its use. It is these small landholders who have made Costa Rica what she is today, and who offer the strongest guarantee for her future.

CHAPTER VIII

THE ESTABLISHMENT OF A CENTRAL AMERICAN FEDERATION

Strength of the Unionist Idea—Breakdown of the First Federation—Attempts to Establish a New Union—Obstacles to the Formation of such a Union at Present—Advantages which would be Derived from Federation—The Attitude of the United States.

THE ideal of uniting Central America under one government has been one of the strongest forces which have influenced internal politics and international relations in the Isthmus from the declaration of independence down to the present day. Realizing that the five countries can never be really independent of one another, and that the interests of all would be best served by joining forces for their common ends, the majority of their statesmen have always been, and are today, perhaps more than ever, desirous of seeing them transformed from a group of small, disorderly republics into one strong nation, able to promote the interests of its people and to command respect from foreign powers. Such a nation, with its five millions of inhabitants, its fertile soil, and its great natural resources, would, they believe, be able to assume a position of importance in the councils of Latin America and to make great strides towards better government and towards a more complete realization of economic opportunities at home. In the last five years especially, increasing contact and occasional friction with other powers have drawn the five states closer together than ever before, for the problems created by the invasion of foreign financial interests and by the intervention of foreign governments in their internal affairs have made them realize more than ever the dangers to which their divided condition and their quarrels among themselves expose them. The pressure from outside has given rise to a stronger sentiment of their common nationality and to a fuller realization of the identity of their interests than could exist while they were still almost shut off from intercourse with other countries.

There are many influences which make the relations between the five countries closer than those which ordinarily exist between neighboring independent states. Their administrative union during the three centuries of Spanish rule and their entry together into the family of nations not only created a strong sentimental tie between them, but also gave rise to political problems common to them all, and to political parties which regarded not individual states but the Isthmus as a whole as their theater of activity. The factions which arose during the years of the Federation kept up an international organization after the dissolution of the central government, and Conservatives in Guatemala, or Liberals in Salvador and Nicaragua, interfered from time to time to promote the interests of their parties in other countries throughout the nineteenth century. Even at the present time, each state has too much interest in the internal affairs of its neighbors to remain indifferent when revolutions or other political changes occur. As a result of this situation, men of the same way of thinking have been brought into closer relations with one another, and have been made to feel, by their co-operation for common political ends, that they were, in fact, citizens of one Central American nation. This feeling has been strengthened by the custom of exiling the leaders of the defeated party after revolutions, which has encouraged travel from one country to another, and by the fact that many of the prominent families of the Isthmus are related to one another by intermarriage. The five republics, moreover, are all confronted with the same economic problems, in developing their natural resources, improving their agricultural methods, and securing capital for the construction of railroads and other public works; and they have much in common in their civilization, and especially in the customs and ways of thought of the upper classes, despite the wide divergences between them in racial and social conditions.

In 1821, when the authority of Spain was thrown off, it was supposed as a matter of course that the provinces of what had been the Viceroyalty of Guatemala would continue to be united under one government. The Constituent Assembly which met after the dissolution of the short-lived union with Mexico was therefore following the logical course laid down for it by the history and the existing political organization of the five countries, as well as by the ideas of the political theorists among its members, when it adopted a constitution providing for a federal republic. The stormy history of the government thus established has already been sketched. The Federation fell to pieces partly because of local jealousies and the conflicts of local interests, and partly because of faults in its constitution and weaknesses in its administration. The civil war which existed in almost all of the states, and the strife between the different departments of the central government itself, made it impossible for the latter to establish a constitutional regime or permanently to exercise any real power. The states, jealous of the control of their affairs from Guatemala, respected the orders of the federal authorities only when it suited their convenience to do so; and these authorities, in order to maintain their position, were forced to intervene in the internal affairs of the states to establish administrations subservient to their wishes. There was thus a series of revolutions and counter revolutions, until within a few years both the national and local governments had become mere despotisms which depended for support solely upon the federal army. It was impossible for a centralized military regime to exist very long in a country where means of communication between the different sections were so inadequate, and where the centrifugal forces were so strong as they were in the turbulent, mutually jealous communities of the Isthmus. The federal government had less and less real power after the first term of President Morazán, and in 1840 it disappeared entirely with the expulsion of its representatives from Central America.

The disastrous failure of the federal republic convinced many of the statesmen of the Isthmus that their countries would be better off as separate states. This feeling was especially strong among the Conservatives in Guatemala, who for more than thirty years were the greatest obstacle to the restoration of the Union. The great families' opposition to a political connection with the other states seems to have arisen from the memory of the expense to which they had been put in supporting the federal authorities before 1829, and of their sufferings at the hands of the Liberals from Honduras and Salvador, who overwhelmed and subjugated them in that year. Costa Rica, at the other extreme of the Isthmus, had also withdrawn formally from the Federation, inspired by motives much similar to those which actuated Guatemala. Unlike the latter country, however, she was able because of her isolated position to remain entirely aloof from the political struggles elsewhere, and only on one or two occasions was forced to take notice of the agitation to which the activities of the Unionist party periodically gave rise.

Salvador, Nicaragua, and Honduras, on the other hand, refused to accept the dissolution of the first union as a final settlement of the relation of the states to one another. Many of the leaders in those countries had taken part in the defeat of Morazán, but they had done so from personal hostility to the federal president rather than from a desire for the destruction of the federal government. The restoration of the Union was championed by the Liberal party, but it was also favored by many of the Conservatives, despite the influence exerted upon the latter by their allies in Guatemala. There were a number of factors which tended to draw the three central republics together. With their *mestizo* population, they resembled one another in their economic and social conditions far more than they resembled Guatemala, with its primitive Indian tribes, on the one hand, or white Costa Rica on the other; and thus no one of them was influenced, as were those countries, by a consciousness that its internal problems were entirely different from those of its neighbors. Furthermore, their jealousy of the superior power of Guatemala, and the alarm caused by Carrera's repeated interventions in their affairs during his dictatorship in that country, greatly strengthened their desire to unite their forces for purposes of mutual defense. Great Britain's aggressions on the East Coast of Nicaragua and Honduras had the same result after 1848. Between 1840 and the invasion of Nicaragua by Walker in 1854, hardly a year passed without the meeting of a congress to discuss plans for forming a union, at least between these three countries. As a rule these congresses adjourned without achieving any definite result, finding their work made hopeless by the intrigues of the separatist party in Guatemala and by the mutual mistrust of the participating states, but twice a federal government in which neither Guatemala nor Costa Rica was represented was actually established. A third attempt to unite the central republics was made forty years later, at the end of the nineteenth century.

The history of these abortive unions affords an instructive illustration of the influences which have kept the five states apart. In 1842, delegates from Salvador, Honduras, and Nicaragua met at Chinandega, in the last named republic, and adopted a treaty providing not so much for a central government as for a confederation, in which each state was left free to manage its own affairs, even to the extent of carrying on diplomatic relations and making war. The only common authority was a council, consisting of one delegate from each republic and presided over by a Supreme Delegate, and a supreme court chosen by the state legislatures. This government sent troops to aid Salvador in a war between that country and Guatemala in 1844, and finally succeeded in bringing the war to an end through the mediation of Frutos Chamorro, the Supreme Delegate. The confederation came to an abrupt and disastrous end in the same year, however, when Salvador and Honduras attacked Nicaragua because the latter had granted asylum to political exiles from these countries.[1]

In 1849, the central republics again signed a treaty of confederation which provided for common action in foreign affairs and a union for purposes of defense. Their action was inspired by the encroachment of Great Britain on the territory of Nicaragua and Honduras on the Mosquito Coast. The council of commissioners to which the management of the affairs of the confederation was intrusted accomplished little; but in 1852, in the face of renewed foreign complications, a diet met at Tegucigalpa to make the union between the three countries closer and to establish, if possible, a real federal government. The diet elected a president, and adopted a constitution giving that official power, not only to represent the three republics in their dealings with foreign powers, but also to intervene by force in the internal affairs of the states, when it was necessary to maintain order. Disapproving of this provision, Salvador and Nicaragua refused to ratify the constitution, and the diet dissolved.[2]

Although the Conservatives of the central republics had been less hostile to the restoration of the federation

[1] See Bancroft, *History of Central America*, Vol. III, p. 188ff., and A. Gómez Carillo, *Compendio de la Historia de la América Central*, pp. 219, 304-305.

[2] Bancroft, III, p. 209; Gómez C. pp. 306-307; J. D. Gámez *Historia de Nicaragua*, 575.

than were the great families of Guatemala, they took little interest in plans for a union after these two failures. During their thirty years' rule in Nicaragua, therefore, that country did not enter into another attempt to accomplish what was regarded as primarily the ideal of the opposite party. With Salvador and Costa Rica, in fact, it opposed and defeated the projects of Rufino Barrios in 1885. It was not until the accession of President Zelaya that the Nicaraguan government again showed itself ready to enter into projects for the restoration of the federation. In 1895, the representatives of the three central republics, meeting at Amapala, drew up a treaty establishing a diet, composed of one member from each country, to which was intrusted the conduct of their relations with one another and with other nations. This body was to elaborate a definite plan for a closer, permanent union.[1] The federation assumed the name "Greater Republic of Central America," and at once took steps to enter into diplomatic relations with the powers.[2] During the next two years a constitution was drawn up, and in the autumn of 1898 an executive council, with far broader powers than the old diet, was installed in Amapala. It had scarcely assembled, however, when the party opposed to the union in Salvador overthrew the government of that state, and declared the federation at an end. The council called upon the presidents of Nicaragua and Honduras to send troops to uphold its authority, but neither executive was willing to make war upon the new government of Salvador. The union was consequently dissolved.[3]

The failure of the federations created by the treaties of 1842, 1849, and 1895 did not indicate that a real union of the five countries would be impracticable, because a

[1] For the text of this treaty, see U. S. Foreign Relations, 1896, p. 390.
[2] President Cleveland recognized the Greater Republic on Dec. 24, 1896. Ibid, p. 369.
[3] Ibid., 1898, p. 172; Gómez C. *op. cit.* p. 310.

real union was not attempted. The political leaders who were in control in Salvador, Honduras, and Nicaragua theoretically favored the establishment of a central government, but they were loath to surrender to it any real power or to confer upon it any right of control over themselves. They insisted upon keeping the management of the state armies, finances, and administrative machinery in their own hands, and they therefore conferred upon the federal officials only an indefinite authority, backed by no military force, which they respected and supported only so long and in so far as it suited their own interests to do so. The unions thus established were not nations, but mere leagues of independent states. Each came to an inglorious end as soon as the rapid changes of Central American politics brought to the front in one of the states an administration which was not in sympathy with the men who controlled the central government.

The apparent impossibility of restoring the federation by the voluntary action of the five republics convinced many of the strongest advocates of a union that their ideal could be realized only by the use of force. It was this belief which led Rufino Barrios, the first great Liberal president of Guatemala, to embark on the disastrous adventure which caused his death. Soon after his accession to power, Barrios endeavored to persuade the presidents of the other republics to agree to some form of federation. The latter declined to enter into any definite treaty, although negotiations upon the subject were carried on intermittently for several years. The United States, when invited to participate in these efforts, declined to interfere, although warmly approving the plan for a union.[1] The equivocal attitude of his neighbors, and their refusal either to agree to or to reject his proposals, finally convinced Barrios that the people of the Isthmus favored his plans, but that the govern-

[1] See U. S. Foreign Relations for 1881 and following years.

ments would consent only if they were compelled to. On February 28, 1885, therefore, he announced that he had assumed command of the military forces of the Central American Federation, and invited the other states to recognize the new government, and to send delegates to a constituent assembly which was to meet in Guatemala City in May of the same year. Honduras expressed approval of his action and placed troops at his disposal, but all of the other countries of the Isthmus at once began to raise armies to defend their independence. President Zaldívar of Salvador, upon whose aid Barrios had confidently counted, yielded to the popular demand for resistance to the aggression of that republic's traditional enemy, and sent an army which defeated the forces of Guatemala at Chalchuapa, on April 2, 1885. The death of Barrios in this battle disheartened his followers, and put an end to a war which could not have failed to have involved every section of the Isthmus if it had continued.

An ambition to place himself at the head of a restored Central American nation has influenced more than one Central American president in his dealings with the neighboring countries. Few have actually gone so far as Barrios did, but the same idea which inspired the Guatemalan leader has often influenced powerful rulers to intervene openly or covertly in the internal affairs of the other states, and has thus frequently been a cause of revolutions and international wars. The most recent attempt to unite the five countries by force was made in 1907. In that year President Zelaya of Nicaragua overthrew the government of President Bonilla in Honduras, and set up a new one, under Miguel Dávila, which was practically controlled by himself. He then proceeded to attack Salvador, inspired by the idea of establishing a Central American union,—an idea which, as he said, was at the time being advocated with enthusiasm by the press of Central America, the United States, and

Mexico.[1] The war which followed was brought to an end by the mediation of President Roosevelt and President Porfirio Díaz.

At the Washington Conference, which met a few months later, the delegates of Honduras, supported by those of Nicaragua, formally proposed that a treaty of union be signed, and stated that the presidents of those countries were ready to lay down their offices if that were necessary to make the execution of the treaty possible. This motion nearly caused the disruption of the conference, for the delegates from Guatemala opposed it, and those from Costa Rica objected even to its being discussed. The representatives from Salvador, who were at first inclined to favor the plan, voted against it as inopportune after receiving instructions to do so from their government, and the matter was finally dropped. The arguments advanced by the advocates and the opponents of this project give a good idea of Central American opinion in regard to the establishment of a union. Señor Fiallos, one of the delegates from Honduras, emphasized the necessity for a federation to put an end to the wars between the states. These, he said, were only civil wars which had crossed the national boundaries, for there were no real antipathies or conflicting interests between the various countries. He dwelt upon the expense of keeping up five separate governments and armies,—an expense which prevented the use of the national revenues for the development of the country. The majority of the committee appointed to consider the matter, on the other hand, admitted that the Union was the greatest and noblest aspiration of Central American patriotism, but affirmed that it could not be brought about until the economic, moral, political, and material conditions of the five republics had been harmonized. It recommended for the present the discussion of measures which might prepare the way for the Union,

[1] See his annual message to the Nicaraguan Congress, Dec. 1, 1907.

such as the improvement of communications, the encouragement of the coasting trade, the establishment of uniform fiscal systems and customs duties, the holding of annual Central American conferences, and the creation of a court of compulsory arbitration.[1]

There seems little probability that a stable and enduring federal government could be established in Central America at the present time. Even a union brought about by the voluntary action of the five countries would almost inevitably fall to pieces sooner or later, however patriotic the spirit which presided at its formation. The centrifugal forces would be no stronger, perhaps, than they were in the North American states before 1787, but they would be fatal because it would be impossible to provide political machinery for settling them. The establishment of a constitutional and orderly administration for the five states together would be as difficult as it has been for each state alone, for the mere fact of union could effect little change in political methods or political morality, and none in the capacity of the people for self-government. The nature of the economic and social conditions in the four northern countries makes it inevitable that any administration under which they were united, if at all centralized, should be a regime of force, similar to that which already prevails in each country. Real elections could no more be held throughout the entire Isthmus than they can be held in any one state today, and in the absence of elections there would be no means of changing the authorities of the federation except by revolution or by a compromise, not between three or four political groups, as in Nicaragua or Honduras today, but between a large number, few of which could be represented in the new government. The unfriendly feeling between different sections, which is still strong among both the upper classes and the common people, and the inevitable jealousy of the small

[1] U. S. Foreign Relations, 1907, II, pp. 669, 721.

states towards the larger ones would sooner or later cause dissatisfaction with the working of the federal system, and quarrels over such questions as the distribution of offices and the expenditure of money on internal improvements. These difficulties would be intensified by the differences in civilization, and consequently in political requirements and in points of view between the more and the less advanced republics. It is hard to see how these conflicting interests could be reconciled by a government whose officials and subjects have as yet never learned the value of compromise, or the necessity of respecting the will of the majority and the rights of the minority.

The obstacles to the formation of a permanent union by the voluntary action of the five states would be still greater in the case of one brought about by force. An able leader, supported by the unionist party in each of the countries, might impose a federal government on the entire Isthmus for a time, but he would meet with immense difficulties in upholding his authority against hostile political groups because of the difficulty of sending troops and supplies from one section to another. While it endured, his regime could only be a personal one. The dissatisfied elements might be held in check temporarily, but they would tear the Union to pieces with the more fury when the ruler who had founded it was forced by his death or by a defeat at the hands of his enemies to relinquish his hold upon the supreme power.

The difficulties in the way of uniting the five republics would not be insuperable if the ruling classes were genuinely ready to co-operate in realizing the national ideal, but the men who enjoy the high offices and the control of the revenues of the state governments show a decided reluctance to giving up any of their power for the common good. The local political groups and the influential families would necessarily be reduced to a position of far less importance if the union were accomplished; and the realization of this fact makes many of those who are most enthusiastic in their advocacy of a Central American Federation slow to take any definite steps towards its realization. It is not difficult for the state authorities to frustrate the endeavors of the Unionist party, because the common people and even the majority of the upper classes show little real interest in the measures which are from time to time proposed for actually bringing the five republics together. Educated and patriotic people, at least in the four northern countries, express themselves in favor of union, but they nevertheless bring little influence to bear on their governments to support projects aiming to bring nearer the time when a Central American nation can be established. The international conferences provided for by the Washington Conventions of 1907, to take a recent example, met regularly for several years to discuss the common interests of the five republics and to formulate plans for bringing them closer together, but they were finally suppressed because the state authorities had failed, apparently from pure indifference, to carry out any of their excellent and for the most part perfectly practical recommendations. The realization of the national ideal will not be possible until this indifference disappears and a broader patriotism takes the place of the jealousy and mistrust which influences the relations of the states to one another at the present time.

Moreover, a permanent union will be all but impossible until a change has taken place in the political conditions of the Isthmus. No central government could long endure unless it commanded the active support of a strong party in every one of the states, and such a party could hardly exist on the basis of cliques, resting largely on local feeling and personal and family ties, such as those which today dominate the political affairs of the five republics. An administration set up under present conditions could only maintain itself by playing off against one another the rival factions in the states, thus bringing about a situation similar to that which caused unbroken turmoil during the life of the first federation. To secure a solid basis for the creation of a Central American nation, the control of politics must be taken out of the hands of the factions as they are at present organized, through an increased participation in the government by the people at large. The spread of popular education and the introduction of foreign ideas throughout the Isthmus makes such a change by no means a distant probability. When it takes place, questions of personal and purely local interests, which are now so prominent in affairs of state, will be relegated to the background, and one of the forces which operates most strongly to keep the states apart will thus be removed.

The relations between the five republics would be closer if the means of intercommunication were better. Although each country possesses railroads and cart roads, which give the majority a comparatively adequate internal transportation system, they are connected with one another only by the roughest of mule paths. Very little commerce passes over these, and journeys overland from one capital to another are beset by many difficulties. Travelers from one country to another, in fact, almost invariably prefer to make use of the expensive and not very comfortable steamers which run at rare and irregular intervals between the ports of the West Coast. This lack of transportation facilities not only tends to isolate the five republics from one another, but also makes much more difficult the problem of establishing a government able to exercise an effective military control over all of them. The gradual improvement of interstate communications will overcome this difficulty, and will also make possible a far greater interchange of products.

The strong unionist sentiment which exists in the four northern countries is not shared by the people of Costa

Rica, who regard the idea of throwing in their lot with that of the other republics with an aversion which makes their participation in the re-establishment of the federation very doubtful. The Costa Ricans, having successfully held aloof from the disorders in other parts of the Isthmus, have little desire to accept any plan which might involve them in the quarrels of their neighbors. They are loath to exchange their free institutions for the military government which prevails around them, or to give up their position as an independent nation to become an unimportant part of a country in which a majority of the inhabitants, and therefore presumably of the voters, would be backward *mestizos* or uncivilized Indians. Rather inclined to be self-centered and self-satisfied, they show little sympathy with the nationalist aspirations of their neighbors, and they are perfectly contented, for the present at least, to continue their peaceful development in their own way.

The free people of Costa Rica could hardly be expected to submit to such a government as social conditions have made inevitable in some of the republics. The differences in the internal situation of the five countries are really the most discouraging obstacle to the realization of the dream of Central American Union. Guatemala, for instance, with forty per cent of the inhabitants of the Isthmus, must under any fair plan of organization have a preponderant influence in the councils of the federation. Her wealth and her dense Indian population, which is more pliable in the hands of the officials than are the *ladinos* of the other countries, would give those who controlled her administrative machinery a dangerous power when dissensions arose within the federation. It is unthinkable that elections there should be anything but a farce for generations to come, for the Indians, untouched for the most part by the changes which are improving the position of the common people in other parts of the Isthmus, must for a period impossible to calculate remain under the political control of the upper classes. For the smaller and weaker countries, therefore, the union would present many very serious dangers. Human ingenuity could hardly devise a form of government able to maintain itself against disaffected factions, and to cope with the conditions existing in the less advanced parts of the Isthmus, which would at the same time be acceptable to the people of the more enlightened sections.

The realization of this difficulty has led many Central American leaders to advocate a confederation, in which each state should be left free to manage its own affairs, rather than a centralized federal government. As we have seen, however, unions of this kind have several times been attempted, and have in every case been a failure. The states which were parties to them showed little respect for the central authorities, and refused to allow the latter to exercise any real power. On several occasions, war broke out between the very states which were parties to the confederation. No Central American Union, while present political conditions continue, can be permanent or beneficial unless the government is given real power, not only to represent the Union in international relations, but also to maintain order and enforce the law throughout its territory. If the individual states retained the control of their military forces, or if they were under administrations which were not in harmony with the national authorities, the federation could only expect a short and stormy life. To establish a decentralized administration would be to invite disaffection and revolution, for each local government would become almost inevitably a center of intrigues against the *status quo*. It is only necessary to recall the history of the first Central American Federation to appreciate the dangers which a half-way measure of union would involve.

The union of the five republics under a central

government strong enough to maintain order and make itself respected would in many ways greatly improve their position. One nation of five million inhabitants, with a rich territory 172,000 square miles in area, would be in a far better position to deal with the rest of the world commercially and diplomatically than five petty states whose quarrels make them one another's worst enemies. If the peoples of the Isthmus were able to present a united front, instead of intriguing with foreign governments against one another's tranquillity or forcing those governments to intervene in Central American affairs by inciting revolutions or engaging in wars against neighboring states, one of the most serious dangers which today threatens their independence would be done away with. Other countries would of course rather deal with one central authority than with five petty ones. The United States especially, which cannot remain indifferent to the disorders arising from the dissensions and the rival ambitions of Central American rulers, because of its immense interests in the Caribbean Sea and the obligations which it assumed in connection with the Washington conventions of 1907, could not but welcome any change which promised to make for peace.

The suppression of the present governments, with their heavy expenditures, would effect an economy which would be of the greatest importance to countries suffering from so many financial difficulties as do those of Central America. In the first place, the cost of maintaining five separate presidents, with their suites, cabinets, and diplomatic corps, which is one of the heavy burdens upon the national treasury today, could be eliminated, and many other unnecessary officials could be dispensed with. Military expenditures could also be cut down, for the armies of the several states are maintained in part at least for use against one another. With the money thus saved, the improvement of means of communication and the development of natural resources could be undertaken on a larger scale than ever before, and could moreover be carried on without encountering many of the obstacles which interstate jealousy now puts in the way. Much more progress than is possible at present could be made in such matters as public instruction, sanitation, and the encouragement of agriculture; and problems like the development of markets for Central American exports and the protection of the national resources against excessive exploitation by foreign capitalists could be dealt with more effectively by united action. To obtain these benefits, however, there must be a central government able to preserve order and to make its authority respected in all parts of the Isthmus, for one which could not fulfill these requirements would be worse than none at all.

Projects for the federation of the Central American republics have always aroused a friendly interest in the United States, where there has been a hope that the Union would promote the stability and the political and economic progress of the Isthmus. As early as 1859, President Buchanan secretly offered to support Juan Rafael Mora, who had just been exiled from Costa Rica, in an attempt to make himself president of a restored Central American Union, promising to aid him by sending two warships as an evidence of moral support. Mora refused, however, on the ground that such a Union, even if it could be established, would in the end be harmful to the best interests of Costa Rica, which would be involved by it in the civil wars of the other countries.[1] Some years later, Secretary Blaine expressed the sympathy of the State Department with Barrios' projects for uniting the five countries, although

[1] Manuel Argüello Mora, the Costa Rican president's nephew and constant companion, gives an account of this interview, at which he was present, in his "*Recuerdos é Impresiones,*" p. 66.

he declined to intervene or to express approval of the use of force in accomplishing them.[1] In 1907, before and after the Washington Conference, there was a considerable amount of discussion of the question in the United States both by officials and by the press.

More recently, the intervention of the United States in the international affairs of the Isthmus, and even in the internal affairs of some of the republics, has made its attitude towards the question of re-establishing the Union more important than ever before.[2] Many of the leading statesmen of the Isthmus believe today that the establishment of a strong and permanent federal government can only be brought about through active aid from Washington. On the other hand, it has been vehemently asserted that the establishment of what is virtually an American protectorate over Nicaragua has made it impossible that the other countries should join in any union with her until the policy of the United States is reversed, since they would subject themselves by doing so to the same foreign domination. Whether this view is entirely justified may well be doubted. In the first place, no permanent political connection between the United States and Nicaragua has been established, or is likely to be established. The government of the North American Republic has indeed intervened in Nicaragua to prevent revolutions, but it seems probable that it would be forced to do as much in any other Central American state where similar conditions existed. The arrangements with the North American bankers, which have aroused so much opposi-

---

[1] See U. S. Foreign Relations for 1881 and the years immediately following, under Guatemala.

[2] According to press dispatches dated August 31, 1917, the five Central American governments are planning to hold a congress in the near future to renew the conventions adopted at Washington in 1907, and to discuss plans for a closer union between the states. It is said that all of the other republics have accepted the invitation of the government of Honduras to send delegates for this purpose.

tion in Central America, are primarily of a financial character. It would be idle to deny that they constitute infringements of Nicaragua's sovereignty, but they can be brought to an end at any time when the Republic is ready to repay the money which its government has borrowed and to buy back the national property which has been sold. It is ridiculous to suppose that either the United States or the bankers have any ulterior political purposes, or that their aim has been other than the improvement of the economic situation of Nicaragua. The treaty providing for American control of the canal route and for a naval base in the Gulf of Fonseca has caused bitter controversies, but it is difficult to see how it can have a permanent adverse influence on the question of the Union. The United States has no interest in Central America more important than that of aiding the five republics to become strong, prosperous, and well-governed commonwealths, and it is therefore impossible to suppose that it will be hostile to any movement which promises to improve their situation.

The unionist idea is one which should command the sympathy of everyone interested in the future welfare of the people of the Isthmus. As we have seen, a stable federation, established upon an equitable basis, and accepted by all of the five republics, could not but greatly improve their situation, making them less exposed to aggression and interference from outside, and encouraging their internal economic and social development. The establishment of such a federation seems impracticable at present, and an attempt to unite the five countries, whether by force or by the voluntary action of their governments, would probably result in more harm than good. But the time when a strong and progressive Central American nation can be founded seems to be drawing steadily though slowly nearer, and the forces which are now at work, changing the internal and the international situation of the five republics, may bring about the consummation which so many of their statesmen desire, sooner than now seems possible. Every friend of the Central American countries must hope that this will be so, in order that the dangers to which they are now exposed through their own divisions and weaknesses and through the inability of some of them to afford protection to the life and property of foreigners may be averted.

CHAPTER IX

THE CAUSES OF CENTRAL AMERICAN REVOLUTIONS

Civil War as a Characteristic Central American Political Institution—Character and Extent of the Conflicts—Forces back of Them: Unfitness of the People for Democratic Government, Oppression by the Party in Power of its Enemies, Rivalry for Office, *Personalismo* and *Localismo*—Indifference of the Mass of the People—Hope for Improvement—Effects of Contact with the Outside World.

THE most important fact in the history of the Central American republics, from their declaration of independence down to the present time, has been the almost continuous civil war from which the majority of them have suffered. Their inability to establish stable governments has retarded their economic and social progress in the past, and is a menace to their welfare and even to their national existence today. The development of agriculture, the building of roads and railroads, and the civilization and education of the masses of the people, have been discouraged, both by strife between factions at home and contests with neighboring governments, and by the misrule resulting from the predominance of the military elements which have been brought to the front by the premium which these conflicts have placed on armed force. The weakness of the five countries, moreover, has frequently exposed them to acts of aggression from foreign powers, and in recent times their very independence has been endangered because the apparent incapacity of most of them for self-government has led to a general belief in Europe and America that they must one day fall under the control of some stronger power. Under modern conditions, it is impossible for a government which cannot maintain order and secure to the lives and property of foreigners the protection which international law demands to expect that its rights of sovereignty, or even its territorial integrity, should be scrupulously respected by governments which are more powerful and better organized. The elimination of internal disorder is therefore one of the most serious problems which confronts the people of the Isthmus.

If one asks the average Central American, whether of the educated classes or of the common people, what has been the principal cause of the revolutions which have occurred in his country, he will almost certainly answer: the ambition of professional politicians and the abuse of power by the government,—the desire of each member of the ruling class to hold office, and the tendency of each administration to use its authority for the personal benefit of those who control its policy and for the gratification of their hatred of their opponents. The force of this reply can be readily appreciated by one who has seen the conditions which exist in some of the five republics, but the causes assigned are nevertheless hardly adequate to explain the extreme prevalence of internal strife in the five republics. There are many countries with perfectly stable governments which are cursed with politicians more ambitious and more selfish than those who have been prominent in revolutions in Central America, and many also where the opponents of those in power are treated with far more severity than falls to the lot of the defeated party there. The reasons given indicate, perhaps, the motives which actuate those who participate in each revolt, but they do not explain the underlying causes which have made uprisings against the government more frequent in Central America than in almost any other part of the civilized world. These causes must be sought, not in the aspirations and immorality of any one relatively small group of men, such as that which figures in Central

American political affairs, but rather in the nature and working of the governmental institutions and in the economic and social condition of the people as a whole.

The way in which revolution became the only means by which the political institutions of the five republics could be worked has already been described. The constitutions which were drawn up for the federal government and for the five states in the years 1823-25 provided, as we have seen, for the choosing of the more important officials by popular elections; but the holding of real elections soon proved to be impossible, because of the ignorance and indifference of the great majority of the people, and the lack of experience in self-government among the ruling classes. The parties which were contending with one another for the control of the government soon yielded to the temptation to employ force and fraud to attain their ends; and the voting for officials consequently became, first an occasion for periodic disorders, accompanied frequently by an appeal to arms, and then a mere farce, in which the triumph of the administration candidate was assured by the pressure exerted by the government. Within a few years after the declaration of independence, force had come to be recognized as the only means by which power was secured and held, and revolution was not only the sole remedy for bad government, but the one way in which a change of officials could be effected. Civil war was thus an indispensable part of the political system.

Revolutions were of almost yearly occurrence throughout the Isthmus during the first half century after the declaration of independence, for the development just described took place in each of the five countries. In some, however, there was early apparent a tendency towards avoiding actual warfare, so long as the established government pursued a policy which made its rule tolerable to the parties not represented in it. Even when disaffection grew so strong that a change was inevitable, attempts were usually made to bring about a compromise. Force still remained the basis of all authority, and potential revolution the only corrective of bad government, but actual fighting between the factions was rare. In Costa Rica, where this tendency was strongest, practically no blood has been shed in political quarrels for nearly sixty years. Nicaragua and Honduras, on the other hand, have had frequent and sanguinary revolutions throughout their history as independent nations. This difference between them and their peaceful neighbor is enough to indicate that other factors, besides the mere impossibility of changing their governments except by force, have contributed to make them turbulent. Before attempting to explain what these factors are, however, it is necessary to understand the nature of Central American revolutions and the character and the motives of the persons who participate in them.

In the first place, it should be borne in mind that the average revolution is not a movement which embraces a very large number of people or which calls into play deep economic or social motives. The countries themselves are very small, for the largest barely exceeds fifty thousand square miles in area. In all of them, except Salvador, much of the national territory is so sparsely settled, and often so impenetrable and unhealthful, that it hardly enters into consideration as a theater of military operations. Of the total population, which is probably not more than 600,000 in Nicaragua, Honduras, or Costa Rica, only a very small portion is sufficiently interested in politics to participate voluntarily in a civil war. Revolutionary armies, therefore, rarely reach any great size, and they rarely need to in order to succeed. The military force of the government is small, ill-equipped, and poorly trained, and not infrequently part of it proves disloyal in a political crisis.

Although it is impossible to estimate with any degree of accuracy how many soldiers are actually under arms at a given time in such countries as Nicaragua or Honduras, it seems very doubtful if the total exceeds two or three thousand, and these are scattered through the country to such an extent that a much smaller revolutionary force, sometimes of less than a hundred men, can seize and hold an important strategic point before the government has time to rally its forces. After an uprising has started, both sides fill their ranks by voluntary recruiting and impressment, but neither is able to raise or to fit out any army which would seem very formidable to a single well-trained regiment. It is only necessary to recall the stand which William Walker, with a few hundred dissolute and undisciplined adventurers, was able to make against the combined military power of the five republics, in order to appreciate the actual force at the disposal of a Central American government. Yet these governments are nevertheless able to suppress the greater part of the revolts which occur against their authority.

The spirit which causes the revolutions is not often one which arouses very much enthusiasm among the people at large. Their leaders are usually inspired by a thirst for offices and spoils or a desire for revenge against political rivals who have oppressed them, and the rank and file are actuated mainly by sectional or class jealousy, but rarely by any genuine political motives. There are of course many men in politics who seek to obtain control of the government, even by revolution, in order to effect economic and social reforms. Generous and patriotic ideas are found both among the chiefs and their followers in all parties, but they play a smaller part in actually bringing about a revolt than do the less creditable but still very human motives upon which the political parties are built up.

Revolutions are rarely the result of a widespread conspiracy among the people. Even a large portion of the active members of the party interested often know little about the plans of the leaders until an armed uprising has already taken place. The procedure followed is much the same in nearly all cases. A group of factional chiefs, with a few score of their more intimate personal followers, raise the standard of revolt with a pronunciamento against the government, naming one of their number as provisional president. An attempt is made either to seize from within some town in which the revolutionary party is particularly strong, or to invade the country from outside, occupying one of the seaports as a base of operations. The latter is perhaps more common, because the important members of the opposition party are generally in exile. The revolution not infrequently gains its foothold, as did that of 1909 in Nicaragua, through the treachery of local authorities who turn over to it the soldiers and the military supplies under their control, or by the disaffection of high officials sufficiently influential to carry with them a considerable part of the army. Arms and supplies are secured from some neighboring government which has reasons for wishing to overthrow the existing administration, or from foreign corporations and speculators who wish concessions or special privileges. A revolt often attains formidable proportions in this way before the government can raise and equip an army to send against it, as it usually starts in regions remote from the capital, where it is able to consolidate its forces before it meets with serious opposition. In the districts still under the control of the authorities, meanwhile, martial law is proclaimed, known or suspected adherents of the party responsible for the revolution are thrown into jail, horses and other property are requisitioned for the army, and every able-bodied man of the laboring and artisan classes, except those who succeed in concealing themselves, is pressed into service as a soldier. The result, of course, is an immediate paralyzation of agriculture and commerce. A revolution thus begun often lasts several months before there is a decision, although only a few battles are fought, and only two or three thousand men, and often less, are engaged on each side. If the rebels win a few successes at the beginning, or if the government is unable to defeat them after a prolonged campaign, the president usually falls, because of his loss of prestige and because of the defection of the always numerous politicians who desire above all else to be on the winning side. When this occurs, there is a complete demoralization of all of the departments of the administration, accompanied, not infrequently, by a split in the victorious party or a counter revolution on the part of the defeated. Order is not restored until one strong leader or group of leaders has established himself or itself in complete military control.

Since these revolutions are the work of so small a proportion of the people, their causes must evidently be sought not so much in any inherent disorderliness and lawlessness of the nation as a whole, as in the questions which have divided the classes interested in politics, and in the conditions which have made it possible for these classes to plunge the community into civil war time after time by their incessant feuds, without being effectually checked by the desire of the rest of the country for peace.

The instigators and leaders of Central American revolutions are in almost every case the pure-blooded, or nearly pure-blooded, descendants of the *conquistadores,* and one of the chief causes of these phenomena must therefore be sought in the characteristics which the creole aristocracy has inherited from its sixteenth century ancestors. Among the Spaniards who founded the colonies on the Isthmus there were a few respectable families, but the majority were adventurers, fugitives from justice, and soldiers who had been left without occupation by the cessation of the wars against the Moors, and came to America in search of excitement and easily gained wealth. In exploring and subjugating the Indian kingdoms, they showed a bravery and an indomitable energy which have few parallels in history, but as colonists they were turbulent, lawless, and unprincipled. Their cruelty towards the Indians has already been described. Their dissensions among themselves, before the government at home had firmly established its military control over them, forecasted what might be expected when the authority of Spain should be withdrawn, for the bloody clashes between rival exploring parties, the vindictiveness and treachery exhibited towards one another by ambitious governors who could not agree upon the extent of their respective jurisdictions, and the occasional uprisings, like that of the Contreras brothers in Nicaragua, among the rabble of the Spanish settlements, made the annals of the Central American provinces during the sixteenth century one long chronicle of bloodshed. After the declaration of independence, it was the descendants of the early colonists who carried on the civil wars which lasted almost without intermission for so many years. The leaders of the political factions,—the men who fill the higher offices when their party is in power and bear the brunt of the opposition at other times,—are still for the most part members of the white upper class, even though the exclusiveness of the old creole aristocracy has been broken down.

It is rather surprising to find the native landholders and merchants, who have more interest than anyone else in the maintenance of order and good government, taking the lead in the civil wars which have made order and good government impossible. But the feuds which have divided the educated and wealthy classes among themselves have been so bitter that it has been impossible down to the present time for their leaders to co-operate with one another in establishing and supporting a stable and efficient government. The custom of proscribing and despoiling political enemies has kept alive and intensified the personal hatred between the members of the rival parties even in those countries where there are no fundamental economic or social questions upon which the ruling classes are divided. After a change of government, the more prominent adversaries of the victorious party are usually exiled or imprisoned; their property is taken from them either by outright confiscation or forced loans; and their constitutional rights are little respected by the officials or by the courts. When an outbreak against the government is attempted or threatened, many of those of its opponents who are still at liberty are seized, and even their wives and children are subjected to imprisonment and mistreatment, and sometimes, as under the government of President Zelaya in Nicaragua, to barbarous tortures. These persecutions, inspired not only by a determination to prevent uprisings against the government, but often by a desire for revenge and for the gratification of individual spite, frequently make the situation of the enemies of the administration so intolerable that they prefer to risk everything in a revolt rather than to submit. This has been especially true in countries where continual revolutions have kept party feeling at white heat, accustoming all classes to regard civil war almost as a normal condition, and forcing the government to take severe measures against all whom it thinks likely to resist its authority by force of arms. Peace can never be hoped for under these conditions. The only republics of Central America which have made any real progress towards stable government are those where the opponents of the party in power are treated with comparative fairness, and where confiscation and imprisonment for political reasons are rare.

Resistance to oppression, however, is by no means the only motive which leads members of the upper classes to engage in intrigues and revolts against the government. The pursuit of office is in itself an attractive occupation, for every member of the small ruling class has a comparatively good chance of becoming president or cabinet minister or of attaining some other honorable and lucrative position. The rewards offered by politics are on the whole greater than those held out by the more solid occupations, especially in those countries where continual disorder make agriculture and commerce a precarious means of securing a livelihood, for very few of the native planters or merchants receive so great an income as they could secure, legitimately or illegitimately, at the expense of the community if they could reach one of the higher positions in the government. Politics, moreover, provides the natural outlet for the energies of those members of the upper class who have no property. This is especially true of the great majority of the lawyers, doctors, and dentists, few of whom secure a respectable living from their overcrowded professions.

Many members of the wealthy and educated classes, however, have always worked for peace, realizing that revolutions not only deprived their property of most of its value, but also lessened their own influence in the community by raising demagogues and purely military leaders to positions of prominence. The influence exerted by this moderate party has depended upon the economic development of each country. In Costa Rica and Salvador, where the cultivation of coffee has been developed until it offers a more attractive field of endeavor than politics, the great landholders have been a powerful factor in bringing about the establishment of stable government. In Guatemala also, the prosperity of agriculture has probably favored peace, although the bitterness of party strife in that country and the backwardness of the Indian population have greatly retarded its political development. Agriculture in Honduras and Nicaragua, on the other hand, being still in a primitive condition, affords a comparatively unattractive occupation, and politics may still be said to be the chief interest of the propertied classes.

Although the landholding and professional classes furnish the leaders, the revolutions would hardly be possible without the participation of the far more numerous other elements in the community. The half-breed artisans in the towns and villages form perhaps the largest part of the factional armies. These laborers, who have little property, and therefore, so far as they can see, little direct interest in the preservation of peace or the economic well-being of the community, find in civil war both a welcome source of excitement and an avenue for personal advancement and profit, for the opportunities for loot during the campaigns, and the rewards distributed among the adherents of the victorious party after a successful revolution, make conspiracy and revolt a more lucrative occupation than hard labor at a trade. There is no way in which the intelligent but unstable *ladino,* little inclined to steady manual or intellectual labor, can so easily achieve wealth and influence as by the pursuit of politics,—a vocation which makes it possible for a boy of the humblest, barefooted, illiterate family, coming from a thatched, one-room hut in the mountains, to rise to a position where he is addressed as " Great and Good Friend " by the heads of the leading nations of the world. Not a few artisans and professional soldiers of this class have actually risen to such a position, and some, especially in the Liberal party, have been presidents of their countries for long periods. Ordinarily, however, they play a less prominent part in affairs than the members of the white aristocracy, who have the advantage of superior education, social prestige, and wealth.

Those who hope to derive some direct individual profit, however, form but a small part of the number of persons engaging in a typical revolution. The rebel leaders would have but little hope of overcoming the advantage conferred on the government by its control of the administrative machinery, and above all of the standing army and military stores, if they did not receive active support from adherents far too numerous to be rewarded by offices or money in the event of victory. The principal motive which brings together the rank and file of a revolutionary army is "*personalismo,*"—the devotion to individual chiefs, sometimes the heads of great families, sometimes professional soldiers, sometimes mere demagogues, whose relation to their followers is usually not so much that of political leaders as of friends and patrons. Ties of blood, friendships, and gratitude for favors received or expected play a much greater part in holding these factions together than community of ideals or principles; and the very nature of the parties consequently makes the strife between them the more bitter and compromise the more difficult. Closely connected with this *personalismo* is *localismo,* the jealousy and rivalry between town and town, which makes the political leaders of each hostile to those in other parts of the country and enables them too often to carry the common people with them in their armed opposition to a government controlled by their enemies. We have already seen how disastrous an influence this spirit has exerted in the history of the Isthmus, and how it has been intensified by continual internal strife and by the persecution of the people of one section by those of another.

Other factors also have often contributed, though usually in a minor degree, to bring about an uprising against the government. Religious questions have been a source of much trouble, although they are less important at present than in the early history of the Isthmus. The Church has now lost its one-time influence through the decline of religious feeling among the people, but in the first half century after the declaration of independence it was often strong enough to instigate a revolt against a government which oppressed it, or, by its own exactions, to cause one against a government which supported it. Abuses of power by the officials, or the adoption of a policy which directly injured a large portion of the people, have sometimes done much to make a revolution possible, and dissatisfaction with the existing administration, apart from any desire to put any other group of individuals in power, always causes many persons to join the ranks of the rebel army. Many others take part merely for the sake of excitement and plunder, —because they wish to fight and to " eat fat cows." The revolutions, when they have once started, naturally attract all of the discontented and adventurous elements in the community. But it is *personalismo* and *localismo* which make it possible for them to start, and which hold the armies participating in them together through the exigencies of the conflict.

Only a small part of the people, however, enter at all into these party conflicts. The great majority, especially in the rural districts, know little and care less about political affairs. They dislike and fear the revolutions, which often involve forced military service for themselves and destruction for their livestock and their little patches of corn and beans, but they have been so accustomed to misgovernment and exploitation ever since their ancestors were conquered by the Spaniards that it never occurs to them to make a concerted effort to check the disorderly tendencies of the politicians. It is this ignorance and indifference of the masses of the people, rather than any disposition to turbulence in the nation as a whole, which has prevented the establishment of stable government in many of the Central American republics, by making it impossible to hold elections and work the constitution by peaceful means, and by permitting rival cliques of professional office-seekers to plunge the country into civil war time after time for the gratification of personal ambitions and feuds, without other restraint than that suggested by their own interests.

It is sometimes asserted that it is the Indian and part

Indian element which is chiefly responsible for the disorders in Central America. This view seems to find justification in the tranquillity of Costa Rica, where the population is almost entirely of Spanish descent, but it is, in fact, very unjust to a race which is on the whole more peaceful, law-abiding, and industrious than the descendants of their conquerors. The Indians rarely participate in a revolution. In Guatemala, where they have retained their racial identity more than in any other part of the Isthmus, they have hardly ever risen against the government since their final subjugation at the beginning of the colonial period, although they have always been forced to serve against their will both in the standing army and in revolutionary forces. The only real popular uprising which has occurred in that republic,—the revolution which placed Carrera in power in 1838, originated not among the Indians but among the ignorant *ladinos* in the districts east of the capital, where the conditions are far more similar to those of Honduras and Nicaragua than to those which prevail throughout the greater part of Guatemala itself. It was among the half-breeds that Carrera secured the followers who enabled him to establish his military despotism, and it was these same half-breeds, under the influence of the village priests, who made the Church so strong a factor during the Conservative administration. In Nicaragua, the semi-civilized rural population in the district of Matagalpa and the villages which have retained their distinctly Indian character in the southwestern Sierras have as a rule remained neutral, so far as they could, in the contests between Leon and Granada, although the Indians of Matagalpa revolted on one occasion, about thirty years ago, when they were forced to aid in constructing a telegraph line into their country. The Indians in the four northern countries, indeed, are responsible for the revolutions only in the sense that they are helpless to prevent them. Their situation is very different from that of the common people of Costa Rica, where the early extinction of the aborigines made possible the development of a compact, homogeneous community of white peasants, among whom it was comparatively easy to establish stable political institutions.

The causes of Central American revolutions, therefore, may be said to be: first, the attempt to impose political institutions copied from one of the world's most advanced democracies upon a country where elections were absolutely impossible; second, what may be called the habit of revolution among the ruling class and the people of many of the towns,—a habit formed during the turbulent years that followed the breakdown of the federal constitution, and perpetuated by the bitterness of personal feuds and sectional jealousy, the pursuit of politics as a money-making occupation, and the mutual persecutions of rival factions; and third, the backwardness of the masses of the people, which has not only made the republican constitutions unworkable, but has also prevented those who in the long run suffer most from civil war from exerting any effective influence for peace.

None of these causes can be said to be permanent. There is no reason to suppose that stable governments will not be attained eventually in all of the five republics, as a result of the education of the people. The public schools, which have been established in the last quarter century even in the remote country districts of the Isthmus, have already done much to improve the situation and enlarge the outlook of the masses of the population, and to hasten the approach of the day when they will be able to assume the control of their own affairs through the democratic machinery which already exists on paper, and to protect themselves against the disastrous consequences arising from the factional quarrels of selfish professional politicians. This influence makes itself felt slowly, but the social and political effects of popular education, once they have asserted themselves, can never be undone. The penetration of foreign ideas and the increase of wealth and improvement of standards of living which have resulted from the development of foreign commerce are also doing their part in changing the situation of the countries of the Isthmus. The landholding classes, as we have seen, are already exerting a strong influence in behalf of peace in the more prosperous countries, for their success in agricultural pursuits has greatly lessened their interest in politics. The laboring classes, also, have found new opportunities for employment and advancement, and are beginning to learn by experience that their own welfare is dependent upon the peaceful development of their country. The factors in favor of stable government have thus been immeasurably strengthened.

Those who hope for the ultimate political regeneration of the Isthmus receive much encouragement from the example of Costa Rica, which started upon her independent existence with the same institutions and the same inexperience in self-government as her neighbors. Costa Rica, it is true, has owed her freedom from civil war largely to her isolation and her homogeneous European population, but the substitution of a popularly elected and constitutional government for the military tyrannies which had existed at first there as well as in other parts of the Isthmus was due primarily to the education of the common people and to the increasing realization on their part of their interest in the conduct of public affairs. There is no reason to suppose that a similar development will not take place eventually in Nicaragua, Honduras, and Salvador, and even among the Indians of Guatemala. The people of those countries have never had the opportunities for peaceful progress which the prosperous peasants of Costa Rica have enjoyed, but there seems little reason to suppose, from observation of the races as they work side by side in schools and public offices, that the Indian or the *mestizo* of the other republics is inherently less capable of advancement or less fitted for self-government than his fellow-citizen of Spanish descent.

The changes brought about by increased intercourse with foreign countries have on the whole favored stability and good government, but in some respects they have been far from beneficial. While agriculture or commerce has been made a more attractive occupation than conspiracy and revolt for many of the great landholders, many others have been driven out of these pursuits and into politics, as the only means of making a living which remained open to them, by the immigration of more efficient foreign planters and business men. We have already seen to what an extent this has taken place in some of the five countries. The interest in peace among the classes who by wealth and education are best qualified to be the leaders of the community has been lessened by the loss of their property, and the number of professional politicians and revolutionists who are almost entirely dependent upon the pursuit of office for support has been swelled by members of many families which formerly devoted their energies to more useful occupations.

Not a few of the foreigners, moreover, have taken part in civil wars and disturbances, for the furtherance of purely selfish aims, and to the great detriment of the native community. The North American or European professional revolutionist, usually an adventurer or a fugitive from justice in his own country, is a type which is all too familiar in the more disorderly countries of the Isthmus. He is rarely anything more than a mercenary soldier, ready to offer his services to the highest bidder, but his presence is a source of annoyance and danger to the constituted authorities, and the viciousness and greed of some who have been rewarded for their assistance in war with official positions has equaled if not exceeded that of the most depraved native leaders. The participation of these men in the armies on both sides of a civil contest, moreover, is often a positive danger to the Central American countries, because of the regrettable readiness of the great powers of the world to protect their citizens in their real or fancied rights even when they are engaged in an occupation so little commendable as that of making war for money against a constituted government. A significant example of the difficulties which arise from this source was afforded by the events which followed the shooting of two American adventurers during the Nicaraguan revolution of 1909.[1]

Still more dangerous to the welfare of the Central American countries are the foreign corporations which, for equally unworthy purposes, often render open or covert aid to a revolutionary movement, in order to assure themselves of the protection and favor of the new government. There is unfortunately little doubt that recent uprisings in Honduras and Nicaragua have been financed and supplied with arms from New Orleans, or that they have owed their success largely to the aid thus received. So long as the resources of the five republics continue to be developed under special concessions and privileges, there will inevitably be a strong temptation for the large fruit companies and other corporations having interests there to intervene in political affairs, because of the great part which official favor or disfavor plays in determining the conditions under which they do business. Such a situation is disastrous to the internal peace of the countries involved, for any discontented faction can usually secure support from some group of investors or speculators who think that they can further their interests or secure valuable concessions by promoting a revolution. In the governments which come into power in this way, however, the influence of the foreign corporations which have aided them is generally far less than might be expected, for Central American political

[1] See Chapter XI.

leaders are none too grateful and none too scrupulous about carrying out obligations which they have entered into; and they rarely lose sight of their distrust of the foreigner in their appreciation of his assistance.

The disturbing influences introduced by intercourse with other countries, however, are offset, and more than offset, by the pressure which foreign governments, actuated by a desire to protect their subjects who have settled or invested capital in Central America, have exerted in behalf of peace. The United States, especially, has been forced to take positive action to prevent civil and international wars in the Isthmus, not only because its commerce and its investments there are larger than those of any other nation, but also because its settled policy not to permit European intervention in the affairs of the weaker American nations has made it necessary to adopt measures which deprive other powers of an excuse for interference. Inspired by a desire to promote the stability and well-being of its neighbors, the United States has in the last ten years taken more and more radical steps to safeguard the peace of the Isthmus, until it has finally reached the point of actually suppressing revolutions in one of the countries by force. Its influence has therefore become the most potent factor, for good or for evil, both in the external and the internal affairs of the five republics. No description of Central American conditions would be complete without a discussion of the way in which this influence has been exercised.

CHAPTER X

THE WASHINGTON CONFERENCE OF 1907

The Increased Responsibilities of the United States in the Caribbean Sea Since 1900—The San José Conference—The War of 1907—The Washington Conference and the Conventions Adopted by it—Their Effectiveness in Promoting Internal and International Peace—Work of the Central American Court—The Central American Conferences and the Central American Bureau.

THE first years of the twentieth century have brought about a decided change in the attitude of the United States towards its neighbors around the Caribbean Sea. The increasing importance of our political and economic interests in those countries has made their domestic prosperity and the maintenance of their independence from European influence more than ever before essential to our own well-being. American investments and trade in the West Indies have attained such great proportions that anything which affects the normal life of one of the countries of that region is felt at once in commercial and financial centers in the United States. The sugar plantations of Cuba and the banana plantations of Central America, to take only two examples, represent many millions of dollars of American capital, and at the same time are important sources of the food supply of the American people. Simultaneously with the expansion of our economic interests, our political interests in the Caribbean have become of paramount national importance. The acquisition of Porto Rico, and much more the building of the Panama Canal, have made it impossible for the United States to remain indifferent when international complications arise which affect the military situation or the political status of countries close to these possessions. The Monroe Doctrine, as applied to the American tropics, has thus become more than ever an indispensable national policy.

At the same time, the maintenance of the Monroe Doctrine has involved increasingly heavy responsibilities and burdens, because the commercial and financial interests of other countries in the Caribbean have also increased as that region has been developed economically and commercially. Even when they have had no ulterior political motives, the European powers have been unable to stand by with equanimity while the security and the interests of their citizens were endangered by the continual revolutions and other disorders which have occurred in some tropical American states. There has consequently been evident an increasing disposition on their part to use force both to secure protection for their nationals and to obtain the payment of debts due to the latter by irresponsible and unscrupulous governments. To such interventions, which necessarily tend to assume a political character, the United States cannot possibly remain indifferent. Neither, however, can it oppose itself to the protection by another country of the lives and property of the latter's subjects. European interference in the affairs of American countries can only be averted if the United States itself assumes the duty of protecting foreigners in the more turbulent of the neighboring republics, and the Monroe Doctrine can only be upheld in the long run if intelligent and disinterested efforts are made to help those republics to remedy the conditions which at present expose them to aggression. As President Roosevelt said in 1905:

"We cannot permanently adhere to the Monroe Doctrine unless we succeed in making it evident, in the first place, that we do not intend to treat it in any shape or way as an excuse for aggrandizement on our part at the expense of the Republics to the south of us; second, that we do not intend to permit it to be used by any of these Republics as a shield to protect that Republic from the consequences of its own misdeeds against foreign nations; third, that inasmuch as by this doctrine we prevent other nations from interfering on this side of the water, we shall ourselves in good faith try to help those of our sister republics which need such help, upward toward peace and order." [1]

The first occasion on which the new policy of the United States became evident in its dealings with the Central American republics was in 1906, when there was a war between Guatemala and Salvador, in which Honduras, as the ally of the latter country, also became involved. The conflict had arisen from the aid furnished by some of the officials of Salvador to a revolutionary movement directed against President Estrada Cabrera. After exerting his influence in vain to prevent the outbreak of hostilities, President Roosevelt invited President Díaz of Mexico to join him in offering mediation. The efforts of the two governments, seconded by those of Costa Rica, resulted in the holding of a peace conference on the deck of the U. S. S. Marblehead, at which representatives of the United States, Mexico, Costa Rica, and Nicaragua were present, as well as the plenipotentiaries of the three belligerents. At this meeting an agreement was signed providing for the cessation of hostilities and the disarmament of the contending forces, and for another conference, to be held later, to conclude a general treaty of peace.[2]

The second conference was held at San José, Costa Rica, in September of the same year. Each of the Central American republics was invited to send delegates, and all did so with the exception of Nicaragua.

---

[1] Quoted by Critchfield (*American Supremacy*, Vol. II, p. 419) from a speech made at Chautauqua.

[2] U. S. Foreign Relations, 1906, I, 834ff. Mexico, *Boletín Oficial de la Secretaría de Relaciones Exteriores*, Vol. 22, p. 235.

President Zelaya declined because he was unwilling to recognize the right of the United States to intervene in Central American affairs.[1] The governments, represented agreed that all differences arising out of the late war should be arbitrated by the United States and Mexico, and that future disputes should be settled by Central American tribunals, specially organized to deal with each case as it arose. They pledged themselves to keep political refugees from other states away from the frontiers of the countries from which they had been exiled, and not to allow their territory to be used as a base for revolutionary movements against their neighbors. Provision was made also for the establishment of a Central American Bureau in Guatemala City and a pedagogical institute in Costa Rica; and general conventions were signed regulating commerce, navigation, and extradition. The work of the San José Conference was superseded by that of the Washington Conference of the following year, when the treaties entered into were reaffirmed and given greater weight by the moral support of the United States and Mexico.[2]

The San José Conference was followed by a year of almost continuous disorder. In December, 1906, a revolution was started in Honduras against the government of Manuel Bonilla. The rebels were operating close to the Nicaraguan boundary, and it was asserted that they were receiving aid from President Zelaya. Whether or not this was so, an alleged violation of Nicaraguan territory by the troops of Honduras soon made war seem inevitable. At the urgent request of the United States and of the other Central American republics, both Zelaya and Bonilla agreed to submit the dispute to the arbitration of a tribunal composed of one member from each Central American republic, which met at once at San Salvador. Before taking up the matter in dispute, this

[1] Nicaragua, *Mem. de Relaciones Exteriores,* '07, p. xxvii, 5.
[2] For the text of these conventions, see U. S. For. Rel., '06, I, p. 857.

body demanded that both parties withdraw their armies from the border. As Zelaya refused to do this, and furthermore declared in advance that he would not accept any settlement which did not make full reparation for the violation of the Nicaraguan frontier, the tribunal dissolved. Zelaya at once declared war on Honduras, and sent forces to co-operate with the revolutionists there. Salvador, on the other hand, assisted the Bonilla administration, at first indirectly and later by sending troops, although her government remained ostensibly neutral. Despite this aid, Bonilla's forces were completely defeated at Namasigue, on March 18, 1907, and not long afterward Tegucigalpa and Amapala, where Bonilla made his last stand, were captured by the Nicaraguan troops and the Honduranean revolutionists. Miguel Dávila was inaugurated as provisional president of Honduras.[1]

By this time, another general conflict seemed inevitable. Zelaya was preparing to attack Salvador, and President Estrada of Guatemala, fearing the extension of Nicaraguan influence, was apparently ready to intervene in defense of his neighbor. The United States and Mexico, however, at the request of the governments of Costa Rica, Guatemala, and Salvador, again exerted their good offices, and finally brought about a conference at Amapala between the ministers of foreign affairs of Nicaragua and Salvador. Here, with the assistance of the diplomatic representatives of the United States, an effort was made to settle the differences between these two countries. The chief question at issue was the presidency of Honduras, for Salvador declared that she could not accept terms of peace which did not assure the existence of a government in that Republic which would be satisfactory to her and to Guatemala, which had now become her ally against Zelaya. After a long discussion of

[1] U. S. Foreign Relations, '07, p. 606; Nicaragua, *Memoria de Relaciones Exteriores*, '07, most of which is devoted to an account of the events here discussed.

various names in an effort to find a candidate who would not only be acceptable to all of the neighboring governments, but who would also be able to maintain himself in power in Honduras, the delegates finally agreed upon General Terencio Sierra, a former president of Honduras, who was then in command of the Nicaraguan forces at Amapala. They accordingly signed a secret treaty, by which they pledged themselves to overthrow the Dávila government and to set up one under Sierra in its place. Nicaragua, however, as the fifth article stated, found it difficult to attack President Dávila, who was her ally, and therefore left this to Salvador. After Dávila was disposed of, both were to join in assisting Sierra, and he was to be considered the ally of both.[1] Having settled this matter, they drew up a general peace treaty.

The terms of these treaties were never carried out. The exigencies of her internal politics prevented Salvador from supporting Sierra, and Dávila was consequently able to establish himself firmly in power. His government, set up by Nicaraguan arms, was of course perfectly acceptable to Zelaya, but the latter nevertheless made the failure of Salvador to carry out the stipulations of the Amapala agreement a pretext for again beginning hostilities against that country. Animated, as he said, by a desire for the union of Central America, he openly aided a revolt against the government of President Figueroa, sending men and supplies to Acajutla on a Nicaraguan gunboat.[2] This expedition was repulsed, and further hostilities were averted by the energetic representations of the United States.

Zelaya's avowed agressive designs against the other states, and his control over the government of Honduras, created a situation which was intolerable to Guatemala

[1] For the text of this treaty, see Nicaragua, *Memoria de Relaciones Exteriores,* '07, p. 405.
[2] Annual message to Nicaraguan Congress, Dec. 1, 1907.

and Salvador. It was soon evident that these countries were planning to attack him, by the usual means of aiding revolutions in Nicaragua and Honduras. The situation became very threatening in the latter part of the summer of 1907, for the four states were already massing armies on their frontiers. In view of the imminent danger of war, Presidents Roosevelt and Díaz jointly offered their mediation, and brought pressure to bear on the various governments to cease their hostile preparations. As a result, it was agreed that a conference should be held in Washington to settle all outstanding difficulties and permanently to establish the relations of the Central American republics on a peaceful basis. The United States and Mexico were invited to appoint representatives " to lend their good and impartial offices in a purely friendly way towards the realization of the objects of the Conference."[1]

The delegates of the five Central American countries met in the Bureau of American Republics on November 14, 1907. The United States was represented by Mr. William I. Buchanan, whose tact and perseverance were inestimably valuable in the negotiations of the succeeding five weeks. Secretary of State Root and Señor Creel, the Mexican ambassador, made speeches at the inaugural session, and the Conference began its work under the most favorable auspices, animated by a spirit of mutual good will and by a genuine desire to bring about peace in Central America. Following the lead of Salvador, each government in turn declared that it had no claims or grievances against its neighbors, and that it was ready to proceed at once to a discussion of plans for a closer union between the republics. A proposal by Nicaragua and Honduras for the immediate establishment of a Central American federation caused a temporary interruption of the prevailing good feeling, but harmony was

[1] Article II of preliminary protocol, signed Sept. 17, 1907. U. S. For. Rel., '07, II, p. 644.

soon restored, and the work of the Conference proceeded smoothly until December 20, when eight conventions, representing the fruit of its deliberations, were signed by the delegates.[1]

The first of these was a general treaty of peace and amity, by which the five governments sought to remove several of the chief causes of revolutions and international wars in the Isthmus, and to provide for a closer co-operation in promoting their common interests. Among its most important provisions were the following:

Article I. " The Republics of Central America . . . bind themselves to always observe the most complete harmony, and decide every difference or difficulty that may arise amongst them, of whatever nature it may be, by means of the Central American Court of Justice created by the Convention which they have concluded for that purpose on this date."

Art. II. ". . . They declare that any disposition or measure which may tend to disturb the constitutional organization " [that is, the existing government] " of one of the Republics is to be deemed a menace to the peace of all."

Art. III. " Taking into account the central geographical position of Honduras, and the facilities which owing to this circumstance have made its territory most often the theater of Central American conflicts, Honduras declares from now on its absolute neutrality in event of any conflict between the other republics; and the latter, in their turn, provided such neutrality be observed, bind themselves to respect it, and in no case to violate the Honduranean territory."

Art. XVI. " . . . Desiring to prevent one of the most frequent causes of disturbances in the Republics, the contracting Governments shall not permit the leaders or

[1] Mr. Buchanan's report, with the text of the conventions, is printed in U. S. For. Rel., '07, pp. 665-723.

principal chiefs of political refugees, or their agents, to reside in the departments bordering on the countries whose peace they might disturb."

Art. XVII. "Every person, no matter what his nationality, who, within the territory of one of the contracting parties, shall initiate or foster revolutionary movements against any of the others, shall be immediately brought to the capital of the Republic, where he shall be submitted to trial according to law."

The other provisions of the treaty aimed to make the relations between the republics closer and more friendly, and to foster their co-operation for the furthering of their mutual interests. It provided for a reciprocal recognition of the validity of judicial proceedings, professional degrees, patents, and copyrights. Citizens of each country, residing in the territory of one of the others, were to enjoy the same privileges as nationals of the latter, and were to be considered as citizens of the latter if they fulfilled other constitutional requirements. Each Republic pledged itself to accredit a permanent legation to each of the others, and agreed that its diplomatic and consular agents in foreign countries should afford the same protection to the persons, ships, and properties of the citizens of other Central American states as to their compatriots. Vessels of any Central American state were to receive the same treatment as national vessels in the ports of others, and an agreement was to be entered into for the encouragement by subsidies of the coasting trade and of foreign steamship connections. The establishment of a practical agricultural school in Salvador, a school of mines and mechanics in Honduras, and one of arts and trades in Nicaragua, as well as the proposed pedagogical institute in Costa Rica and the Central American Bureau in Guatemala, was recommended, although not specifically provided for.

An additional convention to the General Treaty contained radical and rather impractical provisions aiming to make revolutions less frequent:

Art. I. " The Governments of the High Contracting Parties shall not recognize any other Government which may come into power in any of the five Republics as a consequence of a *coup d'état,* or of a revolution against a recognized government, so long as the freely elected representatives of the people thereof have not constitutionally reorganized the country."

Art. II. " No Government of Central America shall in case of civil war intervene in favor of or against the Government of the country where the struggle takes place."

Art. III. " The Governments of Central America, in the first place, are recommended to endeavor to bring about, by the means at their command, a constitutional reform in the sense of prohibiting the re-election of the President of a Republic, where such prohibition does not exist; secondly, to adopt all measures necessary to effect a complete guarantee of the principle of alternation in power."

Another convention established a Central American Court of Justice, consisting of five judges, one to be elected by the legislature of each state. To this tribunal, the five republics bound themselves " to submit all controversies or questions which may arise among them, of whatever nature and no matter what their origin may be, in case the respective Departments of Foreign Affairs shall not have been able to reach an understanding." The Court was also to take cognizance of suits which citizens of one of the contracting parties might bring against the government of one of the others on account of violation of treaties or denial of justice and of the other cases of an international character, including those which two or more of the Central American governments, or one of them and a foreign government, might agree to submit to it. It was to be "competent to determine its own jurisdiction, interpreting the Treaties and Conventions germane to the matter in dispute, and applying the principles of international law." Article XIII provided:

"From the moment in which any suit is instituted against any one or more governments up to that in which a final decision has been pronounced, the Court may at the solicitation of any one of the parties fix the situation in which the contending parties must remain, to the end that the difficulty shall not be aggravated and that things shall be conserved in *statu quo* pending a final decision."

In the exercise of its duties, the Court might address itself to the governments or the tribunals of the respective states, to have its orders carried out, or it might provide for securing their execution through special commissioners, whom the parties were to assist in every way possible. The latter solemnly bound themselves to submit to the judgments of the Court, and agreed "to lend all moral support that may be necessary in order that they may be properly fulfilled."

Every effort was made to secure the complete independence of the Court. It was to sit at Cartago, Costa Rica,[1] where it would be more free from political or personal pressure than in some other parts of the Isthmus. The judges were to serve for five years, receiving a fixed salary paid out of the treasury of the Court, to which each state contributed, and enjoying the privileges and immunities of diplomatic agents; and they were not to exercise their profession or hold public office during their term of service. They were not to consider them-

---

[1] After the destruction of Cartago by an earthquake in 1910 it was moved to San José.

selves barred from sitting in a case to which their own governments were parties, for they were to represent, not the individual states, but the "national conscience of Central America."

An additional article proposed to give the Court "jurisdiction over the conflicts which may arise between the Legislative, Executive, and Judicial powers—when as a matter of fact the judicial decisions and the resolutions of the National Congress are not respected." This provision, which would have authorized the tribunal to intervene in the internal affairs of the contracting powers in times of internal disorder, was never ratified.

The Convention which established the Central American Bureau recognized certain interests as being "those to which special attention should be paid." These were: "the peaceful reorganization of their mother country, Central America"; the establishment of a broad, practical, and complete system of education of an essentially Central American character; the development of commerce and the advancement of agriculture and industry; and the uniformity of civil, commercial, and criminal legislation, customs tariffs, and monetary systems. The functions of the Bureau were to be all those considered necessary and expedient to achieve the objects placed in its care. It was to have an organ of publicity, and was to serve as a center for the distribution of information about Central American conditions both in the Isthmus and in foreign countries.

At the same time, several other conventions were signed. One provided for the extradition of criminals; another for the establishment of a pedagogical institute directed by the government of Costa Rica but supported by all of the others; another for the co-operation of the five countries in making plans for the construction of the Central American sections of the Pan American railway and the improvement of other means of intercommunication. By still another treaty, each of the contracting governments obligated itself to name one or more commissions to study the currency systems, customs tariffs, weights and measures, and other matters of an economic and fiscal nature in their respective countries. After these had reported, delegates were to be appointed to a Central American Conference, which was to discuss the measures recommended by the commissioners, and especially the reform of the various currency systems on a gold basis. Similar conferences were to be held annually thereafter to consider matters which the governments might agree to submit to them.

The Conference's program for the political and economic regeneration of the Isthmus was obviously too ambitious to be carried out at once, for evils arising from deep-rooted habits and fundamental social conditions could not be done away with by mere international agreement, however sincere the contracting parties might be in their desire for peace and for a realization of a closer union. No one could reasonably expect that the five governments would turn at once from their attitude of mutual suspicion and hostility to a harmonious co-operation in undertakings for their common welfare. Neither of the two main objects of the Washington Conventions, —the elimination of civil and international wars and the creation of closer ties between the five republics with a view to uniting them eventually under one government,— seemed to have been realized to any appreciable extent in the years immediately following 1907, and this led many who had hoped that there would at once be a marked improvement in international relations to brand the treaties as a failure. A careful examination of their results, however, shows that the treaties have been very far from a failure, even though their effects have as yet only begun to make themselves felt. Both of the objects of the Conference have been realized to some extent, and there is every prospect that they will be realized more and more fully as time goes on.

At first, indeed, there was little change in the relations between the five republics. Some of the governments, and especially that of Nicaragua, showed little inclination to carry out the obligations of the conventions in good faith. President Zelaya, who already practically controlled Honduras through the Dávila government, continued his machinations against the tranquillity of other neighboring states, directing his efforts mainly towards placing one of his own supporters in the presidency of Salvador. His open assistance to Prudencio Alfaro, who made repeated attempts to invade that republic in 1908 and 1909, finally forced the United States to authorize the commanders of its naval vessels in Central American waters to use force to prevent the launching of filibustering expeditions from Nicaraguan ports.[1] Zelaya's policy created a situation which was intolerable to Guatemala and Salvador, and soon convinced all who were interested in Central American affairs that he was the greatest obstacle to the establishment of permanent peace in the Isthmus. President Taft expressed this belief in his annual message to Congress in December, 1909, when he said:

" Since the Washington Conventions of 1907 were communicated to the Government of the United States as a consulting and advising party, this Government has been almost continuously called upon by one or another, and in turn by all of the five Central American republics, to exert itself for the maintenance of the conventions. Nearly every complaint has been against the Zelaya government of Nicaragua, which has kept Central America in constant tension and turmoil."

In the early part of the summer of 1908, a band of revolutionists invaded Honduras from Salvador, and

[1] See the article by Professor P. M. Brown, at the time U. S. Minister to Honduras, in the American Political Science Review, Vol. VI, Supplement, p. 160.

another band, led by General Lee Christmas, an American soldier of fortune, attacked some of the towns on the north coast of that republic. There was little doubt in the minds of well-informed people that one or both of Zelaya's principal enemies, the Presidents of Guatemala and Salvador, were aiding the revolutionists with a view to striking at him through the government of Honduras. Zelaya at once prepared for war, and the treaties of peace, hardly six months old, seemed to have been forgotten. The United States and Mexico, however, made strong representations to all the parties concerned, and Costa Rica, by a happy inspiration, suggested to the newly established Central American Court that it interpose its influence to prevent the threatened conflict. On July 8, this tribunal addressed a telegram to the presidents of Guatemala, Salvador, Honduras, and Nicaragua, urging them to submit their differences to arbitration. On receipt of this communication, Nicaragua and Honduras made formal complaints to the Court in accordance with the terms of the Washington Conventions,—Honduras charging that Guatemala and Salvador had fomented and assisted the revolution, and had failed to restrain the Honduranean exiles residing in their territory, and Nicaragua appearing as an interested party. The Court acted with promptness and decision. The complainants were asked to submit proofs in support of their charges, and Guatemala, Salvador, and Nicaragua were ordered to refrain from any military movements which might suggest intervention in the internal affairs of Honduras, and to reduce their forces to a peace basis. These messages were transmitted and answered by telegraph, so that within five days of the Court's first note a *modus vivendi* had been established and the immediate danger of a conflict had been dispelled. After Guatemala and Salvador complied with the orders of the Court, the revolution in Honduras subsided. The Court handed down its decision on December

19, 1908. Salvador was absolved of all responsibility for the revolution in Honduras by the votes of the judges representing Salvador, Guatemala, and Costa Rica against those of the judges from Honduras and Nicaragua. Guatemala was exonerated by all except the representative of Honduras. This decision was severely criticised by many persons in Central America, and it lost much of its force from the fact that most of the judges had obviously voted as the interests of the governments which named them dictated. There could be no doubt, however, that the Court had averted a general Central American war, and had thus done a signal service to the cause of peace.[1]

By this time it was clear that the Washington Conventions would have little effect so long as Zelaya continued to be president of Nicaragua. When a revolution broke out against him in the fall of 1909, therefore, it was regarded with more sympathy and favor by those who had been interested in the work of the Conference than was consistent with the spirit, at least, of the Conference's acts. The attitude of the United States and of the other Central American governments, as we shall see in the next chapter, did much to make this uprising a success. Zelaya's defeat naturally involved the fall of Dávila a short time afterward.

After the elimination of Zelaya, the beneficial effects of the Conventions began to show themselves somewhat more than had been possible while the same conditions which had caused the disturbances of the years 1906-7 had continued to exist. It became evident after 1910 that they marked a turning point in the relations of the five republics. Since that year, and in fact, if we except occasional attempts to render covert aid to revolutions, since 1907, there has not been one international war in Central America. It would be difficult to point to an-

[1] For an account of the case, in addition to the official report of the Court, see the Am. Journal of International Law, Vol. II, p. 835.

other ten years in the history of the Isthmus of which this has been true. It is, moreover, hardly conceivable under present conditions, and especially in view of the influence exerted in behalf of peace by the United States, that there should be an armed conflict between two or more of the five republics. The principal object of the Washington Conference may therefore be said to have been realized. The change which has taken place has been in large part due to the fact that the five countries themselves have generally abided by the provisions of the Treaty of Amity and the Treaty establishing the Central American Court, for they have refrained from sending troops to intervene in one another's internal affairs, and have shown a readiness which had been rare before 1907 to submit differences which arose between them to settlement by diplomatic means or arbitration rather than by a resort to arms. Their relations with one another have undoubtedly been improved by the new spirit which the Conference called into being, and their feeling of common nationality and their readiness to co-operate for the realization of their mutual purposes and ambitions have been strengthened by an increasing realization of the external dangers which confront a Central America divided and distracted by internal wars.

The Conventions did less to bring about stability of government in the individual states, but even in this their effect has been by no means negligible. Internal disorders cannot, of course, be done away with while their fundamental causes remain; and the convention providing that governments coming into office by the use of force should not be recognized until after they had received the approval of the voters at a popular election, and that the state constitutions should be so amended as to insure alternation in power, have been entirely disregarded. Nevertheless, revolutionary uprisings have been made decidedly less frequent by the fact that several of the republics have faithfully observed their obligations to exercise surveillance over political exiles from neighboring countries and not to encourage or permit the organization within their territories of attempts to overthrow nearby governments. Enemies of the established order in one of the republics now find it far more difficult than ever before to secure the base of operations and the financial and military assistance which are usually indispensable for the success of a revolt.

The measure of success which the work of the Conference has attained has been very largely due to the energetic support by the United States of the principles which it established. The government at Washington has several times intervened diplomatically, or even by the use of force, to prevent violations of the more important conventions, to which it was practically, if not formally, a party. In doing this, it has usually acted upon the invitation of one or the other of the five republics. It has not hesitated to use any means necessary to prevent unjustified attacks by one country on another, and it has often brought strong pressure to bear to deter the signatory powers from permitting their territory to be used as a base of revolutionary operations against their neighbors. Sometimes North American influence has apparently been the only factor which has secured respect for the obligations imposed by the peace treaty, for one or two of the parties which signed that treaty have shown little disposition to abide by its provisions and have thus endangered the peace of the Isthmus despite the fact that their neighbors were endeavoring to carry out the provisions of the Conventions in good faith.

The Central American Court of Justice, which was to have been the crowning work of the Conference, has not entirely fulfilled the expectations of its founders. It cannot be said to be a tribunal independent of and superior to the five governments, to which any aggrieved person or state may appeal in the confidence of securing justice. Several of the men appointed as judges have been distinguished lawyers of conspicuous ability and undoubted integrity, but at the same time there have been others, sometimes constituting the majority of the Court, who have owed their nominations purely to domestic political considerations. The honor and the large salary attached to them have made the judgeships one of the most attractive positions in the gift of the state governments, and there has consequently been a keen competition for them among prominent politicians, which has made it more difficult to select a man solely on his merits. In addition to this, the importance of controlling the Court as a means of influencing the international politics of the Isthmus has made almost inevitable the appointment of men who could be relied upon to vote as their governments wished when important questions were at issue. The control exerted over the judges by the powers which named them has prevented the Court from becoming in any true sense independent, and has given it the position of a standing commission of distinguished diplomats rather than that of a true court of justice. This was perhaps inevitable, because the states of the Isthmus, which had never known a judicial tribunal not subject in some degree at least to official influence, could hardly grasp the idea of an international body which would be entirely free from the dictation of the authority which created it. There has been, therefore, no strong force of public opinion to support the Court in asserting its right to speak for the " National Conscience of Central America," and even the judges themselves have shown little inclination to seize and hold the position of complete freedom from control with which the Washington Conference had intended to invest them.

That this was true was evident in the first case that was brought before the tribunal. In deciding the suit of Honduras and Nicaragua against Guatemala and Salvador in 1908, each of the judges from the four states interested voted, as we have seen, on the side supported by the country which had appointed him. The general belief that the dictation of the governments involved, rather than the facts as shown by the evidence, had determined the decision of this question, did much to injure the Court and to deprive it of public confidence. Its independence suffered another serious blow as the result of the action taken in another question which arose three years later after the revolution in Nicaragua. The government which succeeded Zelaya failed to contribute its share towards the expenses of the Court, in which the judge appointed by the late administration was still sitting. Now the salaries of the judges, according to the convention founding the tribunal, were to be paid out of the latter's treasury, from a general fund to which each of the states contributed. In this way the Conference had hoped to establish the financial independence of the judges with respect to their governments, but its intention does not seem to have been carried out, for the refusal of Nicaragua to contribute her quota was regarded as the equivalent of withholding her judge's salary. The latter was thus forced to withdraw temporarily from the Court, whereupon that body, instead of calling upon the substitute provided by its constitution, admitted a new magistrate appointed by the Conservative government of Nicaragua. This action entirely disillusioned those who had hoped that the Court would be above party politics and independent of outside pressure, for it established the dependence of the judges on the governments that named them, and constituted a recognition by the tribunal itself of the fact that its members were representatives of the administration in power in their respective countries, rather than magistrates whose tenure was secure without regard to political changes during their legal term of office.

Since its action in averting a general war in 1908, the Court has been more ornamental than useful. It has served as a symbol of Central American unity, and it has kept alive the principle of international arbitration, but it has actually decided very few cases. Three or four suits have been brought against the government of one of the countries by citizens of another, charging violation of treaty rights or denial of justice, but the Court has refused in every instance to adjudicate them, on the ground that the petitioners had not exhausted the means of redress at their disposal in the countries where they claimed that they had been mistreated. It also refused to intervene in the internal affairs of Costa Rica in 1914 to determine the validity of a presidential election. During the two revolutions in Nicaragua, in 1910 and 1912, it endeavored to bring about an agreement between the contending factions, and in 1912 it even sent a commission of its members to confer with the rival leaders; but its efforts came to naught in both cases because the Conservatives, who had the moral support of the United States, were confident of their ability to defeat their opponents, and therefore refused to agree to a compromise.

Its most recent, and in many ways its most important decisions, were those handed down on September 30, 1916, and March 2, 1917, in the suits brought against Nicaragua by Costa Rica and Salvador, which claimed that their rights had been violated by the recent treaty between that country and the United States. The Court refused to declare the treaty void, saying that it had no jurisdiction over the United States, but it held, nevertheless, that the complainants' rights had been violated, thus condemning Nicaragua's action as illegal. This case has raised a very serious question as to the extent to which the authority of the tribunal will be recognized. Despite Nicaragua's refusal to appear as a party to the case or to accept the verdict, there can be no doubt that the Court had jurisdiction over the question at issue, or that Nicaragua is bound, by the Washington Conventions, to respect its decision. Whether she will do so, however, seems very doubtful. If she continues in her refusal, and is supported in her attitude by the Government of the United States, the prestige of the Court will be seriously impaired, if, indeed, its very existence is not endangered. It is already rather unpopular because of the expense which it involves and because it has accomplished so little, and it seems probable that it would have been disbanded before this if the United States had not exerted a strong influence in behalf of its continuance.

The measures planned by the Conference for promoting closer economic relations between the five republics have only been carried out in part, and their results have been far from satisfactory. Although the provisions for granting citizens of each Central American state the rights of citizens in all the others, and the mutual recognition of professional degrees, patents, and copyrights, have undoubtedly done much to encourage travel and commerce and to promote good feeling, the more ambitious projects outlined in the Conventions have been almost, if not quite, fruitless. Few of the educational institutions which the Conference contemplated have been established, and those which individual states have founded as a result of its recommendations have not attained a truly international character because of the reluctance of other governments to appropriate money for their support. The Central American conferences met annually for five years, drawing up conventions for the reform of the currency and fiscal systems, the establishment of free trade, the adoption of a comprehensive unified system of education, and the improvement of interstate communications; but they were finally discontinued because none of their work had been given any practical effect by the governments. The Central American Bureau (Oficina Internacional Centroamericana) has perhaps been the only institution provided for at the meeting in 1907 which has thus far fully justified its creation. This office, which has been sort of a clearing house for statistical and other data, has done much useful work in distributing commercial information in Central America and abroad, and has also served as an international agency for elaborating plans for joint action on subjects of general importance. Its organ, "Centro America," is the most important periodical published in the Isthmus.

It is still too early to attempt a final estimate of the results of the Washington Conference, or to judge of the ultimate economic and political effects of its work. Some of the stipulations of the conventions adopted by it have never been carried out, and others have been rendered obsolete by the events of the last ten years, but in the main the agreements entered into are still in force, and are by no means without practical value. The provisions restraining the states from interfering in one another's affairs and binding them to submit their disputes to arbitration cannot but make a great change in the political conditions of the Isthmus, if the five countries continue to observe them and if the United States continues to exert its influence to secure respect for them. The spirit of Central American unity, which inspired the actions of the Conference, is growing stronger daily as the states realize more fully their dependence upon one another and the importance of presenting a united front to the world. It seems not improbable that the meeting in Washington in 1907 will be looked back upon in the future as a turning point in the history of the Isthmus, marking a first and decisive step towards the elimination of the international and internal wars which had hitherto been so frequent and so destructive.

CHAPTER XI

THE INTERVENTION OF THE UNITED STATES IN NICARAGUA

The Revolution of 1909—Attitude of the United States—Victory of the Conservatives—Financial and Political Difficulties Confronting the New Government—The Dawson Agreement and the Loan Treaty—Reform of the Currency, Establishment of the Customs Collectorship, and Reorganization of the Foreign Debt by the American Bankers—The Joint Claims Commission—Failure of the Loan Treaty—The Revolution of 1912 and the Intervention of the United States—Support of the Government Since 1912 by American Marines—New Loans and Purchase of the Railroad and Bank Stock by the Bankers—The Election of 1916—The Canal Treaty—Objections of Costa Rica and Salvador—Decision of the Central American Court—Opposition to Our Policy in Nicaragua and the Influence of Our Policy on Our Relations with the Other Central American States.

IN October, 1909, a band of Nicaraguan Conservatives started a revolution at Bluefields. They won over Juan J. Estrada, the governor of the province of which that city is the capital, by proclaiming him provisional president, and thus secured control of most of the East Coast of the Republic. Money and supplies were obtained from some of the other Central American countries, and also from the foreign colony on the Coast, whose interests had been injured by certain concessions which President Zelaya had recently granted. This assistance, and the protection afforded by the wild country which separated Bluefields from the rest of the Republic, enabled the revolutionists to raise a considerable army and to organize a *de facto* government before the constituted authorities were able to attack them.

The uprising was from the first regarded with sympathy throughout Central America and in Washington, for Zelaya's continual encouragement of revolutions in other countries had made him obnoxious to all of his neighbors, and had led to a general belief that his administration was the principal obstacle to the establishment of peace in the Isthmus. The relations between Nicaragua and the United States had been strained for some time, because of the friction caused by Zelaya's violations of the Washington Conventions, and because there had been a number of unpleasant diplomatic incidents, including the prolonged dispute over the so-called Emery claim,[1] which had culminated in the withdrawal of the American minister from Managua. Nevertheless, both the United States and the other Central American countries remained at first ostensibly neutral in the contest. In November, however, the execution by Zelaya's troops of two American soldiers of fortune, who held commissions in the revolutionary army, caused President Taft to break off diplomatic relations with the Liberal administration entirely, and to give the revolution his open, if indirect, support.

The attitude of the American government was set forth in a note addressed by Secretary of State Knox to the Nicaraguan Chargé d'Affaires at Washington. "Since the Washington Conference of 1907," it stated, "it is notorious that President Zelaya has almost continuously kept Central America in tension and turmoil." The Liberal administration was described as "a regime which unfortunately has been a blot upon the history of Nicaragua." The murder of American citizens was but the culmination of a series of outrages which had made friendly relations between the two governments impossible. Moreover, the United States was convinced "that the revolution represents the ideals and the will of a majority of the Nicaraguan people more faithfully than does the Government of President Zelaya." The revolution, the Secretary said, had already attained serious proportions on the East Coast, and new uprisings were reported in the West. This tended to produce "a condition of anarchy which leaves, at a given time, no

---

[1] See U. S. Foreign Relations, 1909, under Nicaragua.

definite, responsible source to which the Government of the United States could look for reparation for the killing of Messrs. Cannon and Groce, or indeed, for the protection which must be assured American citizens and American interests in Nicaragua. In these circumstances, the President no longer feels for the Government of President Zelaya that respect and confidence which would make it appropriate hereafter to maintain with it regular diplomatic relations, implying the will and the ability to respect and assure what is due from one state to another." Both factions were to be held responsible for the protection of American life and property in the sections under their control. The United States would wait, before demanding reparation for the murders, until it saw whether or not the government which was in power after the revolution was "entirely dissociated from the present intolerable conditions." Meanwhile it reserved the liberty to take such action as it saw fit to preserve its interests, and the State Department would continue to receive unofficially both the former Chargé d'Affaires and the representative of the revolution.[1]

This note brought about Zelaya's fall, for he realized that he could not hope to maintain himself against the open opposition of the United States. After vainly attempting to come to an understanding with Secretary Knox, the Nicaraguan ruler yielded to the advice of President Díaz of Mexico and to the pleas of his friends at home, and resigned his position to Dr. José Madriz, one of the most distinguished citizens of Leon. The Liberals had hoped to placate the United States by making president a civilian of known ability and honesty, but their expectations were disappointed, for President Taft refused to recognize the new executive.[2] The revo-

[1] For the text of the note, see U. S. Foreign Relations, 1910, p. 455.
[2] The events leading up to Zelaya's fall are discussed in U. S. Foreign Relations, 1909, President Taft's message to Congress on Foreign Relations, December, 1909, and Zelaya's book, "La Revolución de Nicaragua y Los Estados Unidos."

lutionists also declined his offer to open peace negotiations.

For a time, nevertheless, it appeared probable that President Madriz would be able to restore order. On February 22, 1910, a revolutionary army which attempted to invade the lake region was defeated and almost destroyed, and Estrada and the other leaders, with the remnants of their troops, were forced to retire to Bluefields. The government at once prepared to attack that city vigorously by land and by sea, proclaiming a blockade of the port, and occupying the Bluff, where the customs house was situated. The final reduction of the rebel army, however, proved impossible. The officers of the American warships, which had been sent to the port at the outbreak of the war, refused to allow the blockading squadron to interfere with American ships or ships carrying American goods, and denied the right of the Government officials to collect customs duties at the Bluff, permitting Estrada to establish a new customs house in the territory under his control. When the Liberal commanders, thus prevented from cutting off the supplies or the revenues of the insurgents, prepared to take the town by assault, the American commander forbade them to attack it from the land side, and threatened to sink the gunboats if they shelled the rebel trenches. This action, taken on the ground that a bombardment or fighting in the streets would destroy the property of Americans and other foreigners, rendered certain the defeat of the Government army, which could not long remain encamped far from its base of supplies in the hot and unhealthful coast district outside of the city. Within a few weeks the besiegers were forced to withdraw into the interior.

The Liberals in control at the capital, who had already lost the sympathy of many of Zelaya's former supporters by their wholesale political arrests and their partisan policy, were completely discredited by their failure to take Bluefields, and their government collapsed entirely when Estrada again approached the interior with a reinforced army. There were new outbreaks at several points in the lake region which it was impossible to suppress. Madriz left Managua on August 20, 1910, and the revolutionists entered the city on the following day.

The revolutionary forces were composed mainly of adherents of the wealthy Conservative families of Granada, but there were also many Liberals, some of whom had been prominent leaders in the revolt, who had joined the uprising either from personal hostility to Zelaya or from the hope of gaining something for themselves. The new provisional president, Juan J. Estrada, was a member of the artisan class of Managua, who had been raised by Zelaya to the position of governor of the East Coast province, and whose leadership had been accepted by the Conservatives only because the success of their plot at the beginning depended upon his betraying his patron and turning over to them the garrison at Bluefields. Another Liberal, General José María Moncada, who had for several years been an opponent of Zelaya, became minister of *gobernación* in the new government, and was one of the most trusted advisors of the provisional president. The minister of war, General Luís Mena, had formerly been a follower of the Chamorro family, but his military exploits during the recent struggle and his influence with the army had given him a prestige which threatened to eclipse that of his former patrons, and had made him the most powerful figure in the administration. None of these men were liked or trusted by the old Granada aristocracy, who had hoped through the success of the revolution to regain the power which they had enjoyed during the thirty years before Zelaya became president. Even the *Granadinos,* however, were not entirely united among themselves, for there was no little jealousy between some of the great families. General Emiliano Chamorro, who had for many years been the leader of Conservative revolts against Zelaya, had a strong following among the members of his party in all sections of the Republic, but he was opposed by a faction headed by the Cuadra family, who subsequently became very powerful through their alliance with President Adolfo Díaz. It is necessary to bear in mind these rivalries between the different leaders and groups in the new administration, in order to understand the political difficulties which confronted it during the two years following its accession to power.

The agreement by which the Liberals had turned over the government to the revolutionary leaders had provided for a general amnesty, for a free election to be held within one year, and for the recognition of the debts contracted by both parties during the struggle. Little or no attention was paid to the two former articles, but the debts of both parties,—to members of the revolutionary forces,—were fully recognized, and, in so far as the condition of the treasury permitted, paid. Each person who had taken part in the revolt received fifty hectares (about 123 acres) of the national lands, and vast sums were awarded to prominent members of the Conservative party who had suffered under the Zelaya regime from confiscation or forced loans, or even from "moral" injuries, such as the death of a close relative. A large sum which had been left in the treasury by Dr. Madriz was soon exhausted, and new issues of unsecured paper money were resorted to. By April, 1911, the government admitted that the already depreciated currency had been further inflated to the extent of 15,000,-000 pesos, and in the autumn of the same year 10,000,000 pesos more were secretly put into circulation.[1] Some of this money was necessarily used to meet the current expenses of the government, for the revenues had suffered a serious decline since the revolution, but the greater

[1] See Messrs. Harrison and Conant's Report Presenting a Plan of Monetary Reform for Nicaragua, pp. 10, 11.

part seems to have gone to those in power and to their friends and relatives.

The emptiness of the treasury, accompanied by the inflation of the currency to twice its former quantity, made worse the already desperate economic situation of the country. The revolution had paralyzed agriculture and commerce, not only by taking thousands of workers away from their fields and shops, but also by the actual destruction of cattle and crops, and by the complete disorganization of the transportation system. The discontent caused by these conditions made the position of the new government very precarious, for the Liberals, who outnumbered the Conservatives in the country at large, had no intention of accepting their defeat as final. They felt that they had been beaten, not through the superior strength of their enemies, but by the intervention of the United States; and they were encouraged to keep up an active opposition to the government by the hope of returning to power through the dissensions which soon appeared among the different chiefs of the Conservative party. The opposition press, which for a few months enjoyed and abused an unwonted liberty, kept party feeling at the boiling point, and the bitterness between the two factions was greatly intensified by a bloody clash between government troops and the members of a peaceful Liberal parade at Leon in November, 1911. The Conservative administration, bankrupt and divided within itself, seemed for a time utterly unable to cope with the situation.

The Republic was saved from falling into a condition of complete anarchy only by the assistance rendered to the new government by the United States. In October, 1910, the State Department sent Mr. Thomas C. Dawson to Managua to study the situation and to bring about an understanding between the Conservative leaders. Through his good offices, the so-called Dawson agreement was signed on November 5 by the principal leaders of the revolution. This arrangement provided for the continuance of Estrada at the head of the government, for the appointment of a commission containing American members to pass on all claims against the government arising out of the recent war and out of the cancellation of concessions granted by Zelaya, and for the negotiation of a loan treaty in the United States.[1] A constitutional convention which met on December 31 elected Estrada provisional president for two years, and Adolfo Díaz vice-president. The new administration was at once officially recognized by the United States.

Estrada's position was by no means an easy one. He could rely neither upon the military power, which was entirely in the hands of General Mena, nor upon the Constitutional Convention, which was composed chiefly of followers of Emiliano Chamorro. The rival ambitions of the different leaders soon broke down the political arrangements established by the Dawson agreement. When the Convention framed a constitution which would have made itself rather than the president the actual authority in the state, Estrada dissolved it, thus breaking with Chamorro, who left the country. Estrada later attempted to remove from office and imprison General Mena, who had used his control of the army to fill a new constituent assembly with his personal followers. The military leaders remained loyal to their chief, and prepared to secure his release by force. Only the intervention of the United States minister averted fighting in the streets of Managua. Estrada and Moncada, the minister of *gobernación*, resigned, and Díaz succeeded to the presidency, with the consent of Mena. The minister of war was for some months the real head of the government.

Meanwhile the plans for the financial reorganization of the Republic, which had also been a part of the Dawson agreement, had assumed definite form. Early

[1] See U. S. Foreign Relations, 1910, pp. 764-6.

in 1911, a study of the situation had been made by a financial advisor appointed by Estrada at the suggestion of the State Department. The pecuniary difficulties which confronted the new government were growing very serious. Foreign creditors, supported by their governments, were urgently demanding the payment of interest on the bonded debt, and several claimants were seeking compensation for concessions which the revolutionists had cancelled or violated. The treasury was practically empty, and the repeated issues of paper money which had been resorted to to provide funds had disorganized the currency to such an extent that fluctuations in the rate of exchange made foreign commerce almost impossible.[1]

On June 6, 1911, a treaty was signed with the United States, by which that country agreed to assist Nicaragua in securing a loan from American bankers for the consolidation of its internal and external debt and for other purposes. The loan was to be secured by the customs duties, which were to be collected, so long as the bonds remained unpaid, by an official appointed by Nicaragua from a list presented by the fiscal agent of the loan and approved by the President of the United States.[2] The treaty was similar in every way to that signed in January of the same year by the United States and Honduras, and, like it, was never ratified by the United States Senate. On September 1, while it was still under consideration by the Senate, contracts were signed by which Brown Brothers and Company and J. and W. Seligman and Company, of New York, agreed to lend the Republic fifteen million dollars when the treaty went into effect. The bankers were to purchase the Republic's bonds, bearing five per cent interest, at 90½ per cent of their face value, and the money thus received was to

[1] The rate of exchange rose from 913% in December, 1909, to 2,000% at the end of 1911. See the Report of Messrs. Conant and Harrison, p. 15.

[2] The text of the treaty is printed in the Americal Journal of International Law, 1911, Supplement, p. 291.

be employed for the reform of the currency, the construction of railroads from the interior to Matagalpa and to the Atlantic Coast, and the refunding of the external and the internal debts. As there was little hope of immediate action on the loan treaty, for the United States Congress had adjourned, the bankers agreed to purchase of the Republic six per cent treasury bills to the amount of $1,500,000, in order to provide funds for the most needed reform, an immediate reorganization of the currency. These were guaranteed by the customs revenues, which were to be administered until the notes were retired by a collector general designated by the bankers. The Republic agreed that any dispute relating to this contract should be referred to the Secretary of State of the United States for final decision. The treasury bills were to be retired at once if the fifteen-million-dollar bond issue took place.[1]

The product of this loan was spent by the bankers for the benefit of the Republic. The reorganization of the monetary system was intrusted to the National Bank of Nicaragua, an institution incorporated in the United States with capital supplied from the loan. This was to be managed by the bankers until such time as the treasury bills should be paid. On March 20, 1912, a new currency law was passed by the Nicaraguan Congress, putting into effect a plan which had been worked out by two distinguished American financial experts, who had been sent by the bankers to report on the situation.[2] A unit called *Córdoba,* equal in value to one dollar United States currency, was instituted, and the National Bank was authorized to issue paper and silver money of the new denominations in such quantities as it might consider expedient. This was to

[1] These and the later contracts between the bankers and the Nicaraguan Government have been published in the annual reports of the ministry of *Hacienda y Crédito Público.*

[2] Their report was the above cited Report Presenting a Plan of Monetary Reform for Nicaragua. The Monetary Law is printed in the report, p. 71.

be exchanged for the old *billetes* at a rate to be fixed by agreement between the President of Nicaragua and the bankers. The bank-notes which were to form the greater part of the new circulating medium were to be kept at par by the sale of drafts against a reserve fund maintained in New York by the Republic with its own money, but managed by the National Bank. The latter was to have full control of the currency reform as the agent of the Republic, and was to have an exclusive right to issue paper money.

Meanwhile it had been found that additional funds would be necessary if the currency reform were to be carried out, because the secret issues of paper money made during the autumn of 1911, even after the signature of the treasury bills agreement, had greatly increased the probable expense of the reform. The bankers therefore agreed to open a credit of $500,000 to provide the reserve fund contemplated in the plan of reorganization, and agreed also to lend the Republic an additional $255,000 in small monthly amounts for current expenses. Both of these advances were to bear interest at the rate of six per cent, and were to be repaid when Nicaragua received the money which was due to it, as will be explained below, from the Ethelburga Syndicate. Payment was due on October 15, 1912, but the bankers agreed to grant an extension of time both for these loans and for the treasury bills, if the Republic were then unable to pay them. In return, the Republic agreed to cut down its budget and to raise the customs duties by collecting them at a new rate of exchange. At the same time, it granted the bankers an option on fifty-one per cent of the stock in the National Railway, the management of which was to be turned over to a corporation formed in the United States. This company was to be entirely controlled by the bankers until they had received all money due them from the Republic.

As soon as the plan for the currency reform was

completed the government began to purchase and destroy the old paper money, in order to reduce the rate of exchange, for the expert commission had decided that a conversion at the prevailing rate of twenty to one would work a serious injustice to some classes in the community in view of the rapidity with which the rate had risen during the past twelve months. This proceeding, although justifiable from a broad social point of view, involved a heavy expense to the government, and at the same time proved extremely profitable to those who had shared in the distributions of paper money, which had taken place since the victory of the revolution. The National Bank was established in the summer of 1912, and early in 1913 the new money was in circulation. The old *billetes* were gradually retired, being exchanged at a fixed rate of 12½ to one. In November, 1915, they ceased to be legal tender.

Meanwhile the Customs Collectorship had been installed in December, 1911, under the direction of Colonel Clifford D. Ham. This gentleman has administered the service ever since, in accordance with the terms of the treasury bills contract and of the later agreement with the holders of the Republic's foreign debt. The Collector General, in his own words, has regarded himself not so much as an employee of the Nicaraguan Government as a "trustee, with obligations to four parties—the Republic of Nicaragua, the Secretary of State of the United States, certain citizens of the United States, and certain citizens of England."[1] In accordance with this view, he has declined to recognize the right of the Tribunal of Accounts and other governmental agencies to exercise any authority over him, and he has been in the main supported in this position by the higher Nicaraguan officials. By the terms of its arrangements with the bankers, the Republic is debarred from reducing its tariff without the latters' consent,

[1] See his official report, December, 1914, p. 12.

or from taking any other action which might lessen the value of the guarantee afforded by the customs revenues. The collectorship, and the readjustment of the foreign debt which its establishment made possible, may perhaps be said to be the one conspicuously successful feature of the American bankers' operations in Nicaragua. The Collector General, who has entire power to appoint and remove his subordinates, has reorganized and reformed the service, and has succeeded in eliminating most of the corruption and inefficiency which had prevailed under native administration. Foreign importers and customs agencies who had enjoyed special privileges or improper exemptions have in some cases opposed the new regime very bitterly, but the majority of the business men of the country have had good reason to welcome the substitution of a fair system for one which exposed them to continual extortion and fraud. The amount of revenue secured, in proportion to the imports, has been greatly increased, although the paralyzation of trade during the war of 1912 and the commercial stagnation which has prevailed since the beginning of the European war have prevented the receipts from reaching an amount much greater than that secured in the days of Zelaya. Nevertheless, the collections during 1913, the only year since the establishment of the new system in which normal conditions prevailed, were the largest in the history of the Republic.[1]

Negotiations with the holders of the Republic's foreign debt were completed in the first months of 1912, when an arrangement highly beneficial to both parties was

[1] The following table, compiled from the Reports of the Collector General for 1911-13 and 1915, shows the total receipts, reduced to American gold, for the years 1904-15:

1904	$ 910,627.27	1910	$ 854,547.29
1905	1,282,246.86	1911	1,138,428.89
1906	1,595,219.53	1912	1,265,615.12
1907	1,246,844.85	1913	1,729,008.34
1908	1,027,437.16	1914	1,234,633.54
1909	976,554.15	1915	787,767.11

brought about by the American bankers, acting on behalf of the Nicaraguan Government. Zelaya had refunded the then existing foreign debt in 1909, by placing bonds to the amount of £1,250,000 at seventy-five per cent of their face value, bearing six per cent interest, with the Ethelburga Syndicate in London. As the service of this loan had been suspended after the revolution, and the British Government had already intervened diplomatically on behalf of the bondholders, the need for a readjustment had been pressing. A contract was signed on May 25, 1912, between the American bankers and the Corporation of Foreign Bondholders, by which the latter agreed to a reduction of the interest on the loan to five per cent, on condition that the interest and amortization charges be made a first lien on the customs receipts of the Republic, and that those receipts should continue to be collected under the control of the bankers. This agreement not only effected a saving in money and an improvement in the credit of the Republic, but it also secured for the government the use of a sum of £371,000, representing part of the proceeds of the sale of the 1909 bonds, which had been held in London when the service of the loan had been suspended. About one-third of this money was used for the payment of interest already due, but the remainder was available, in accordance with an agreement made on the same date between the American bankers and the Republic, for the fortification of the currency reform and the repayment of a part of the obligations of the government to the bankers.

The Claims Commission provided for by the Dawson agreement began its sessions on May 1, 1911. It was authorized by legislative decree to adjudicate without further appeal all unliquidated claims against the government, including especially those arising from the late war and from the cancellation of concessions and other contracts made by former administrations. Of the three commissioners, one was a Nicaraguan citizen appointed by the Nicaraguan Government and the other two were Americans, one named by the Republic on the recommendation of the United States and the other designated by the State Department. The commission continued its labors until late in 1914, and passed on 7,908 claims for a total of $13,808,161 gold. Its awards amounted to $1,840,432.31, about two-thirds of which was for small claims presented by natives. The American holders of concessions, who demanded $7,576,564.13, received only $538,749.71. The original intention had been to provide for the payment of these awards with the money received from the proposed fifteen-million-dollar bond issue. It was impossible after the failure of the loan treaty for the government to do this, but a sum of $158,548 was nevertheless provided from the customs receipts for the payment of 4,116 of the smallest claims, which were mainly for losses of livestock and similar property by poor persons during the civil wars of 1909-10 and 1912.[1] Even though the plan for the refunding of the internal debt could not be carried out, it was a decided advantage both for the government and for the holders of the claims to have them passed on by an impartial tribunal, in order that the former might know definitely how much it owed, and that the latter might secure the recognition of their claims as acknowledged obligations of the treasury.

These measures had been carried out by the State Department, and by the bankers at the request and with the co-operation of the State Department, in anticipation of the ratification of the loan treaty by the United States Senate. Their effect was practically to put into operation the most important features of that agreement,—the customs collectorship, the adjustment

[1] For the work of the Commission, see the article by Mr. Schoenrich, one of its members, in the American Journal of International Law, Vol. 9, p. 958.

of the external debt, and the reform of the currency,—despite the opposition to the State Department's policy which defeated the treaty in the Senate. The rejection of the treaty, however, made it impossible to secure money for the complete execution of the reforms which had been inaugurated by the Treasury Bills Agreement, for the bankers were naturally unwilling to make the large loan which had been planned for without an adequate guarantee of the protection of their government. Their situation and that of the Republic was thus made very difficult. The foreign debt remained in English and French hands; the creditors of the government at home remained unpaid; the projected railroads could not be built; and the general improvement in the condition of business and agriculture, which had been expected to result from the solution of the government's financial difficulties and the payment of its obligations to planters, merchants, and officials, did not take place. The poor credit of the Republic made it impossible for it to secure additional loans from the bankers except on onerous terms, while its pressing necessities forced it to embark on a hand-to-mouth policy of mortgaging or selling all of its available resources in order to secure funds. The bankers, on the other hand, had been drawn into a business which promised little profit or credit to themselves, but from which they could not well withdraw. Instead of underwriting a large bond issue, and aiding in an ambitious project for the economic regeneration of Nicaragua, as they had expected to when they first entered into the contracts of September, 1911, they have become involved deeper and deeper in the financial support of a virtually bankrupt government.

While these financial operations were being carried out, the political situation had become more threatening than ever. General Mena had caused the Assembly to elect him President of the Republic, in October, 1911, for the term beginning January 1, 1913, notwithstanding the protests of the United States Minister and of the Granada Conservatives, who asserted that this action was a violation of the Dawson agreement. The strength of the opposition to this proceeding encouraged President Díaz to attempt to throw off the control of the minister of war. On July 29, 1912, he summarily removed the latter from office, and appointed Emiliano Chamorro general-in-chief of the army. Mena fled to Masaya, with a large part of the troops and of the city police of the capital. Most of the national stores of artillery and ammunition had been gathered in Masaya and in Granada, where Mena's son was in command of the barracks. The revolutionists were reinforced by a large number of Liberals, for Benjamín Zeledón, formerly minister of war under Zelaya, assumed the leadership of one of their armies, and the people of Leon revolted and seized control of that city and of the neighboring provinces. Mena's distrust of his old enemies, however, and his refusal to send arms and ammunition to the Leon leaders, prevented effective co-operation between the two factions, and probably saved the government from defeat.

As it was, the government could not expect to hold out long, with little ammunition and few troops, while the rebels controlled practically all the approaches to the capital. The United States, however, could hardly permit the overthrow of the Conservative authorities. Mena, who had fallen seriously ill, had been forced to let the leadership of the revolution pass almost completely into the hands of Zeledón and the Leon chiefs. If Zelaya's followers regained control of the government, all of the efforts of the State Department to place Nicaragua on her feet politically and financially would have been useless, and the interests of the New York bankers, who had undertaken their operations in the country at the express request of the United States Government, would be seriously imperiled. The American Minister, therefore, demanded that President Díaz guarantee effective protection to the life and property of foreigners in the Republic. The latter replied that he was unable to do so, but asked the United States to assume this responsibility itself. In compliance with this request, American marines landed at Corinto, and assumed control of the National Railway, which ran from that port through Leon, Managua, and Masaya to Granada. This, as we have seen, was the property of the government, but was held and operated by the bankers as a partial guarantee of their loans. By September 8, traffic had been resumed between Corinto and Granada, although the rebels still held all of the more important cities along the route with the exception of Managua. On September 18, the United States Minister, Mr. Weitzel, made public an official declaration that the United States intended to keep open the routes of communication in the Republic and to protect American life and property. His government, he said, had been opposed to Zelaya not only as a person but as a system, and it would exert its influence, at the request of President Díaz, to prevent a return to that system and to uphold the lawful authority. This pronouncement disheartened the revolutionists and caused many to withdraw from the uprising. On September 25, General Mena surrendered at Granada to Admiral Sutherland, the commander of the American forces, and the rebels were confined to their positions at Masaya and Leon. A few days later, Admiral Sutherland ordered Zeledón to evacuate the Barranca Fort, overlooking Masaya, on the ground that his position threatened the railway. When the Liberal leader refused, American troops stormed and took the position. The war soon afterwards came to an end with the surrender of Leon to another American officer. Seven American marines and bluejackets had lost their lives.[1]

[1] Report of the Navy Department, 1912, p. 13.

After the revolution, it was necessary to decide upon the election of a president for the term 1913-1917. The greater part of the Conservative party supported the candidacy of General Chamorro, but Díaz, who controlled the machinery of the administration, desired to succeed himself in power. An agreement was effected through the intervention of Mr. Weitzel, who insisted that the *Chamorristas* accept Díaz, while Chamorro was given the position of minister at Washington. At the election, which was held while a large part of the American marines were still in the country, the three or four thousand voters who were allowed to participate unanimously approved the official ticket, which was the only one in the field.

Since 1912, the Government of Nicaragua has practically been maintained in office by the support of the United States, for a legation guard of one hundred marines is kept in one of the forts at Managua and a warship is stationed at Corinto as reminders that the United States will not permit another uprising against the constituted authorities. One hundred well-trained and well-equipped soldiers are in themselves no inconsiderable force in a country like Nicaragua, and their influence is increased by the recollection of the events of 1912. Without their moral backing, the administration could hardly have remained in power. Although President Díaz dealt with his opponents more justly and humanely than has been customary in Nicaragua, and showed great liberality in his attitude towards the expression of political opinion in the press and in private conversation, his administration did not have the whole-hearted adherence of any of the larger political groups, and was for this reason decidedly unpopular. Not only the Liberals and the friends of General Mena, but even most of the Conservatives, were dissatisfied. General Chamorro himself co-operated loyally with the president, but he was unable to prevent many of his followers from conspiring to place their own faction in power. There were, therefore, continual intrigues and frequent petty revolts, which lessened the government's prestige and exhausted its energy and resources. The outbreak of another civil war was prevented, apparently, only by the determined attitude of the United States.

Two of the causes which contributed most to the weakness of the Díaz government were its inability to meet its current expenses and the increasing unpopularity of its relations with the New York bankers. At the time of Mena's revolt, the difficulties confronting the treasury had seemed in a fair way to solution, but the expense and the loss of revenue due to the war made matters worse than ever. The government was forced to ask further advances from the bankers, and to turn over to them, as security, and in the hope of improving its financial situation thereby, the collection of all of its internal revenues.[1] These were administered by the National Bank for a year, after which the arrangement was abandoned as unsatisfactory, because of the difficulties encountered by the American administrators in obtaining the enforcement of the fiscal laws and the prevention of the clandestine manufacture of *aguardiente*. It was reported in October, 1916, however, that the internal revenues had again been taken over by the bankers.

As there was no improvement in the financial condition of the Republic, contracts providing for further assistance by the bankers were signed on October 8, 1913. The latter agreed to purchase another issue of treasury bills to the amount of one million dollars, bearing interest at six per cent, and at the same time bought fifty-one per cent of the stock of the National Railway for one million dollars, thus becoming the owners of property which they had in fact held and operated for more than a year. The Republic agreed to employ a part of the two million dollars thus received in the pay-

[1] See the contracts of Oct. 31, 1912, *Memoria de Hacienda*, 1912-13.

ment of all its outstanding obligations to the bankers and to the National Bank, including the sums still due on the 1911 treasury bills and the supplementary loans, and in the addition of $350,000 to the currency reserve. At the same time it was to subscribe $47,000, while the bankers subscribed $153,000, for an increase in the capital of the National Bank, which was to be raised from $100,000 to $300,000. The remainder of the money, amounting approximately to three quarters of a million dollars, went to the Republic for its current expenses. Since the bankers acquired fifty-one per cent of the stock of the National Bank as well as of the Railway by these contracts, it was arranged that they should name six, the Nicaraguan Minister of Finance two, and the United States Secretary of State one, of the directors of both corporations.

Before these new treasury bills fell due, the outbreak of the European war put an end to all hope for the immediate financial rehabilitation of the Republic. The economic situation of the country at large was already very bad before this final disaster occurred. The exhaustion and demoralization which had resulted from two unusually destructive civil wars, combined with the reduction of military forces in the rural districts from motives of economy, had led to a great increase in highway robbery and crime, which caused general unrest and discouraged internal commerce. Matters were made worse by the continual political agitation. The crops, moreover, had been severely damaged by droughts and by a plague of grasshoppers, and in many districts the agricultural population had been reduced to a pitiable state of want. The merchants in the cities had suffered great losses from the failure of the Government to pay for large amounts of supplies purchased or requisitioned by it, and from the inability of the treasury to meet the salaries of the public employees, who made up a large part of the city population. When the outbreak of the war cut off the European credits upon which both the coffee growers and the merchants had depended, foreign and domestic commerce came almost to a standstill. The income of the national treasury was greatly reduced, for the receipts from the customs duties declined from $1,730,603.22 in 1913 to $1,237,593.33 in 1914 and $789,716.76 in 1915, and the other revenues decreased at the same time to an alarming extent. It was manifestly impossible for the government to meet even the most necessary of its current expenses, if it had to discharge its obligations to foreign creditors at the same time, and it would have faced absolute bankruptcy had not the bankers again come to its assistance. The payment of interest on the treasury bills was suspended, by contracts made in October, 1914, and the bankers used their good offices to secure a similar suspension of charges on the English debt, in order that the Republic might use all of the reduced customs revenue for its own needs. These arrangements have since been renewed from time to time for short periods, always on condition that the Republic should so far as possible resume the service of the loans if it should receive the three million dollars due to it in accordance with the canal treaty with the United States.

The conditions created by the war put a severe strain upon the new currency system. The replenishment of the reserve fund became well-nigh impossible just at the time when the disorganization of international credit, which forced exchange upon European centers to an unprecedented figure throughout the Western Hemisphere, caused an abnormal drain upon it. The National Bank, therefore, was forced to suspend the sale of the drafts by which the par value of its notes had been maintained. At the same time there was a strong popular demand for new issues of money to supply funds for the government and to finance the coffee growers, who were unable to secure the usual advances from abroad for moving their crop. As a result of this, a contract was signed on December 2, 1914, by which a new issue of 1,500,000 Córdobas was provided for,— C1,000,000 to be used for making loans to agriculturalists and exporters, and C500,000, which was to be guaranteed by the proceeds of a new capital tax collected by the National Bank, for the payment of salaries and other obligations of the government. At the same time, the Bank was authorized to pay its depositors with additional notes, secured by mortgages and other securities. All of these issues were to be retired as rapidly as the loans were repaid and the profits of the capital tax were received. The interest upon the loans to planters and merchants, which was to be at the rate of twelve per cent, was divided between the government and the Bank,—an arrangement highly profitable to the latter, considering that the notes were exclusively obligations of the Republic. So long as these issues were still in circulation, the Bank was not to sell drafts against the reserve fund, and the government was to be relieved of its obligation to maintain that fund at the amount required by previous contracts. The new issues of paper and the suspension of the sale of exchange constituted of course a temporary abandonment of the gold standard. The premium on New York drafts rose to thirty per cent during the first months of 1915, but in May of that year it was greatly reduced by the operations of an English bank in Managua. Some months later, the National Bank itself resumed the sale of drafts with its own funds, thus raising its notes again to their par value.

Early in 1916, all parties in the Republic turned their attention to the coming presidential election. In the campaign which preceded this, the various political groups enjoyed a very unusual amount of freedom in carrying on their propaganda, and each one founded clubs and published numerous newspapers to support its candidate. The chief factions which took part in the campaign were:

the government party, which had few friends outside of official circles; the old Conservatives, with their chief strength in Granada, who were in the main enthusiastic followers of Emiliano Chamorro; and the Liberals, who, though by no means entirely at harmony among themselves, were nevertheless united in their determination to regain control of the government. There were also one or two lesser groups, which had hopes of coming into power as the result of a compromise between the more extreme parties. The Liberals, with the support of the great city of Leon, and with a strong following in each of the other important cities except Granada, were probably more numerous than all of their opponents together. It was clear from the beginning, however, that the outcome of the election would depend not so much upon the will of the majority as upon the attitude assumed by the United States. The administration, which had made Dr. Carlos Cuadra Pasos the official candidate, obviously intended to perpetuate its own regime, relying on the support of the American marines to prevent armed opposition to its plans. The Chamorristas, on their side, believed that the United States would insist that the Government accept their candidate, who had won general respect during his service as minister at Washington. The security of American interests in Nicaragua was in very large measure dependent upon the continuance in power of the Conservative party, of which Chamorro was undoubtedly the most popular leader; and the latter had strong additional claims to consideration because of his loyal support of the constituted authorities, after the disappointment which he had suffered in 1913, and despite the discontent of his own followers with the Díaz administration.

The Liberals, on the other hand, believed that any fair solution of the situation would restore them to power. They unquestionably constituted a majority of the people of the Republic, and they were on the whole more united than their Conservative opponents. For several years they had been endeavoring to secure the withdrawal of the marines from Nicaragua, believing that they would easily obtain control of the government as soon as the existing administration should be deprived of foreign support; and they had been carrying on an extensive campaign in Central America and in political circles in Washington with a view to arousing sentiment against the intervention of the United States in the internal affairs of Nicaragua. Their leaders desired first of all to secure the withdrawal of the American marines, but many were willing, if this proved unobtainable, to accept American supervision of the presidential election, which would have reduced somewhat the possibility of the exercise of pressure and the employment of fraud by the government. Whatever chance the Liberals might once have had to secure the recognition of their right to participate on equal terms in the election, however, was forfeited when they nominated as their candidate for president Dr. Julián Irías, Zelaya's most trusted minister, who had been closely associated with the dictator in all of the acts which had aroused the hostility of the United States between 1906 and 1909. Although Irías was one of the ablest and most popular leaders of the Liberal party, it was hardly possible that a man whose election would mean a restoration of the old regime should become president of Nicaragua with the consent and assistance of the United States.

The United States could not well escape the responsibility for deciding which of the three candidates should become president for the ensuing term. A policy of non-intervention except to prevent disorder would have meant the election of Dr. Cuadra, against the wishes of the great majority of both parties. A supervised election, on the other hand, supposing that it could have been conducted with any fairness, which seemed unlikely, would probably have placed in office a president whose avowed object was to expel the American bankers from the Republic and to terminate American influence in the government. It was almost inevitable under such circumstances that the Conservative party should receive the open support of the American minister. By the time of the election, it was evident that General Chamorro was to be the next president. Dr. Irías had been prevented from entering Nicaragua when he came home to conduct his campaign in August, and the Liberals had been warned that no candidate who had been associated with the Zelaya regime would be recognized by the United States if elected. Somewhat later Dr. Cuadra withdrew his candidacy. The election was held in October, and the new president, General Chamorro, was inaugurated in January, 1917.

After the attempt to secure the ratification of the loan treaty had been finally abandoned, the hopes of the Nicaraguan Government for the eventual solution of its financial problems were centered upon a new agreement signed in February, 1913, which provided for the payment by the United States to Nicaragua of three million dollars in return for an exclusive right to construct a transisthmian canal through the San Juan River and the Great Lake and for the privilege of establishing a naval base in her territory on the Gulf of Fonseca. After Mr. Bryan assumed office as Secretary of State, this treaty was modified by the addition of an article by which Nicaragua agreed not to declare war without the consent of the United States, or to enter into treaties with foreign governments affecting her independence or territorial integrity, or to contract public debts beyond her ability to pay, and by which she recognized the right of the United States to intervene in her affairs when necessary to preserve her independence or to protect life and property in her domain. This so-called protectorate plan failed of ratification in the United States Senate, and a new treaty, without it, was signed on

August 5, 1914. Despite the strong opposition which this also encountered in the Senate, it was finally ratified with some amendments, and was proclaimed on June 24, 1916. The principal provisions of the treaty as ratified were as follows:

I. " The Government of Nicaragua grants in perpetuity to the Government of the United States, forever free from all taxation or other public charge, the exclusive proprietary rights necessary and convenient for the construction, operation, and maintenance of an interoceanic canal by way of the San Juan River and the Great Lake of Nicaragua, or by way of any route over Nicaraguan territory. . . .

II. ". . . The Government of Nicaragua hereby leases for a term of ninety-nine years to the Government of the United States the islands in the Caribbean Sea known as Great Corn Island and Little Corn Island; and the Government of Nicaragua further grants to the Government of the United States for a like period of ninety-nine years the right to establish, operate and maintain a naval base at such place on the territory of Nicaragua bordering upon the Gulf of Fonseca as the Government of the United States may select. . . .

III. " In consideration of the foregoing stipulations and for the purposes contemplated by this Convention and for the purpose of reducing the present indebtedness of Nicaragua, the Government of the United States shall . . . pay for the benefit of the Republic of Nicaragua the sum of three million dollars . . . to be applied by Nicaragua upon its indebtedness or other public purposes for the advancement of the welfare of Nicaragua in a manner to be determined by the two high contracting parties. . . ."

Even before this treaty had been made public, unofficial reports revealing its provisions had led Costa Rica and Salvador to protest vigorously to the United States and to Nicaragua against what each considered to be a grave infringement of its own rights. Their opposition had led the United States Senate to add to the treaty a proviso declaring that nothing in the Convention was intended to affect any existing right of Costa Rica, Salvador, or Honduras. This, however, did little to conciliate those states, and the efforts of the State Department to secure their approval of the new condition of affairs created by the treaty by an offer to make similar agreements with them, to safeguard their rights and to indemnify them with pecuniary compensations, proved unavailing. After the treaty had been proclaimed, Costa Rica and Salvador took their protests to the Central American Court of Justice, requesting that tribunal to enjoin Nicaragua from carrying out its provisions. The Court decided to take cognizance of the matter, despite Nicaragua's refusal to be a party to any action before it.[1]

Costa Rica's case was a simple one, based upon treaty provisions. By the boundary treaty between her and Nicaragua, signed in 1858, she had been given perpetual rights of free navigation in the lower part of the San Juan River, and the Nicaraguan Government had agreed to consult her before it entered into any contract for the construction of an interoceanic canal. There had been some dispute about the terms of this treaty, which had led in 1888 to the submission of the questions at issue to the arbitration of President Cleveland. The latter had held the treaty valid, and had expressly declared in his award that: " The Republic of Nicaragua remains bound not to make any grants for canal purposes across her

[1] Costa Rica protested to the United States on April 17, 1913, and to Nicaragua on April 27, 1913. Salvador protested to the United States on October 21, 1913, and to Nicaragua on April 14, 1916. The notes exchanged in regard to the treaty are published in Costa Rica, *Memoria de Relaciones Exteriores*, 1913, 1914, etc., and in Salvador, *Libro Rosado* for the same years. The documents accompanying the cases presented before the Central American Court have been published in English by the legations of the two countries at Washington.

territory without first asking the opinion of the Republic of Costa Rica." Costa Rica asserted that the construction of the proposed canal would interfere with her navigation of the San Juan River, thus infringing her rights under the convention of 1858 and also under those provisions of the Washington Conventions of 1907 which granted to each Central American Republic the free navigation of the waters of the others; that it would injuriously affect her own territory on the banks of the San Juan; and finally that the Canal Treaty had been signed and ratified before she had even been informed of its provisions, and without her assent being asked at any stage of the proceedings. Nicaragua refused to answer the complaint of Costa Rica, and declared that she would neither recognize the competence of the Court to assume jurisdiction in the matter nor abide by its decision when rendered. She denied that the treaty was either a concession for the construction of a canal, or an agreement for the sale of the San Juan River, saying that it was only an option granting to the United States the privilege of building a canal, under an additional contract, at some future time.

Salvador's case was based upon broader political grounds, and her protests were directed chiefly against the establishment of the naval base in the Gulf of Fonseca, in close proximity to one of her most important ports. "It must be patent to every one," her complaint stated, "that the establishment, by a powerful state, of a naval base in the immediate vicinity of the Republic of El Salvador would constitute a serious menace—not merely imaginary, but real and apparent—to the freedom of life and the autonomy of that Republic. And that positive menace would exist, not solely by reason of the influence that the United States, as an essential to the adequate development of the ends determined upon for the efficiency and security of the proposed naval base, would naturally need to exercise and enjoy at all times in connection with incidents of the highest importance in the national life of the small neighboring states, but would be also, and especially, vital because in the future, in any armed conflict that might arise between the United States and one or more military powers, the territories bounded by the Gulf of Fonseca would be converted, to an extent incalculable in view of the offensive power and range of modern armaments, into belligerent camps wherein would be decided the fate of the proposed naval establishment—a decision that would inevitably involve the sacrifice of the independence and sovereignty of the weaker Central American States, as has been the case with the smaller nations in the present European struggle under conditions more or less similar."

Furthermore, Salvador asserted that the treaty violated her proprietary rights in the Gulf of Fonseca. As successors of the Central American Federation, she said, Salvador, Honduras, and Nicaragua exercised a joint ownership over the Gulf, which clearly gave her the right to object to the use of its waters for military purposes by a foreign power. Her contention was somewhat weakened by the fact that the three republics in question had divided all of the islands of the Gulf between them, and that each in practice exercised jurisdiction over a portion of it; but it was nevertheless impossible to show that any treaty to which Salvador had been a party had ever put an end to the community which the three adjacent republics had inherited from Spain and the Central American Federation. Salvador also asserted that the treaty was prejudicial to the general interests of Central America, which despite temporary political separation was nevertheless a definite political entity of which each of the states was still a part. The alienation of Central American territory by one country was a violation of the rights of the others. Such alienation was at the same time, by a rather far-fetched interpretation, claimed to be a violation of the article in the Washington Peace Treaty of 1907 which declared any alteration in the constitutional order of one of the states a menace to the welfare of all. Finally, it was maintained that the treaty could not legally have been concluded under the Nicaraguan constitution, and was therefore void.

The Court handed down its decision in the case of Costa Rica on September 30, 1916. It declared that Nicaragua had violated Costa Rica's rights by making the treaty, but it declined to declare the treaty void, as it had no jurisdiction over the United States. On March 2, 1917, it handed down a similar decision in the case of Salvador. Its action has been disregarded by Nicaragua, and by the United States. The decision has undoubtedly created an extremely embarrassing situation. There can be no doubt that the Court had jurisdiction over the question at issue, under the terms of the Washington conventions, or that the other Central American countries, and particularly Costa Rica, had strong cases against the convention, based not only upon international law and treaty provisions, but also upon the necessity for protecting their vital national interests. If the treaty is still put into effect, after what has happened, both the Court of Justice and the Washington Conventions will have ceased to be of practical value, and our government will be committed to a policy which involves the entire disregard of what the Central American republics consider to be their rights. It may well be doubted whether even the great military value of the proposed naval base, or the theoretical value of an option on another canal route, are worth the permanent alienation of Central American public opinion and the abandonment of the considerations of justice and good will which have hitherto governed our relations with the five republics.

The policy pursued by the United States Government

in Nicaragua since 1912 has caused bitter resentment throughout Central America. The Nicaraguan Liberals and most thinking people in other parts of the Isthmus feel that the intervention of American marines in the revolution of 1912 and the subsequent maintenance of the administration by armed force have reduced Nicaragua to the position of a subject country and have gravely jeopardized the independence of the other republics. The Díaz government has been regarded as a mere creature of the State Department, and it is denied that the agreements made by it are in any sense acts of the Nicaraguan nation. Both the contracts with the American bankers and the canal convention are regarded as evidences of an intention in the State Department to exploit the present situation for the benefit of American capitalists and for the promotion of an aggressive policy of political expansion. It is perhaps rather difficult for Americans, who realize how far any purpose of territorial expansion is from the minds of those who control our foreign policy, to comprehend the feeling of suspicion and fear which recent events have aroused among the more intelligent and patriotic classes in Central America. That feeling is nevertheless in large measure justified. No country can be said to enjoy independence when it is constantly in danger, as the events of the last five years have shown all the Central American republics to be, of arbitrary and sometimes undiscriminating intervention by an outside power in their political and financial affairs. Although the United States has been actuated in the policy which it has pursued solely by a desire to promote the peace and prosperity of the Central American countries, neither the necessity for the action which it has taken nor the purity of its motives has been fully appreciated in the Isthmus. The result has been a misunderstanding and a sentiment of hostility which threaten, unless steps can be taken to regain their confidence, to make the people of the five republics regard their North American neighbor as their most dangerous enemy.

It will be difficult to convince the Central Americans of the sincerity of our good will or the disinterestedness of our intentions so long as we continue to uphold a minority administration in Nicaragua by force of arms. The maintenance of the established authority has thus far been unavoidable because the only alternative was the abandonment of Nicaragua to a renewal of the civil wars which reduced her to so pitiable a condition before 1912. Peace was the first and absolute necessity if the country were to be saved from utter ruin. But it is unthinkable that the United States, in the name of constitutional government, should permanently identify itself with any one faction or that it should continue indefinitely to use its power to exclude from all share in the administration the party to which a majority of the people of the Republic profess allegiance. Ultimately, an attempt must be made, either to hold a fair election or to effect an agreement between the various parties by which a president accepted by all can be placed in office.

Any adjustment of the political situation must necessarily involve measures to protect the interests of the American bankers, who have invested about two million dollars in their efforts to preserve Nicaragua from bankruptcy and to improve her economic condition. Brown Brothers and Company and J. and W. Seligman and Company entered upon their dealings with Nicaragua at the explicit request of the State Department, and it would be impossible to expose them to the partial or total loss of their investments by withdrawing the support of the government. The first thought of a Liberal administration would be to undo so far as it could the situation created by the loan contracts. Actual confiscation of property would of course be impossible, but both the bankers and the holders of the English bonds, which are now secured by the American collection of the customs duties, might suffer serious losses at the hands of an unfriendly president. For this reason, an agreement in regard to the future status of the bankers, or an adjustment of the debts due to them from the Republic, would be an essential part of any arrangement which aimed to terminate the American intervention.

The motives and methods of the bankers, like those of the State Department, have been severely impugned by the Nicaraguan Liberals and by the leaders of public opinion in other parts of Central America. One constantly hears charges that they are co-operating with a corrupt and subservient administration to defraud the people, and that they have taken advantage of the needs of the government and the greed of the officials to secure control of all of the more valuable national property. Those who make these accusations point to the fact that the Republic has become heavily indebted to the New York firms, and that the National Railway, the National Bank, the customs houses, and the collection of the internal revenues have at the same time passed into their hands, while the government apparently has nothing to show in return. The more serious of these charges spring entirely from ignorance or from partisan political motives. The Liberals are ready to use any means and to make any statement likely to discredit the Conservative administration or to arouse public sentiment in Nicaragua or in the United States against the policy which has enabled their rivals to remain in power; and the patriotic fervor of their efforts to free their country from alien domination receives at least a part of its force from the fact that they hope thereby to gain control of the government for themselves. Few of them, moreover, have taken the trouble to investigate the financial operations of the bankers in order to substantiate the accusations which they make. The writer was unable, during a stay of six months in Nicaragua, to find one prominent Liberal who had even read the loan contracts.

For this, and for the statement frequently put forth that the Government and the bankers have carried on their operations in secret and in an underhand manner, there is no excuse, for every one of the more important contracts has been published in the reports of the Minister of Finance, which are easily accessible to the public. It must be remembered, however, that there are very few persons in Nicaragua who are fitted by training or experience to form an intelligent opinion from the perusal of these documents.

The bankers' investments in Nicaragua so far have been as follows:

1913 Treasury Bills	$1,000,000
51% of the stock in the National Railway	1,000,000
51% of the stock in the National Bank	153,000
Total (exclusive of accrued interest)	$2,153,000

Earlier loans were, as we have seen, repaid or refunded with the 1913 treasury bills. These bear interest at the rate of six per cent, which is certainly not excessive if we consider the desperate condition of the Republic's credit. The par value of the bankers' holdings in the capital stock of the railway is $1,683,000. Since the total net profits of the line were $244,706.62 Cordobas in 1913-14, and $251,320.56 in 1914-15,[1] it is evident that it will be a valuable property under foreign management and protection, although the return thus far has not been great considering the dangers attending investments in such enterprises in countries where revolutions, with their consequent destruction of material and paralyzation of traffic, are of frequent occurrence. It should be remembered, moreover, that the Government still owns forty-nine per cent of the stock and thus receives nearly half of the profits, so that it is a direct beneficiary from the improvement in the property and

[1] Nicaragua, *Memoria de Hacienda*, 1915, p. 750.

the increase in the profits which resulted from the reorganization. The Republic shares similarly in any profits which may be made by the National Bank. This institution, founded primarily for the purposes of the currency reform, has apparently not made large profits up to the present time, because of its small capital, its not very efficient management, and the heavy enpenses involved in maintaining three separate branches besides the central office. It has received small sums for its services in connection with the currency reform, and it has in addition loaned considerable amounts to the government and to private individuals, charging both twelve per cent interest, which is rather less than the prevailing rate in Nicaragua. The wisdom, and perhaps the propriety, of some of its operations have been open to criticism, but its services in connection with the currency reform and its extension of credit to the government when the latter has been in difficulties have certainly justified its institution.

The charge that the United States Government has been guided in its financial policy in Nicaragua by a deliberate intention to exploit the people of that country for the benefit of American capitalists is of course simply ridiculous. Equally so is the idea that two great financial institutions of the standing of Brown Brothers and Seligman and Company would compromise their reputation and devote their time and energy in schemes for defrauding Nicaragua of a few thousands of dollars a year. The bankers have necessarily sought to protect their own interests, and in order to do so have imposed rather onerous conditions upon the Republic; but it must be remembered that they have been dealing with a practically bankrupt country, which is at the present time unable to meet any of its foreign obligations, and that their investments are rendered doubly insecure by the bad economic situation and by the uncertainty of political conditions. The sums involved and the possibilities of illegitimate profits may well seem immense to citizens of a country whose total annual budget is only two or three million dollars; but no one who sees the matter in its true proportions can well believe that the bankers have been enriching themselves very rapidly at the expense of Nicaragua.

On the other hand, it must be admitted that the loan contracts have contained much that is objectionable from the point of view of the patriotic Nicaraguan citizen. The situation which they have created cannot but be humiliating to a people which values its national independence. The collection of the public revenues by foreigners, and the sale of the most valuable national property, however necessary for the good of the country, has naturally been exceedingly distasteful to public opinion. Moreover there has been a suspicion, apparently too well founded, that some of the money received from the bankers has benefited certain high officials rather than the nation as a whole, and there is no doubt at all that large profits were made by members of the party in power as the result of the currency reform. The men sent from the United States to take charge of the various interests acquired by the bankers have not always shown tact or ability, and some of them, for this reason or from causes lying entirely beyond their control, have become very unpopular. The raising of rates by the railway, and the refusal to grant free passes to all persons of social or political prominence, have caused much dissatisfaction; and the National Bank has been severely criticised for its failure to make loans to everyone who was in need of money. The currency reform was bitterly opposed at first because of the inconvenience which the conversion caused and the apparent shortage of money which resulted, and it was generally regarded as a failure when the bank-notes fell below par at the outbreak of the European war. It has since become more popular. The financial reforms as a whole, however beneficial in the long run, have involved expenses which the nation could ill afford. The expert commission which worked out the currency reform, the mixed claims commission, the officials of the customs service, and other Americans who have been appointed to official or semi-official positions since 1912 have received remunerations which have seemed inordinately large as compared with the incomes of the native officials; and the publication of their salaries and their expense accounts has given rise to many charges of extravagance.

It is easy to point out how insignificant these grievances are as compared with the benefits conferred by the adjustment of and the reduction of charges on the foreign debt, the immense improvement in the operation of the railway and in the customs service, and the establishment of a currency system on a stable basis in place of the depreciated, fluctuating paper of former times. It is also easy to prove that the vast majority of the people have been inestimably better off through the maintenance of order, which has been entirely due to the military and financial support of the government by the United States, than they would have been if the bloody party strife and the wars with Central American neighbors which marked the last years of the Liberal regime had been allowed to continue. But this does not alter the fact that the situation which exists in Nicaragua today is inherently and fundamentally wrong, and that it cannot form a basis for a permanent settlement satisfactory either to that country or to the United States. Our government cannot continue to uphold by force a minority administration and to support that administration in a financial policy which is opposed by the great majority of the Nicaraguan people, if it wishes to eradicate the suspicion in Central America, and in fact throughout Latin America, that its ultimate intention is to deprive Nicaragua, and eventually her neighbors, of their position as independent nations.

CHAPTER XII

COMMERCE

Principal Exports of the Isthmus: Coffee, Bananas, and Precious Metals—Other Products—Imports—Condition of American Trade—Effects of the European War.

THE foreign commerce of Central America is based upon the exchange of coffee, bananas, precious metals, and a few other products of minor importance for manufactured articles from the United States and Europe. The most important export, from the Central American point of view, is coffee; for the banana farms, which belong to foreign corporations and are cultivated by foreign laborers, are situated in districts so far away from the centers of population that they play a small part in the economic life of the country, and the gold and silver mines are also with few exceptions the property of European and North American capitalists. The mining companies give employment to many natives at wages somewhat greater than those paid in agricultural enterprises, but otherwise they do little to add to the general prosperity of the community. The owners of the coffee plantations, the majority of whom are natives, reside in Central America and spend their income there, and all employ exclusively native labor. Except in Honduras, where it is cultivated only for local consumption, coffee is the chief export of the mountain region on the West Coast where the great majority of the inhabitants of the Isthmus live.

Central American coffee is of an excellent quality, and brings a high price in the European markets, to which the greater part of it has always been sent. The product of Costa Rica is a favorite in England, while "Coban" and other Guatemalan varieties are well known in

Germany and on the continent. The product of the Isthmus has not been so popular in the United States, where it has been unable to compete with the lower-priced, but inferior, coffee of Brazil or with certain other superior grades which have secured a better foothold in our markets. Table V indicates the disposition of the crop of each country of the Isthmus in normal times, and to some extent the change which has been brought about in export conditions by the European war.

TABLE I
EXPORTS OF CENTRAL AMERICA, 1913.
(Value in U. S. Gold.)

	Guatemala	Salvador	Honduras	Nicaragua	Costa Rica
Coffee	12,254,724	7,495,214	116,302	5,004,449	3,605,029
Bananas	825,670		1,714,398	429,802	5,194,428
Precious Metals		1,495,805	886,591	1,063,077	1,021,473
Hides	455,476	95,870	159,820	326,599	132,883
Timber	247,759		12,617	321,869	141,361
Rubber	100,323	18,092	14,289	278,763	44,482
Sugar	349,052	72,852		31,805	
Chicle	142,108				
Balsam of Peru		89,476			
Cocoanuts			219,968		
Indigo		52,984			
Cacao				39,828	105,034
Live Cattle			251,361	288,009 [1]	

The ripe berry is prepared for the market at a cleaning and drying plant called a *beneficio*. The larger growers, who produce the greater part of the total crop, ordinarily have their own *beneficios* on their plantations. Those who have not been able to install the rather expensive machinery which these plants require either ship their coffee partly cleaned, in the shell, or else have it prepared for the market on the plantation of a neighbor or at establishments which exist for the purpose in such cities as Guatemala and Managua. The small landholders, many of whom have a few trees from which they

[1] Figures of Costa Rican government for imports from Nicaragua.

Note. These figures are compiled from official statistics, or from the United States Daily Consular and Trade Reports, which in turn are based upon the official statistics of the Central American governments. They are inexact, because the statistics upon which they are based are rarely entirely trustworthy.

secure a money income to supplement their food crops, ordinarily sell their coffee in the berry to the owners of the *beneficios*. The exportation is frequently, perhaps usually, undertaken by the planter himself, who ships his crop directly to an importer in some European city or on consignment to an agent in Hamburg or London, to be sold in the open market. This seems to be the general though not the universal practice in Costa Rica, Salvador, and Nicaragua. In Guatemala, on the other hand, there are several German and North American houses which buy the coffee from the grower and export it on their own account. Certain companies in the United States, with agencies in Central America, have done a large business of this kind, especially since the beginning of the European war.

The majority of the coffee plantations of the Isthmus belong to native Central Americans. This is true even in Guatemala and Nicaragua, where, as has been said in preceding chapters, nearly all of the largest and best equipped *fincas* are the property of Germans or of other aliens.[1] In Salvador and Costa Rica there are few foreign owners. Even in these countries, however, the tendency which has been so strong in Guatemala, for the more valuable plantations to pass gradually into the hands of investors from abroad, has been at work in recent years. Foreign influence, moreover, is by no means confined to the ownership of the plantations themselves, for the native planters frequently have financial connections with European banking houses in the Central American capitals or in Hamburg or London which give the latter a large measure of control over the sale of

[1] Special Agent Harris, in his Report on "Central America as an Export Field" (U. S. Dept. of Commerce, Special Agents' Series, No. 113), gives the following figures in regard to the ownership and production of the coffee plantations of Guatemala:

Nationality	No. of Plantations	Product in quintals
Guatemalan	1,657	525,356
German	170	358,353
North American	16	19,285
Other	236	143,242

their coffee and even over their methods of production. A very large proportion of the plantations is heavily mortgaged to these concerns, and even the annual crop is often hypothecated or sold to the banker several months before it is harvested, and is handled by him when ready for market. The terms of these arrangements are usually anything but favorable to the planter. In Guatemala, for example, the banker ordinarily not only receives interest on the sums advanced at the prevailing rate of ten or twelve per cent, but at the same time takes an option upon the entire crop, under which he can purchase it at twenty-five cents per bag less than the market price at the time of the harvest. This option alone is equivalent to the payment by the planter of about three per cent of his entire gross receipts, in addition to the interest. Under these conditions, especially in view of the improvidence and inefficiency of many of the native landowners, it is not strange that the most desirable plantations are passing one by one into the hands of Germans and Englishmen, who are able either to finance themselves or to secure money for moving their crops upon better terms.

TABLE II
THE WORLD'S EXPORTS OF BANANAS, 1911.
(From U. S. Daily Consular and Trade Reports, Dec. 26, 1912.)

Central America—
Costa Rica .... 9,309,586 bunches.
Honduras .... 6,500,000 "
Nicaragua .... 2,250,000 "
Guatemala .... 1,755,704 "

Total .... 19,815,290 bunches.

Other Countries—
Jamaica .... 16,497,385 bunches.
Colombia .... 4,901,894 "
Panama .... 4,261,500 "
Canary Islands .... 2,648,378 "
Cuba .... 2,500,000 "
Mexico .... 750,000 "
British Honduras .... 525,000 "
Other Countries .... 1,037,516 "

Total .... 33,121,673 bunches.

Grand Total .... 52,936,963 bunches.

Total imports into United States, 1911, 44,699,222 bunches. (Commerce and Navigation of the U. S., 1911.)

Second only to coffee in the value of the total amount exported, and far more important so far as the United States is concerned, are bananas. In 1913, nearly twenty-two million bunches, or between two and three billions of bananas, were exported from Costa Rica, Honduras, Guatemala, and Nicaragua. Nearly all of this immense amount, which was about forty per cent of the total commercial production of the world, went to the United States. Less than fifty years ago, Mr. Minor C. Keith, who was building a railway from Puerto Limon to the interior of Costa Rica, began the cultivation of bananas along the line in order to provide freight for the road during the years which must elapse before it could reach the inhabited part of the Republic. Until this time, the hot and unhealthful forests along the East Coast of Central America had been an uninhabited and undeveloped jungle, but they proved so well adapted to the growing of bananas that the fruit farms soon became more valuable than the railway. Meanwhile other planters had engaged in the same business in Jamaica and elsewhere in the West Indies, and the banana, which had hitherto been a curiosity, was coming into general use in the United States. The more important producers around the Caribbean Sea joined in forming the United Fruit Company, which is now by far the most important business concern in tropical America. Its immense plantations in Central America, Jamaica, Cuba, Colombia, and Panama are traversed by hundreds of miles of railway, and their products are carried to the United States and Europe by a great fleet of its own steamers, which are the principal, and since the beginning of the European war almost the only, carriers of freight and passengers between Central American ports and the eastern part of the United States. Besides the numerous lines built expressly for carrying bananas from the farms to the wharves, the Fruit Company, or concerns allied to it, control the entire railway system of Guatemala, a large part of that of Salvador, and the most important road, from San José to Puerto Limon, in Costa Rica. The few independent growers along its lines are completely at its mercy, for they have no alternative but to sell their fruit to it under the conditions which it dictates. In Honduras and Nicaragua, there are a number of ostensibly competing companies, with their own railway lines and ships, but many of these are said to be actually under the control of the greater corporation. The latter has on more than one occasion shown itself ruthless and unscrupulous in dealing with real competitors, over whom it has every advantage through its control of the facilities for shipping fruit.

In the last few years, the bananas have been attacked by a disease which apparently shows itself in nearly all plantations after a certain period of cultivation. Its appearance has made it necessary to abandon large tracts of developed land and many miles of railway, especially in some portions of Costa Rica. No means of checking it has yet been discovered, and it has been found easier to plant new farms than to fight it where it has obtained a foothold. At present the disease does not seem likely to decrease materially the total production, for there are still immense tracts of virgin land suitable for banana growing around the shores of the Caribbean Sea, but it is a very grave menace to the prosperous communities which have grown up on the coast as a result of the fruit trade. Unless it is overcome, or unless some other product, such as cacao, can be grown on the abandoned farms, there seems to be serious danger that many sections of the East Coast will sink back into jungle.

Among Americans who have been on the Coast and have but a slight acquaintance with the interior, there is a tendency greatly to exaggerate the influence of the United Fruit Company in Central America. As a matter of fact, that corporation plays a smaller part than might be expected in the economic and political life of the five republics. On the Coast, especially in Costa Rica, it is all-powerful, for it absolutely controls the industry and the export and import trade of the banana country, and is the employer of the greater part of the population; but in the interior, where the great majority of the people live, its influence is confined to its control of the railway lines. These are not owned and operated directly by the Fruit Company, but by corporations closely connected with it. There are also many other enterprises, including street railways, mines, and electrical plants, which have been financed by some of the capitalists who are prominent in the Fruit Company, so that the total Central American investments of what are known as the "Keith interests" are very great. These investors, however, apparently interfere little in politics. Their relations with the governments, sometimes cordial, sometimes the opposite, are not so close that they can be said to exercise any important influence on the internal affairs of any of the five republics, and the native officials are apt to be jealous of their power and to regard with suspicion any concession which seems likely to increase their influence.

Notwithstanding the immense development of the banana trade, the full possibilities of this fruit in providing cheap fruit for the people of the temperate zones are still far from being realized. Exportation from Central America and other producing countries is at present limited to the amount necessary to meet the demand for the fresh fruit in the United States, because the European market has as yet been little exploited, and few facilities have been provided for exporting bananas from the Caribbean to transatlantic ports. A considerable proportion of the product of Costa Rica was sent to England in the years immediately preceding the war, but the total was insignificant in comparison with the consumption in the United States.[1] Millions of bunches of fruit now go to waste every year, for the amount cut each week on the plantations is arbitrarily limited with a view to the state of the market and the facilities for shipping, and thousands of bunches are rejected at the train or at the steamer as being overripe or otherwise defective. It ought to be practicable to convert this waste product into dried bananas or banana flour, both of which are now commercially possible, but few attempts have so far been made to do so. The two or three factories which have been established in Central American ports for this purpose have had little success, apparently from poor management or lack of proper equipment.

The precious metals, which rank third in the list of exports, are found in all parts of Central America, but as yet they have been exploited on a comparatively small scale. There are a few gold and silver mines, operated by foreign capital, in each of the republics except Guatemala, but the total exportations of the Isthmus, according to customs reports, amounted to less than four and one half millions of dollars in 1913.[2] The investment of foreign capital in mines has been discouraged by the disorder which has prevailed in some of the five republics, and the lack of adequate transportation facilities has been an obstacle to the introduction of heavy machinery and to the exportation of the product. These difficulties, which have held back the production of gold and silver, have of course made impossible the exploitation of the other mineral resources of the Isthmus, although these are known to be great. With the estab-

[1] 2,763,111 bunches were exported from Costa Rica to England in 1913. (Costa Rica, *Anuario Estadístico*, 1913, p. 279.)

[2] It is probable that more than this was actually produced. Large amounts are said to be smuggled out of certain countries every year to avoid paying the export tax, and this assertion is to some extent borne out by a comparison of the export statistics with the import statistics of the United States.

lishment of internal stability and the building of good roads to the metalliferous districts, however, mining should easily become a much more important industry than it is at present.

In comparison with coffee, bananas, and the precious metals, the other exports of Central America are of little importance. The herds of cattle, which are one of the principal forms of wealth in Honduras and Nicaragua, provide some horns and hides for shipment to foreign countries, but the quantity has hitherto been very small. The live animals are the chief articles of commerce between Honduras and Nicaragua on the one hand and their more densely populated neighbors on the other, but they have never been exported to any extent to other countries. Mahogany, Spanish cedar, and other forest products, such as rubber and chicle, which is used in making chewing gum, are exported, chiefly by foreigners, from the low country along the coasts. Sugar in various forms and cacao are grown in large quantities, but almost entirely for local consumption. Besides these products, typical of any tropical country, there are others which have importance in certain localities as articles of foreign commerce. Thus, some millions of cocoanuts are shipped from the North Coast of Honduras, and indigo and balsam of Peru from Salvador. None of these minor exports have received very much attention, because the interest of the native community has been centered in the production of coffee and of the staple food crops, and foreign capital has been invested chiefly in mines, banana plantations, and railways. With the comparatively good transportation facilities that now exist, it would seem that there should be a great opportunity for the cultivation of such products as cacao, vanilla, and rubber, or for the shipment to the United States, on the fast banana steamers, of some of the countless delicious tropical fruits which have hitherto been almost unknown in our markets. Countries of such rich and varied agricultural possibilities, with such easy access to the Gulf ports of the United States, must eventually acquire an importance far greater than that which they now have in supplying our markets with many kinds of food which we cannot ourselves produce.

TABLE III

SHARE OF THE UNITED STATES, GREAT BRITAIN, AND GERMANY IN THE COMMERCE OF CENTRAL AMERICA.

EXPORTS.

	United States	Great Britain	Germany	Total
Guatemala, 1913	3,923,354	1,857,105	7,653,557	14,449,926
1915	6,881,410	1,322,271	50,237	11,566,586
Salvador, 1913	2,676,637	668,823	1,611,085	9,411,112
1915	3,096,277	341,920	9,945	8,812,387
Honduras, 1913	2,974,000	18,000	164,000	3,421,000
1915	2,987,000	1,000	690	3,858,000
Nicaragua, 1913	2,722,385	998,564	1,887,698	7,712,047
1915	3,079,810	438,500	......	4,567,201
Costa Rica, 1913	5,204,429	4,319,085	504,506	10,324,149
1915	4,864,803	4,438,233	13,225	9,971,582
Total for Central America, 1913	17,500,805	7,861,577	11,820,866	45,318,234
1915	20,909,300'	6,541,924	74,097	38,775,756

(Compiled from official reports of the Central American governments. The values are given as in American gold, calculated at the prevailing rate of exchange for the year in question.)

Even before the beginning of the European war, the United States bought the greater part of Central America's exports. Nearly all of the bananas went to American ports, as did by far the greater part of the gold and silver from the mines. With the coffee, the situation was different, but the partial closing of the European markets forced the planters to seek a market for this in the United States. This was especially true in Guatemala, where American buyers were almost the only ones in the field during 1915 and 1916. In the countries which had been less dependent on the German market, the change was not so marked, but all of them nevertheless shipped more coffee to the United States in those years than ever before. Costa Rica, however, retained her privileged position in the London market, at least during 1915, and Salvador found valuable new customers in the Scandinavian countries and Holland. The necessity for finding new purchasers has naturally involved a considerable loss for the Central American planters. Their coffee has on the whole met with a favorable reception in the United States, but the prices which they have received have not been so high as those to which they were accustomed in the markets in which they had long established connections, and they have encountered no little difficulty in making shipments because of the withdrawal of many of the steamers which formerly called at the ports of the Isthmus.

TABLE IV
IMPORTS OF COFFEE INTO THE UNITED STATES, 1913 and 1915.
(From Commerce and Navigation of the United States, 1915, p. 75.)

	1913	1915
Guatemala	18,544,228 lbs.	44,605,039 lbs.
Salvador	8,756,267 "	15,823,350 "
Nicaragua	2,915,239 "	6,430,600 "
Honduras	239,114 "	665,912 "
Costa Rica	1,474,397 "	6,770,964 "

TABLE V
COFFEE EXPORTS OF CENTRAL AMERICA, 1913 and 1915.
(Figures in quintals of 100 lbs. Spanish or 46 kg. From Central American government publications.)

	Guatemala		Salvador		Nicaragua		Costa Rica	
	1913	1915	1913	1915	1913	1915	1913	1915
U. S.	211,886	386,080	107,796	142,337	36,753	62,439	16,032	38,969
England	106,666	.....*	34,151	29,127	32,854	40,816	231,382	204,711
Germany	432,329	.....*	121,201	994	75,634	......	25,451	1,304
Austria-H.	42,054	.....*	35,574	381	......	......	......	......
France	......	.....*	159,559	90,502	103,012	57,379	......	......
Italy	......	......	95,389	76,147	......	30,095	......	......
Holland	......	......	......	92,763	......	......	......	......
Scandinavian countries	......	......	......	218,619	......	......	......	......
Total exports	875,337	775,622	625,942	663,216	243,324	198,533	283,023	265,355

* Figures not available.

The imports of Central America are those of all tropical countries which have no manufacturing industries of their own. Machinery and tools for agricultural purposes; textiles; flour, lard, and other food products which are produced in insufficient quantities in the Isthmus; and in general, manufactured articles of all kinds, must be purchased abroad. The greater part of these are for the use of the upper classes, but even the ordinary laborers, whose standard of living in many places is otherwise little better than it was in the days when the country had no foreign commerce, use some foreign goods, such as cheap textiles and machetes.

In the import as well as the export trade, the United States easily occupies the leading place, supplying the greater part of the foodstuffs, hardware, and machinery, and a very considerable part of the textiles. Our share in the total, even before the war, was well over fifty per cent, with Great Britain and Germany respectively second and third. Tables VI, VII, and VIII will give an approximate idea of the nature and origin of the imports of the Isthmus in normal times. The predominance of the United States was due primarily to proximity and superior steamer connections. The Caribbean ports of the Isthmus, which are less than fifteen hundred miles from our Gulf ports, were connected with those ports by regular lines of swift steamers, whereas they had no adequate means of communication with Europe. The Pacific ports, on the other hand, although they were visited regularly by the small steamers of the German Cosmos Line, relied chiefly upon the service of the Pacific Mail between San Francisco and Panama.

This gave American trade an advantage which would have been even greater than it was if transatlantic manufacturers had not been favored by several factors which to some extent offset their geographical handicap. Freight rates to Europe, however, were not proportionately greater than rates to the United States, even in cases where the goods must be transshipped at a North American port. Furthermore, European merchants controlled the greater part of the import and wholesale trade in each of the five republics, and natu-

TABLE VI

SHARE OF THE UNITED STATES, GREAT BRITAIN, AND GERMANY IN THE COMMERCE OF CENTRAL AMERICA.

IMPORTS.

(Compiled from Central American government publications; values in American gold.)

	United States	Great Britain	Germany	Total
Guatemala, 1913	5,053,060	1,650,387	2,043,329	10,062,327
1915	3,751,761	577,206	146,053	5,072,476
Salvador, 1913	2,491,145	1,603,846	713,855	6,173,545
1915	2,478,322	1,054,838	41,136	4,182,922
Nicaragua, 1913	3,244,008	1,150,611	619,212	5,770,006
1915	2,592,799	302,294	36,960	3,159,219
Honduras, 1913-14	5,262,000	460,000	522,000	6,625,000
1914-15	5,177,000	303,000	96,000	5,875,000
Costa Rica, 1913	4,468,946	1,289,181	1,341,333	8,867,280
1915	3,031,997	548,810	42,979	4,478,782
Total for Central America, 1913	20,519,159	6,154,025	5,239,729	37,498,158
1915	17,031,879	2,786,148	363,128	22,768,399

TABLE VII

PRINCIPAL IMPORTS OF GUATEMALA, 1913 and 1915.

(From U. S. Commerce Reports and Guatemalan official statistics; values in American gold.)

	1913.	1915.
Cotton goods, total	1,734,832	758,570
United States	503,920	
Great Britain	778,278	
Germany	337,181	
Linen, hemp, and jute manufactures (in large part coffee sacks). Total	222,320	252,481
United States	20,788	
Great Britain	80,954	
Germany	111,141	
Woolen manufactures, total	253,107	52,308
United States	30,938	
Great Britain	64,635	
Germany	111,866	
Silk manufactures, total	263,448	68,525
(Mostly from Japan, China, and France.)		
Manufactures of iron and steel, total	685,548	121,198
United States	384,094	
Great Britain	97,434	
Germany	181,538	
Glass, crockery, earthenware, etc., total	106,825	27,859
United States	24,783	
Germany	58,944	
Leather goods, total	156,688	94,661
United States	110,318	
Germany	30,244	
Foodstuffs, total	566,856	538,236
United States	260,854	
Great Britain	54,859	
Germany	86,923	

278 THE FIVE REPUBLICS

TABLE VII—Continued

	1913.	1915.
Stationery, paper, etc., total	179,798	147,243
United States	87,420	
Germany	60,491	
Drugs and medicines, total	268,523	108,666
United States	99,359	
Germany	62,375	
Wheat flour, from United States	394,931	506,510
Agricultural and industrial machinery, total	350,366	127,433
United States	175,683	
Great Britain	86,456	
Germany	78,711	
Lumber, from United States	179,880	78,667
Railway material, total	426,826	121,843
United States	424,235	
Petroleum, from United States	184,936	110,925
Wines, liquors, etc., total	347,752	125,583
United States	73,752	
Germany	73,415	
Other articles, total	1,636,678	732,449
United States	1,079,007	
Germany	406,214	
Great Britain	50,298	

TABLE VIII

PRINCIPAL IMPORTS OF COSTA RICA.

(From Costa Rican official statistics, quoted in U. S. Commerce Reports, Dec. 9, 1916. Values in American gold.)

	1913.	1915.
Live cattle, from Nicaragua	323,067	95,964
Cotton goods, total	828,948	466,699
United States	243,802	266,333
Great Britain	355,042	129,848
Germany	124,699	4,491
Coal, total	261,975	106,953
United States	258,329	92,039
Drugs, total	150,142	115,903
United States	76,173	85,194
Germany	29,690	4,065
Electrical material, total	150,339	95,176
United States	121,416	86,773
Flour, total	258,407	224,480
United States	257,457	209,662
Lard, total	200,362	144,181
United States	194,968	142,270
Railway material, total	296,772	62,387
United States	272,242	59,725
Rice, total	143,391	108,649
United States	31,621	93,283
Germany	82,088	......
Wheat, from United States	219,487	323,567
Coffee sacks, total	88,958	98,531
United States	11,161	13,220
Great Britain	69,424	83,919

rally bought articles from export houses in their own country, whenever they could, not only for sentimental reasons, but because they received better terms and longer credits. Even at the present time, when the war has caused a great reduction in the exports of all of the belligerent countries, the people of the Isthmus still continue to buy certain classes of goods from French or English manufacturers which might just as well be imported from the United States if American manufacturers made an effort to secure the trade.

That they have not done so seems to be due chiefly to indifference. The reasons why American exporters fail to make a better showing in Latin American markets have been discussed so often and so fully in the last three years that there is little object in repeating them here. It is sufficient to say that the same story of carelessness in filling orders and in packing goods, of failure to send well-equipped salesmen, and of refusal to comply with the custom of the country in such matters as credits and accommodations, are heard in Central America as elsewhere. Since the European war has forced the importers of the Isthmus to depend more than ever before upon American manufacturers for their supplies, one hears many complaints of inconsiderate or discourteous treatment, and of general inefficiency in handling trade.

One of the chief obstacles to the increase of American trade in Central America has been the lack of banking facilities. Most of the banks which exist in the larger cities of the Isthmus at the present time are purely local institutions, and their operations are rarely such as to make them a strong force for good in the economic life of the community. They speculate in the rate of exchange, issue more or less depreciated paper money, engage in financial transactions with the government which consume a large part of their available funds, and make loans to planters and merchants at rates of interest which vary from ten per cent, with first-class security, to thirty or forty per cent in cases where the element of speculation is greater. These conditions, which are perhaps inevitable in a country where capital is so scarce and where the instability of political affairs makes the element of risk in all credit transactions so great, seriously detract from their usefulness. Unfortunately, moreover, there are some institutions which are not managed in accordance with the principles either of sound banking or of ordinary honesty, and these are necessarily a source of weakness to the whole financial community. Within the last five years, two of the largest banks in Central America have failed, under circumstances which aroused very grave suspicions of mismanagement and defalcation. The banks cannot afford adequate facilities for financing the export and the import trade, for they have neither the available funds nor the connections abroad which are necessary for this purpose. Moreover, they can obtain such high profits in other forms of operations that there is little inducement for them to engage in ordinary commercial transactions. Many of them are engaged in the coffee export business or in other forms of trade themselves and are consequently little inclined to aid other merchants who may wish to compete with them. The establishment of branches of American banks, dedicated to a legitimate banking business, and especially to the financing of American trade, would perhaps do more to stimulate commerce with the United States than any other one influence.

The question of credits has been another serious obstacle to the development of our trade. The average Central American merchant must have from three to six months to make payment for goods which he imports, because he in turn must grant a considerable time to the small retail dealers whom he supplies. American manufacturers are as a rule unwilling to grant credits for so long a period, and they have sometimes exposed themselves to heavy loss when they have done so because of the difficulty of ascertaining which of the local importers were deserving of confidence. This difficulty also could to a great extent be obviated if reliable American banks could be established in the five republics.

That our commerce holds first place in Central America despite these drawbacks is due partly to the fact that there are certain articles, such as flour, railway material, and petroleum, which the people of the Isthmus must almost inevitably purchase in our markets, and partly to the activity of a few great corporations which have stores or permanent agencies in Central America, and handle a very large amount of imports from the United States. The United Fruit Company and other fruit companies in Honduras and Nicaragua, as well as most of the mining companies, maintain commissaries where American goods are sold in great quantities. Grace and Company, in co-operation with the American International Corporation, does a considerable business in merchandise on the West Coast, and has offices in most of the important cities of the Isthmus. Several well-known American manufacturers also are more or less adequately represented by permanent agents in the important commercial centers.

Although our share in the total imports and exports of the Isthmus has been greater than ever before, since the beginning of the European war, the total of our trade has not been so large as might have been expected, because of the partial paralyzation of the commerce of the five republics. At the outbreak of hostilities the foreign credits upon which the normal business of the Central American community had depended were entirely cut off, and exchange on European centers rose to a prohibitive figure, especially in the countries which were not on a gold basis. Merchants were thus unable to obtain goods or even to pay their debts. At the same time, the purchasing power of their customers was seriously decreased, because the rise in the rate of exchange made prices inordinately high in the local currency, and because the planters, unable to secure advances from abroad to move their crops, were forced to cut down their expenditures and in some cases to lay off their workmen. Most of the governments, also, were in severe financial difficulties, for their revenues, which consisted chiefly of the import duties, had declined, and their expenditures, of which the money for the service of the foreign debt constituted an important part, had increased with the advance in the cost of foreign drafts. Some of them were thus unable to pay their employees, and the poverty of the latter intensified the general financial depression. For a time, the sale of foreign goods almost ceased. When it was found, however, that the products of the Isthmus could still be sold abroad, even if at somewhat lower prices, confidence began to return and commerce recovered to some degree, but imports are still far below normal, and seem likely to remain so for some time.

After the close of the war, it seems probable that the position lost by English and German exporters since 1914 will be regained by them, unless their American competitors make a more successful effort than they have yet made to secure a permanent foothold in the market. The European houses which control the import business of the Isthmus will probably turn back to their former correspondents at the first opportunity, for their experience with American firms in the last three years has not been such as to encourage them to continue it after they are able to resume their old connections. Many of the difficulties which merchants in Central America say they have encountered in dealing with American exporters have undoubtedly been due to war conditions in the United States and to an ignorance on both sides of the other's methods of doing business, but many others can only have resulted from carelessness and indifference to new trade opportunities.

Nevertheless, there is every prospect that the share of the United States in the commerce of Central America will continue to increase in the future as it has in the past. Proximity and the excellent steamer connections created by the banana trade give our manufacturers an advantage against which European importers will find it increasingly hard to compete. The North American element in the Isthmus as a whole is increasing more rapidly than any other foreign element, especially in the banana towns on the East Coast, and North American investments are probably already greater than those of any other country. The richer classes among the Central Americans themselves, moreover, travel more and more in the United States rather than in Europe, and thus acquire a taste for articles of North American manufacture, where they formerly demanded French or English products. A great increase in our trade with the five republics waits only upon the establishment of proper banking facilities and upon the awakening of American exporters to a realization of their opportunities.

CHAPTER XIII

CENTRAL AMERICAN PUBLIC FINANCE

Sources of Revenue—Defects of the Fiscal Systems—Floating Debts—Brief History of the Bonded Debt in Each Republic—Depreciation of the Currency Systems—The Monetary Situation in Each Country—Need for Financial Assistance from the United States.

FEW factors have done more to retard the economic progress of the Central American republics than the defects of their fiscal systems. The inability of the governments to meet the current expenses of efficient administration or to discharge their obligations to foreigners, and the demoralization of the monetary systems which has resulted from attempts to make the depreciation of the currency a source of revenue, have been a serious drawback to the investment of capital and the development of commerce in the Isthmus, and have involved some of the five countries in rather serious diplomatic complications. This financial weakness has been due partly to the nature of the governments' incomes, partly to defects in administration, arising from ignorance or dishonesty, and partly to general economic and political conditions.

Each of the five republics obtains its revenues principally from customs duties, on exports and imports, and from the rum monopoly. Other sources of income, of which the most important are tobacco and powder monopolies and stamp taxes, amount to very little as compared with these two great items. Direct property taxes, the introduction of which has at times been attempted in Guatemala, Nicaragua, and Costa Rica, have met with very little success, and have been very unpopular.

This fiscal system has many bad features. The duties upon imports, upon which the chief reliance is placed, are so high that they seem in many cases to discourage commerce. This is especially true in regard to the cheap textiles and other articles used by the working classes, for the imposition of the duty according to the gross weight of the package, and the failure to make adequate distinction between different qualities of the same category of articles, raises the prices of some goods to a point where consumption is materially lessened. There are still stronger objections to the second great source of revenue, the manufacture and sale of *aguardiente,* or rum, for as in other countries where similar monopolies have existed the temptation to stimulate the consumption of the liquor has in some cases proved stronger than consideration for the welfare of the community. In view of the relation between drink and vice and crime, which is nowhere more directly evident than among the working classes of the Isthmus, it is hard to understand how the public authorities can not only permit but encourage the unrestricted sale of what is little more than a low grade of alcohol. Some of the governments, indeed, have endeavored by raising the price of the *aguardiente* to check its consumption, and have done so without materially decreasing their own income, but with the majority the object has seemed to be to sell a large amount at a low price rather than the opposite.

The following table shows the revenues of each of the five republics in 1913, the last year before the general financing disorganization caused by the European war:

Revenues in 1913. (Approximate equivalent in American gold.)

Source of revenue	Guatemala	Honduras	Salvador	Nicaragua	Costa Rica
Import duties	1,930,000	1,130,000	2,900,000	1,680,000*	2,500,000
Export duties	1,275,000	88,000	600,000	......	112,000
Liquor and other monopolies	450,000	775,000	1,200,000	1,368,000	1,150,000
State owned railways, telegraphs, postal service, etc. (Gross income)	200,000	140,000	285,000	......	500,000
Miscellaneous	325,000	377,000	615,000	317,000	208,000
Total revenues	4,180,000	2,500,000	5,600,000	3,355,000	4,470,000

* Includes export duties.

The way in which the Central American governments spend their income has already been described. The heaviest outlays are those for military purposes and for the service of the foreign debt. The following table shows roughly the division of the expenditures between the different departments of the administration:

Expenditures in 1913. (Approximate equivalent in U. S. gold.)

Department	Guatemala	Honduras	Nicaragua	Salvador	Costa Rica
Gobernación	220,000	320,000	208,000	860,000	380,000
Public works	130,000	287,000	902,000	600,000	695,000
Public instruction	180,000	152,000	159,000	354,000	635,000
War and marine	520,000	720,000	410,000	1,600,000	627,000
Finance and public credit	475,000	185,000	385,000	2,150,000	1,320,000
Charities	.....*	.....*	9,600	500,000	80,000
Judiciary	.....*	70,000	127,000	280,000	325,000
Miscellaneous	695,000	26,000	2,800,000	126,000	211,000
Total expenditures	2,320,000	1,750,000	4,809,000	6,470,000	4,273,000

* Not specified.

Note. The miscellaneous expenditures include items of nearly $500,000 for "exchange," i. e. for buying drafts on foreign places, in Guatemala, and of $1,680,000 for paying claims arising from recent revolutions in Nicaragua.

The revenues are decreased, and the expenditures are increased, in some countries to an alarming degree, by inefficiency and corruption in their administration. The control of the public funds is almost entirely in the hands of the President and his subordinates, for the voting of taxes and of the budget by Congress is a very perfunctory matter even in those countries which have most nearly attained constitutional government in other respects. The income is derived from sources which remain much the same from year to year, and its disposition is subject to little control by the Congress, because the annual financial legislation does not always appropriate specific sums for specific purposes, but simply divides the estimated expenditure between the various departments. The administration, moreover, does not seem to regard itself as bound to keep within the general limits laid down if it can obtain funds for additional outlays. The Congress, which is rarely in a position to oppose itself to the wishes of the executive in this or in other matters, usually ratifies excess expenditures or proposed changes in the budget with little question.

In some of the countries, there is undoubtedly a large amount of corruption in the management of financial affairs. The traditions of the public service encourage rather lax conduct on the part of the officials, for custom and public opinion tolerate many practices which are now considered improper in countries which have had a longer experience in self-government, and those who are unscrupulous are aided in defrauding the government by the inadequate provision which is made for the supervision of accounts. The commonest forms of graft are those which imply a rather loose standard of official morality rather than actual theft or dishonesty, but it cannot be denied that there are many officials, some of whom occupy the highest positions in their respective countries, who have enriched themselves during their tenure of office by means which nothing could excuse. Few such men, fortunately, occupy positions of power in the five republics at the present time.

The chief fault of Central American public finance is the indifference shown in regard to the balancing of revenues and expenditures. The governments frequently pay salaries and other obligations with receipts rather than with money. This practice gives rise to many abuses, for often the receipts can be cashed only by persons having influence with the authorities of the treasury department, and thus become a source of graft. Certain governments, indeed, make it a practice to buy their own promises to pay at a discount, after depreciating them by refusing to redeem them at their face value. The floating debt, which ordinarily bears a very high rate of interest, is always an indefinite but steadily increasing quantity, comprising a great variety of obligations. It includes claims for salaries and for supplies furnished to the government, for damage to property during revolutions, for violated concessions and contracts, and other demands of every degree of validity. Some of these are paid off from time to time as the condition of the treasury permits, but no provision is made for the service or amortization of the internal debt as a whole.[1]

Each of the five republics has also a bonded debt, held for the most part in England. In most cases this dates back to the loan of £163,000 contracted in London by the officials of the first Central American Federation. Costa Rica and Salvador paid off their share of this after they became independent, but the other states, after defaulting for several years, eventually made arrangements for refunding the bonds with new loans. At the same time, further issues were made, chiefly for the construction of railways, during the period of prosperity and inflation which accompanied the first development of the coffee plantations in the seventies and eighties. These were often accompanied by fraud, in which both the officials of the Central American governments and the companies which floated the bonds participated, and which in some cases reached immense proportions. The service of the foreign debts became very difficult when the coffee prices fell, and when the decline in the price of silver, upon which the monetary systems of the Isthmus were based, greatly increased the amount of the debt in terms of the national currency without proportionately increasing the national revenues. During the decade 1890-1900, nearly all of the republics found

[1] The internal debt of each of the republics, according to statistics compiled from their Treasury Reports and from the 1915 Report of the Council of the Corporation of Foreign Bondholders, was as follows on December 31, 1914.

(Figures in American gold.)

Guatemala	3,880,986
Salvador	4,563,676
Nicaragua	6,676,662
Honduras (July 31, 1914.)	1,844,585
Costa Rica	2,692,215

it impossible to maintain regular payments of interest. New arrangements were therefore made with the creditors, who were forced to accept successive reductions of their claims, amounting in some cases to a large proportion of the total, in order to obtain any payment at all. These readjustments, with the partial repudiation which they involved, naturally injured severely the credit of the five countries.

Guatemala has until very recently been involved in almost continuous difficulties with her creditors. Her share of the debt of the Central American Federation remained in default until 1856, when it was refunded with the accrued interest into a new five per cent loan of £100,000. In 1869 another loan of £500,000, issued at 70½ and bearing interest at six per cent, was issued through a London banking house. Both loans went into default in 1876. They were refunded in 1888 by a bond issue of £922,700, bearing four per cent interest, and another issue was made at the same time to consolidate the internal debt. The Republic again failed to meet its obligations to its creditors in 1894, and the latter were forced to accept a further reduction of their claims. By an arrangement made in 1895, both the external and internal bonds were refunded by a new issue of £1,600,000, at four per cent, secured by a special tax of $1.50 gold on each bag of coffee exported. These bonds now constitute the principal foreign debt of the Republic. The government soon violated the terms of the agreement under which they were issued, for the the coffee export tax was reduced in 1898 and 1899, and its proceeds were used for other purposes than the service of the loan. Payments of interest were suspended from 1898 to 1913. After several fruitless attempts to reach an agreement, the bondholders finally secured the resumption of payments through the energetic diplomatic intervention of the British government, and the interest has been met regularly since 1913. The principal, on December 31, 1915, amounted to £2,357,063.[1]

Salvador had paid off her share of the federal debt in 1860, by a compromise with the holders of the bonds. In 1899, a loan of £300,000 at six per cent and in 1892 another of £500,000 at six per cent were obtained from bankers in London for the purpose of extending the railway line from Acajutla to Santa Ana and San Salvador. These were secured by mortgages on the railway. In 1894 the service of the loans was assumed by the Central American Public Works Company, which took over the railway for eighty years in return for a promise of an annual subsidy from the government and a guarantee of a minimum annual profit. In 1899 this company entered into another contract with the Republic, by which it agreed to retire on its own account all of the 1889 and 1892 bonds, converting them into five per cent mortgage debentures of the Salvador Railway Company, which had been formed to take over the concessions held by the Public Works Company. The Railway Company was to receive a fixed annual subsidy of £24,000 for eighteen years. In this way the bonds ceased to be obligations of the Republic. The only foreign bonded debt of Salvador at the present time is the issue of six per cent sterling bonds secured through two London banks in 1908. On January 1, 1916, £756,900 out of the original £1,000,000 were still outstanding. The service of these was suspended after the outbreak of the European war, but an arrangement was made with the bondholders by which the coupons from August, 1915, to August, 1919, were to be funded into new bonds bearing seven per cent interest.

Costa Rica, which had paid off her share of the Central American debt in full immediately after the

[1] These and other details in regard to the bonded debts of the Central American Republics are for the most part based on information in the 1915 Report of the Council of the Corporation of Foreign Bondholders in London.

dissolution of the Federation, contracted two loans in London,—one of £1,000,000 at six per cent in 1871, and the other of £2,400,000 at seven per cent in 1872,— during the first years of General Guardia's administration. From the two, it is said that the Republic received a total sum of £1,158,611, 18 s, 5 d,[1] the rest being kept by the speculators who arranged the transaction. The service of the debt was suspended in 1874. In 1885 a new arrangement was made through Mr. Minor C. Keith, by which the old bonds were refunded at one half their face value by a new issue of £2,000,000 at five per cent. The interest was to be paid by Mr. Keith until 1888, in return for concessions in regard to the railroad which he was building, and after that date by the government. The service of the debt was suspended from 1895 to 1897, when a new agreement was made by which the rate of interest was reduced and the unpaid coupons were exchanged for certificates at forty per cent of their face value. Payments were resumed and were maintained until October, 1901, when a financial crisis caused by high rates of exchange and falling coffee prices again forced the government to suspend them. For nearly ten years the bondholders were put off, usually on the ground that the Republic was unable to pay as much as its creditors asked. Each administration made an effort to settle the matter by securing a reduction of the debt, but refunding contracts made with Speyer and Company in 1905 and with the National City Bank of New York in 1909 were rejected by the Congress. Finally, however, the pressing need for refunding the internal debt, which bore ruinous rates of interest and was increasing alarmingly every year, led the government to make a new contract with Mr. Minor Keith in 1911. This provided for a bond issue of £1,617,200, bearing four per cent interest for the first ten years and five per cent thereafter, to refund entirely the principal and the unpaid interest

[1] Message of President Jiménez to Congress, 1911.

of the old debt, which, even with the numerous previous reductions, amounted to £2,710,293 by the end of 1910. The creditors accepted the arrangement, and the bonds were taken by an international syndicate, formed by bankers in New York, London, Hamburg, and Paris. The interest was secured by the customs revenues, the administration of which was to be taken over by the syndicate in case of default. As soon as the Congress had ratified this agreement, another loan of 35,000,000 francs at five per cent, issued at eighty, and secured by a mortgage on the *aguardiente* monopoly, was arranged in Paris for the payment of the internal debt. Since 1911, the service of these obligations has been maintained with scrupulous regularity. The total foreign debt of the Republic on December 31, 1915, was 31,478,392.27 colones, or $14,641,112.68 American gold.[1]

In Nicaragua, £285,000 in six per cent bonds secured by a mortgage on the National Railway had been issued in 1886. Payments were suspended on these in 1894, and an arrangement was made in 1895 by which the interest was reduced to four per cent. In 1904, another six per cent loan, to the amount of $1,000,000 gold, was negotiated with Mr. Weinberger of New Orleans. Both of these debts were paid in 1909 by means of an issue of £1,250,000 at six per cent contracted for by the Ethelburga Syndicate of London. The interest on the Ethelburga loan was reduced to five per cent in 1912, through the good offices of the two New York banking firms which had undertaken the reorganization of the currency, on condition that these firms continue to administer the customs revenues of the Republic, by which the bonds were secured. The total foreign debt of Nicaragua on December 31, 1915, was as follows:[2]

---

[1] Costa Rica, *Memoria de Hacienda*, 1915. This sum includes certain minor obligations to correspondents in New York, London, and Paris.

[2] This does not include the accrued interest, which now amounts to a considerable sum, as the service of the loans has been suspended since 1914.

Ethelburga bonds (£1,179,620) $5,740,131
Debt to Brown Brothers and Seligman 1,060,000

Total $6,800,131

Honduras is now the only one of the Central American republics which has not effected some adjustment of its foreign debt. This country, on January 1, 1916, owed to foreign creditors the immense sum of £25,407,858,[1] arising from loans contracted in London and Paris in the years 1867-70. Bonds to a nominal value of £5,398,570, and bearing from five to ten per cent interest, were issued at that time for the construction of an interoceanic railroad from Puerto Cortez to the Gulf of Fonseca. The greater part of the money received from the investors in these securities seems to have been divided between the officials of the Republic and the promoters, with the result that the sum which finally found its way into the national treasury was sufficient only to build ninety kilometers of the railroad. The payments of interest, which until that time had been made out of the principal of the loan, were suspended in 1872, and the quotation of the bonds on the European exchanges dropped rapidly from 85½% to 1¼% of their face value.[2] A few half-hearted efforts to enter into negotiations with the bondholders have been made during the years which have since intervened, but the Republic has shown little inclination to make good its obligations, and there have even been occasional propositions to repudiate the debt altogether, because of the fraud which accompanied its flotation. Meanwhile the government has been unable to make arrangements for the extension of the National Railway into the interior, because of the lien held by the bondholders upon the line, and it

[1] Report of the Council of the Corporation of Foreign Bondholders, 1915, p. 207.
[2] Honduras, Boletín Legislativo, April 19, 1911. (Quoting from the Moniteur des Rentiers of Paris.)

has also been unable to obtain new loans for carrying out other internal improvements. The foreign debt has thus been one of the principal factors which have retarded the Republic's economic advance.

Early in 1909, a plan for the settlement of the debt was arranged by the British minister in Central America, but its consummation was prevented by the protest of the United States, which insisted that provision must at the same time be made for the adjustment of certain American claims. An arrangement suggested by J. P. Morgan and Company was therefore substituted for the British scheme. The New York bankers agreed to purchase the old bonds at the rate of £15 in cash for each £100 of the old bonds with their accrued interest, on condition that the United States government be a party to the agreement under which this was done. After some delay, a treaty was signed on January 10, 1911, by Secretary of State Knox and the Minister of Honduras at Washington, in accordance with which the United States was to assist Honduras in obtaining a loan secured by her customs duties, which were to be administered, until the bonds were paid, by a collector general nominated by the State Department. The treaty was rejected by the Honduranean Congress on January 31, 1911.[1] After the Bonilla revolution, another attempt was made to arrange for the loan, but there was such strong opposition to the treaty in the American Senate that nothing could be accomplished. In February, 1912, J. P. Morgan and Company withdrew from the negotiations, and a syndicate of New Orleans bankers took their place. The treaty, however, was never ratified, and the plan for a new loan was finally abandoned.

At the Pan American Financial Conference in May, 1915, the delegates from Honduras announced that their

---

[1] The treaty was exactly similar to that signed in the same year by the United States and Nicaragua. For the text, see the American Journal of International Law, Vol. 5, supplement, p. 274.

government was ready to increase the customs duties and the banana export tax to a point where they would yield an additional sum of $410,000 gold each year, which might be set aside for the service of the foreign debt. As the holders of the bonds have indicated their willingness to negotiate upon this basis, there seems to be reason to hope that an adjustment will eventually be brought about which will place the credit of the Republic on a sound basis.[1] Until this is done, it will be impossible to build railroads or to carry out the other internal improvements which are indispensable for the development of the country.

The failure of the Central American governments to fulfill their obligations to foreign creditors is not due entirely to a listless sense of national honor, for in many cases there has been serious doubt whether these obligations should be regarded as entirely valid. The circumstances under which the majority of the public debts were contracted were such that the governments have felt a strong reluctance to recognize their duty to repay them in full. The bonds, bearing heavy rates of interest, were usually purchased in the first place at a considerable reduction from their face value, and the speculators who floated them took advantage of the ignorance or the cupidity of the agents with whom they negotiated to defraud the borrowing governments of large sums. A large part of the product of the issue, in fact, seems in many cases to have been retained by the underwriters or divided by them with the Central American officials. Subsequent administrations were naturally unwilling to repay sums from which the country as a whole had never received the benefit, especially as the service of the loan involved a heavy and in some cases intolerable burden upon the impoverished treasury and deprived the government of resources which were sorely needed for the

[1] See the 1915 Report of the Council of the Corporation of Foreign Bondholders.

maintenance of order and the promotion of internal improvements.

One of the influences which have most disastrously affected the government finances and the credit of the Central American republics during the last generation has been the depreciation of their currencies. Until the last decade of the nineteenth century, the money of the Isthmus had been based upon the silver dollar, subdivided into eight *reales* or one hundred cents. Each of the five countries had its own coinage, but foreign money, especially from other Latin American states, was ordinarily accepted at its face value. When the market price of silver declined, as it did with great rapidity after 1890, there was a serious disturbance both of the foreign commerce and of the finances and credit of the five governments, and this disturbance was intensified by a further depreciation of the currency, in Guatemala, Costa Rica, and Nicaragua, by the issue of irredeemable paper money. For a number of years, rates of exchange fluctuated widely, with a general upward tendency, and it became increasingly difficult for merchants to pay their bills in foreign countries and for the governments to meet the service of their loans. Costa Rica, and later Nicaragua, succeeded in establishing a currency on a gold basis, but in the other republics the situation grew more and more difficult until the outbreak of the European war in 1915. This catastrophe caused the rate of exchange upon New York to rise from 25 to 100 per cent in each of the five countries, and made necessary a suspension of payments upon the foreign debt in two of them.

Several causes have contributed to the disorganization of the Central American currencies. The fallacies which have at times caused unfortunate experiments with the monetary systems of other countries have been as attractive in Central America as elsewhere, and every financial or commercial depression has seen demands, which have usually been acceded to, for an increase in the circulating medium. The banks, whose notes form the larger part of the currency in each state, have been subject to little effective regulation, and have in some cases been abetted by the governments in flooding the country with worthless paper money. By unscrupulous speculation in foreign exchange, moreover, they have often done much to cause unnecessarily violent fluctuations in the premium on gold. At the present time, laws relieving the banks of their obligation to exchange their notes for gold or silver are in force in Guatemala, Salvador, Nicaragua, and Costa Rica. The factor which has done most to disorganize the monetary systems of the five republics, however, has been the inability of the authorities to resist the temptation to use the depreciation of the currency as a source of revenue. There is no easier method of raising money for pressing needs than the issue of government paper or the granting of special privileges to the banks in return for loans; and few of the countries have as yet learned that such a policy in the long run does far more harm than good.

The worst currency system of the Isthmus is that of Guatemala, where silver coin has entirely disappeared from the circulation within the last twenty years. On assuming office in 1898, President Estrada Cabrera found himself confronted by serious financial difficulties arising from the extravagance of his predecessor and the business depression from which all of the Central American countries were at the time suffering. In order to provide funds, the new administration resorted to what was practically an issue of unsecured paper money. In return for a large loan, drawn in part from the reserves which guaranteed their circulation, the banks were relieved of their obligation to redeem their notes in silver, and a large issue of new notes, guaranteed solely by the claims of the banks against the government, was made at the same time through the so-called *Comité Bancario*.

Subsequent decrees made all debts payable in paper even though the contracts expressly provided for payment in silver. The redemption of the bank-notes has never been attempted, and further issues have been made from time to time until the amount in circulation, on January 1, 1916, was more than $160,000,000.[1] The money depreciated rapidly. Just before the outbreak of the European war, the paper *peso* was worth about five cents in gold, but in August and September, 1914, the difficulty of obtaining drafts on foreign countries forced the rate of exchange from 20 to 1 to 40 to 1. It has remained approximately at this point since that time, although it has fluctuated considerably, sometimes rising or falling as much as thirty per cent within a few weeks.

The circulating medium is now in a very bad condition. The notes of the smaller denominations are dirty and torn almost beyond recognition, and in quantity they fall far short of supplying the necessities of commerce. The subsidiary coinage, which consists of nickel and copper pieces of $12\frac{1}{2}$ and 25 cents, is also insufficient in quantity, and it is supplemented in ordinary transactions by tokens issued by business houses and municipalities, tram-car tickets, and postage stamps. This state of affairs naturally causes great inconvenience to persons engaged in commerce on a small scale.

The fluctuations in the rate of exchange make business transactions very difficult, for merchants who handle imported goods must change their prices from day to day if they are to avoid loss, and must at the same time face the greatly decreased purchasing power of the masses of the people when the money in which wages and salaries are paid depreciates. There is a growing tendency to quote prices and make transactions in United States currency, of which there is a large amount in circulation.

[1] U. S. Commerce Reports, Supplement 29a, September 2, 1916.

Proposals for reforming the currency have been made from time to time, but none of them have been taken up by the government. The reintroduction of a metal standard, in fact, has been opposed by one of the most influential classes in the community. The coffee planters and other employers of labor have benefited greatly by the rising rate of exchange. Despite the depreciation of the currency, they have raised the wages of their employees comparatively little, and the latter, bound by contracts from which the decline in their earning power made it more difficult than ever for them to escape, have been unable to protest. The result has been an enormous increase in profits, for wage costs have been reduced, while the coffee has continued to be sold for gold in the European and North American markets. The government also benefits by the present situation, for the revenues from the customs houses are received in gold, and the employees are paid in paper, with the result that there is a yearly increasing surplus in favor of the treasury. The effect of this condition on the morality of the underpaid officials has already been mentioned.

In Nicaragua, monetary conditions were much similar to those in Guatemala before the reform carried out by the New York bankers in 1912. President Zelaya had driven the silver out of circulation early in his administration by the issue of legal tender treasury notes, and the value of the *peso*, after his fall, had sunk to about five cents gold. The establishment of a new currency, under the 1911 treasury bills agreement, has been described in Chapter XI. At the beginning of the European war, the new money was exchangeable at par for sight drafts on New York. The inability of the government to replenish the exchange fund against which these drafts were drawn forced the National Bank to suspend their sale for a time, with the result that the premium on American exchange rose to thirty per cent early in 1915. More recently, however, the National

Bank has resumed the sale of drafts at par with its own funds.

Honduras is still upon a silver basis. Silver coin circulates at its intrinsic value, and bank-notes, which are generally used in commerce, are accepted at par in the cities and towns, although the country people as a rule prefer to use specie. The Republic has coined little money of its own, but a considerable part of the silver of Guatemala and Nicaragua found its way over the border when those republics fell under a paper regime, and *pesos,* or dollars, from Salvador, Chile, and Peru are in general use. The monetary system of the Republic is thus better than that of the majority of its neighbors, but it can nevertheless hardly be said to be sound. The rise and fall of the price of silver in the world's markets involves fluctuations in the rate of exchange which are only less violent than in the case of an unsecured paper circulation, and cause much inconvenience and danger to merchants dealing with foreign countries. A part of the Republic's imports, which for several years past have exceeded the exports, are undoubtedly paid for in silver coin, despite the restrictions on the export of specie. This tends to leave only subsidiary coins, of a lower standard of fineness than that of the *pesos,* in circulation, and to make it more difficult also for the banks to maintain their metallic reserves. Since the beginning of 1916, especially, the scarcity of exchange on New York, combined with the high price of silver in the foreign markets, has threatened to drain the country of its circulating medium, and has forced the government to forbid entirely the exportation of coin.

The currency of Salvador was until very recently on a silver basis, but in August, 1914, the banks, whose notes formed a large part of the circulating medium, were allowed to suspend silver payments in order to safeguard their metallic reserves, and the exportation of specie was forbidden. Silver coin has now almost disappeared from circulation, and bank-notes and small nickel coins have taken its place in all transactions. The fact that the banks still maintain a large reserve for the resumption of specie payments after the war, however, has prevented a serious depreciation, although the rate of exchange has fluctuated considerably.

In Costa Rica, the depreciation of the currency had begun as early as 1882 with the issue of government paper and bank-notes which gradually drove silver coin out of circulation. Rates of exchange rose slowly until 1896, when President Rafael Yglesias procured the passage of a law which provided for the establishment of a gold standard. A unit called the *colón,* worth about 46½ cents in United States currency, was adopted, and certificates were gradually exchanged for the old money at the rate of one *colón* for one *peso.* On July 15, 1900, the government was able to begin the redemption of these certificates in gold coin. A new law, meanwhile, had required the banks to guarantee their notes by adequate reserves of specie, so that the currency of the Republic was placed upon a sound basis. At the outbreak of the European war, however, the government relieved the banks of their obligation to redeem their notes in gold. A little later, finding that its revenues were falling off, and being unable to arrange for a loan with the existing banks, it granted to a new institution, the Banco Internacional, the privilege of issuing inconvertible notes secured by government bonds. The result was a rapid depreciation of the currency. The rate of exchange on New York rose from 218 on August 1, 1914, to 260 in January, 1915, and to nearly 300 a few months later. It has been reduced somewhat since that time, and a metallic reserve has gradually been accumulated by the Banco Internacional, so that there seems to be ground for hoping that the paper will be redeemed at par when normal conditions are restored.

The Central American republics will have to depend

upon the assistance of foreign capital both for the readjustment of their foreign debts and the reorganization of their monetary systems,—reforms for which the need will become pressing soon after the conclusion of the war. The problem of placing their credit on a sound basis is one of the most important which confronts them today. If their economic development is to continue, they will require new loans from abroad, not only for refunding old obligations and stabilizing their depreciated and fluctuating currencies, but also for building railways and roads, improving ports, and making other internal improvements. These new loans, probably, can be obtained to best advantage only in the United States, with the aid of the American government, for no other country has the interest which we have in the solvency and the economic welfare of the Central American nations, and no other, while the Monroe Doctrine is maintained in its present form, is really in a position to guarantee to its bankers the full measure of protection which is necessary to make loans to the republics of the Isthmus a safe investment.

CHAPTER XIV

THE INFLUENCE OF THE UNITED STATES IN CENTRAL AMERICA

The Economic and Political Interests of the United States in Central America—Intervention in the Internal Affairs of the Five Republics—Antagonism in Central America—Beneficial Effects and Shortcomings of Our Policy—How the United States can Assist in Promoting Good Government and Economic Development—Moral Influence of the United States—The Ultimate Object of Our Policy.

THE events of the last ten years have made it clear that the relations between the United States and Central America must inevitably be closer than our relations with countries whose well-being is of less vital importance to us. However much we may dislike interfering in the internal affairs of our neighbors, we cannot remain indifferent when disorder and misrule paralyze agriculture and commerce and threaten to provoke European intervention in a region where our political and economic interests are so great as they are in the republics bordering on the Caribbean Sea. Both for our own security and for the sake of helping neighbors with whom we are united by powerful ties of proximity and common interests, we must inevitably use our influence more and more to aid the Central American republics in developing stable political institutions which will insure their prosperity and their continued independence.

The interests of the United States in the Isthmus are far greater than those of any other foreign power. In the first place, like the other countries around the Caribbean Sea, the five republics are one of the most promising fields for the expansion of American commerce and the investment of American capital. While no one of them is an important customer of itself, together they make up a market which will one day be of very great value. Our exports to them have increased greatly in recent years and especially since the beginning of the European war, and our imports from them are growing steadily. Only a very small part of the food-producing possibilities of the tropics, moreover, has as yet been realized, and economists say that it is not improbable that the people of the temperate zone will be forced to rely upon their equatorial neighbors for an increasingly large proportion of their provisions in the not distant future. If this is so, the development of that part of the tropics which is naturally tributary to us commercially cannot be a matter of indifference. This development can only take place with the improvement of political conditions, and with the introduction of capital from wealthier countries which the establishment of peaceful government will make possible.

The establishment of peaceful government in the Isthmus is a matter in which we are deeply interested for political reasons. The Monroe Doctrine must always be a paramount principle of our foreign policy, at least in so far as it deals with the countries of the Caribbean, because the exercise of political influence in that region by a foreign power could not but be a constant menace to our peace and security. Several European nations, however, have extensive and legitimate interests in Central America, for many of their citizens reside and own property there and most of the foreign debt of each of the five republics is held in London or Paris. It is impossible to expect that they should remain inactive when these investments are made worthless by internal disorders or by the arbitrary action of irresponsible native rulers. Whatever one may think of the morality of the protection of foreign investments by intervention and the collection of public debts by force, this is the established practice of most civilized nations, and it is a practice which finds much justification in the conditions which exist in certain Central American countries. The landing of troops and the seizure of ports by a foreign power, so near our shores and in the immediate vicinity of the Panama Canal, can hardly fail to endanger the most vital interests of the United States, because of the manifold opportunities which such measures afford for exerting an influence over internal politics. The control of the policy of one of the Central American governments by a European chancellory or the grant of special economic privileges would of course be intolerable to the United States. That such consequences might follow even a simple intervention to enforce the payment of debts, is all too evident from events which have occurred in other parts of the world. The American government cannot, however, oppose measures adopted by European powers for the protection of the legitimate interests of their nationals without itself assuming a certain responsibility for the safeguarding of foreign life and property. Even supposing that it were sufficiently powerful to prevent other governments from intervening, it could hardly allow its protection to be made a cloak for the confiscation of foreign property and the repudiation of bonded debts by unscrupulous professional revolutionists like those who have at one time or another been in power in each of the Central American countries.

The United States has already gone very far in its attempts to assist its Central American neighbors to attain political and financial stability. At first it limited its efforts to friendly advice and mediation. By participating in the Washington Conference of 1907, however, it became in a measure responsible for the enforcement of the conventions drawn up by that body, in so far, at least, as they related to the discouragement of revolutions, the compulsory arbitration of disputes, and the neutralization of Honduras.[1] The continual violation of the provisions of the Washington Treaties by President Zelaya of Nicaragua led President Taft to break off relations with him in 1909 and to intervene in the revolution of that year in such a way that the fall of the Liberal administration was inevitable; and the financial and military assistance which it was necessary to render to Zelaya's successors, in order to prevent the Republic from falling into a state of anarchy, imposed new and still greater responsibilities upon the United States. Since 1912, when a revolt against the established authorities was suppressed by American troops, the Conservative government at Managua has been kept in office by the presence of a force of American marines, and the State Department has become deeply involved in assisting the Republic to adjust its financial affairs. The United States has recently acquired new interests in the Isthmus by the treaty giving it the right to construct an interoceanic canal through Nicaragua and to establish a naval base in the Gulf of Fonseca. Meanwhile outbreaks of disorder have been discouraged in all parts of the Isthmus by the influence exerted by the authorities at Washington against violations of the 1907 conventions and by their refusal to recognize governments which came into power through revolution.

The policy of the United States has aroused strong antagonism in Central America. The people of the Isthmus are by no means convinced of the disinterestedness or the friendly intentions of their powerful neighbor, and it would be difficult to persuade them that the interference of the latter in their affairs will ultimately be for their own good. Their hostility is due partly to the inevitable opposition among a proud and sensitive

[1] "The Treaties and Conventions of Washington of 1907, . . . were conceived, debated, and concluded through the friendly intervention of the Government of the United States of America. These conventions have, therefore, the moral guaranty of that great nation." (Case of Costa Rica against Nicaragua before the Central American Court of Justice, 1916, p. 9.)

people to foreign intervention in their domestic concerns, and partly to the failure of the American government to convince the Central Americans of the altruism of its aims. Our State Department has had no definite, well-understood, and energetically enforced policy, but has been forced from step to step by circumstances as they have arisen, and its course of action has not always been such as to inspire confidence in the purity of its motives. The attitude of the American government in the revolution of 1909-10 in Nicaragua, for example, was hardly consistent in view of its championship of the Washington Conventions, notwithstanding the excellent reasons which the United States as well as the Central American countries had for desiring President Zelaya's fall. The "Dollar Diplomacy" of Mr. Taft's administration was regarded throughout the Isthmus as the opening wedge for the political absorption of the five republics by the United States. This feeling caused the emphatic rejection of the proposed loan treaty by the Honduranean congress, and aroused a violent opposition to the financial policy of the Conservative government in Nicaragua,—an opposition which was greatly intensified by the fact that the authorities who signed the loan contracts and who turned over to American banking concerns the control of the customs houses, the currency system, and the national railways, were maintained in office by the armed forces of the United States. The steps taken more recently in connection with the canal treaty have been regarded by many Central Americans as final proof of the aggressive intentions of the American government.

The United States has nevertheless achieved one of its main objects, in that revolutions and international wars have been checked throughout the Isthmus. There has been no very serious disturbance of the peace since the suppression of Mena's revolt in Nicaragua in 1912. This has been due partly to the efforts of the State

Department to secure the strict observance of those provisions of the Washington Conventions which restrain the Central American republics from intervening in one another's internal political affairs, and from allowing their territory to be made the base of operations against neighboring governments, but more to a fear on the part of native political leaders that a renewal of the disorderly conditions which formerly existed would lead to American intervention and to the domination of their affairs, as in Nicaragua, by an outside power. This apprehension has exerted a most valuable restraining influence on enemies of the established order in many countries which had hardly ever known five years of continuous peace before 1912. There were, it is true, small revolts in Nicaragua and Guatemala in 1915 and 1916, but they were easily suppressed by the authorities, and they hardly disturbed the tranquillity of the greater part of the territory of the republics in which they occurred. Their insignificance showed that no large or influential section of the opposition party had participated in them. As the result even of this short era of peace, there has been a marked improvement in economic and political conditions in many sections of the Isthmus.

The policy of refusing to recognize any forcible change of government, however, is a very difficult one to carry out consistently. It would be manifestly impossible to prevent all revolutions. An attempt to do so would involve continual armed intervention in the internal affairs of the Central American republics, which would be as burdensome and distasteful to the United States as it would be intolerable to the people of the Isthmus. It is often equally impossible, and sometimes exceedingly disastrous, to refuse to recognize a government which has sprung from a revolution. After one administration has fallen and its successor has established itself firmly in power, the refusal of the United States to recognize the new authorities only weakens them, and thus opens the way for a complete disintegration of the political organization, without advancing appreciably the cause of constitutional government. The restoration of the old regime is rarely either possible or desirable. The ousted authorities, if they themselves secured office, like almost all Central American administrations, as the result of a successful revolution or an election controlled by the government, can hardly lay claim to a higher degree of legality than their successors, and a president who has once lost his prestige and his following is not often able to re-establish a strong and efficient government, even with foreign support.

The prevention of chronic civil war is indeed the first great requisite for the improvement of political conditions in Central America, but even peace will be a doubtful blessing in the long run if it is secured by the maintenance in office by outside influence of presidents who are responsible to no one and who have nothing to fear from popular opposition. The mere discouragement of revolutions offers no solution for the most serious of Central America's political problems, for it provides no guarantee of good government and no peaceful method of removing authorities whose rule may have become intolerable.

The responsibility resting upon the United States is the more serious, because the American government is not infrequently called upon actually to decide who shall be president of one or the other of the five republics. Even an intervention to protect foreign life and property often determines, as a matter of fact, the outcome of a civil war, and the influence upon internal politics is still greater when the United States uses diplomatic pressure or force to prevent a revolution or to bring about an agreement between the contending factions. In either case, the United States practically imposes upon the country affected the rule of one or the other political group. It is impossible to intervene merely to prevent disorder, and then leave to the people the choice of their own rulers, for elections, as we have seen, are nothing more than a form for putting into effect the choice of the government already in office. It would be foolish to attempt to force democratic institutions upon the less advanced republics of the Isthmus at the present time. No president of one of those countries, however sincere he might be in his purpose, could really hold a free election, and any attempt to do so would probably end in bloodshed and disaster. An election supervised by the United States, which was proposed as a solution of the recent presidential problem in Nicaragua, would be equally unsatisfactory as a means of establishing a new administration. Aside from the difficulty of ascertaining the wishes of a nation where the majority of the voters have no interest in political affairs, there are so many opportunities for fraud and for the exercise of pressure by the government and by the local officials at every stage of the campaign, as well as in the election itself, that it would be practically impossible to guarantee the opposition party a fair chance. An administration which has once obtained military control can perpetuate itself indefinitely under constitutional forms until its opponents become sufficiently strong to overthrow it by force of arms.

The United States, therefore, can hardly assist one party in securing and holding the control of the government, without assuring itself that the men whom it thus keeps in office are acceptable to the people under their rule, and that they administer the affairs of their country with at least a reasonable degree of honesty and efficiency. This can only be done by establishing an administration which fairly represents the best elements in the community. It should not be impossible to secure such an administration by an agreement between the party leaders, who for all practical purposes represent the country in political affairs. Compromise between the various factions, which is the only practicable means, except revolution, of changing the higher officials, is the end towards which the diplomatic efforts of the United States should be directed in cases where circumstances make a reorganization of the government inevitable. The more respectable and patriotic leaders of all parties would far prefer an adjustment of this kind to a continuation of civil war, and even those who might be unwilling to subordinate their own ambitions to the general welfare would probably accept it rather than incur the danger of armed intervention by the United States.

The friendly mediation of the United States would do much to improve the political conditions of the Isthmus if it were directed towards strengthening the influence of the better element in the educated class. Numerous intelligent and patriotic men of high political ideals are to be found in each country, but they have not hitherto had so large a share in the direction of affairs as they should because the revolutions have brought to the front military leaders and demagogues rather than statesmen. Even where men of the highest character have been at the head of the government, as has not infrequently been the case, they have found themselves forced to place corrupt or unworthy men in office for political reasons, because they have been unable to free themselves from dependence upon the support of the professional politicians. With the greater stability in the government which will necessarily result from the discouragement of revolutions, however, the less turbulent elements should become more and more prominent, especially if they are supported by the influence of the United States.

The United States can at the same time materially assist its Central American neighbors by aiding them in securing new loans for the reorganization of their finances and the development of their natural resources.

The unenviable record of Central American bonds makes it unlikely that any bankers, whether American or European, would lend money to one of the five republics, unless it were on the most onerous terms, without an effective guarantee of the protection of their government in case of default. Considering the close relation between the solvency of the countries of the Isthmus and the maintenance of the Monroe Doctrine, it is evident that the United States must eventually exert its good offices in cases where it has been impossible to reach an agreement with foreign creditors by any other means.

In Santo Domingo and Nicaragua, the service of loans made by American bankers has been guaranteed by placing the administration of the customs duties in the hands of officials appointed by or at least approved by the State Department. This is far from being an entirely satisfactory solution of the problem. The collectorships thus far established have provided a highly satisfactory guarantee for the foreign creditors, and have decidedly increased the efficiency of the customs service, but their existence has been very distasteful and of doubtful advantage to the native community. Graft is abolished in the customs houses themselves, but there is nothing to prevent that portion of the receipts which is not used for the service of the foreign debt from being misspent. Revolutions are not done away with, for revolutionists fight, not, as is sometimes said, for the possession of the customs houses, but rather for the control of the appointing power and of the revenues, which the customs officials must necessarily turn over to them when they become the *de facto* government. The chief result is the imposition upon the American government of a heavy burden of responsibility which forces it to intervene continually in the internal affairs of the native governments, and which often leads to friction with the officials and to a feeling of dislike towards the United States in the community at large. The acceptance of foreign financial control, moreover, inevitably involves a lessening of the sense of international responsibility and a certain loss of national self-respect which cannot but react unfavorably upon internal politics.

It may well be questioned whether the bondholders could not be satisfactorily protected by other methods. If, for instance, the foreign loan were secured by the hypothecation of the customs revenues or of some other easily collected source of revenue, with a promise of the protection of the State Department in realizing the guarantee of the loan in case of default, the interests of the creditor would be adequately protected, while the Central American governments, so long as they dealt honestly by the bondholders, would be spared the humiliation of having to place one of their principal functions in the hands of a foreign official who was in no way subject to their control. This is the basis upon which Costa Rica's external debt rests at present, except that no foreign government participated officially in the arrangement. There would probably be little difficulty about maintaining the service of the loan under such conditions. The majority of the Central American governments have shown little regard for their credit in times past, but they would probably manifest little inclination to default if their debts were reorganized on a fair basis, and if they were aware that a failure to pay would involve the seizure of their customs houses.

It is highly desirable that the United States should exercise a measure of control over the operations not only of American bankers but of other American corporations which do business in the Isthmus. The economic development of the last twenty-five years has created a situation in which some of the five republics are almost powerless to protect themselves against the oppression and greed of foreign interests, for corporations like the great fruit companies and the railroad companies are able to bring to the support of their projects financial resources which far exceed those of the local government or of any group of natives. Some of these concerns, by the corruption of officials or by the unscrupulous use of their control of transportation facilities, have obtained special privileges which have been an obstacle to the legitimate business of other foreigners and to the development of the community as a whole. Moreover, serious international difficulties have not infrequently arisen when subsequent governments have attempted to annul or to modify these concessions. Only a more careful supervision of the contracts entered into by American concerns with native officials, who are not always above temptation and who are in any event rarely in a position to ascertain the financial responsibility of the concerns with which they are dealing or the ultimate effects of the privileges which are asked, can insure the United States against the possibility of being forced to use its power to protect unscrupulous speculators and predatory corporations in the exercise of rights which, even though legally acquired, are in many cases extremely unfair and injurious to the countries which have granted them.

The same interests which have obtained inequitable concessions by dishonest methods have too often sought to secure influence with the native governments by fomenting and assisting revolutions against presidents from whom they cannot obtain what they desire. In recent years influences of this kind have done even more to cause internal disorder in some of the republics than the intervention and intrigues of other Central American governments. Honduras has been the chief sufferer, for the numerous outbreaks which occurred in that Republic between 1907 and 1911 seem to have been financed in many cases by interests in New Orleans, and to have received valuable assistance from the foreign colony on the North Coast. In Nicaragua also the indiscriminate granting of concessions on the one hand and the dissatisfaction among the foreign interests which were injured by these grants of special privileges on the other was one of the primary causes of the revolution of 1909-10. If permanent peace is ever to be established in the Isthmus, the encouragement of revolutions from outside, whether it be for the satisfaction of the ambition or the jealousy of petty despots in neighboring republics or for the pecuniary profit of unprincipled foreigners, must be repressed by every possible means.

Much can be done to promote stable government in Central America by the consistent enforcement of the principles of the Washington conventions, for few revolutions, except those which originate in genuine popular discontent with the existing regime, would attain formidable proportions if they were not allowed to use neutral territory as a base and if they received no assistance from other Central American countries or from friends in the United States. If the American government exerts its influence to secure the observation of the 1907 treaties, and at the same time adopts effective means for restraining its own citizens from disturbing the peace of the Isthmus, the position of constituted governments throughout Central America will be greatly strengthened. To be effective, such a policy must be vigorously enforced, and its one end,—to prevent revolutions and international wars in Central America,—should be pursued in such a way that there can be no suspicion of selfish objects or ulterior political purposes.

Much depends upon the character and the ability of the men who are sent to represent the United States diplomatically in the Central American capitals. Unless they are fitted for their positions by disposition and by training, their relations with the native governments can never be entirely satisfactory. An acquaintance with the character of the people and a command of Spanish are of the first importance, for Central American political methods and the motives which govern the action of men and parties, incomprehensible at best to the average American, are entirely beyond the understanding of one who does not speak the language and is thus barred from association with any but a very small portion of the people. The cordiality of our relations with the republics of the Isthmus depends to a very great extent upon the capacity of our agents to win the confidence and friendship of their people; and the extremely important position occupied by the United States minister in these countries, where he is forced to play a part far more influential than that which falls to the lot of the average diplomat, makes it an act of injustice to the Central American countries themselves to send ministers who are not properly qualified for their position.

The influence and authority of the United States in Central America are very great, for there are few educated men in the Isthmus who do not realize that the future of their countries will be determined almost entirely by their relations with their northern neighbor. The people of the five republics have always admired our civilization and our institutions, and they have often turned to the American government, not only for protection against European powers, but also for aid in adjusting their domestic difficulties. They have bitterly resented the policy of the last five years, which they have regarded as a menace to their independence, but their hostility to American intervention would to a great extent disappear if they were convinced that it was actuated by a desire to assist them and not by any purpose of expansion. Even those elements which are most jealously opposed to foreign control at present would not object so strongly to the exercise of foreign influence if they themselves profited by it, and most of the more intelligent and patriotic political leaders avow that they would welcome the assistance of the American

OF CENTRAL AMERICA 317

government in securing peace and stability in the Isthmus and in bringing about the Central American Union.

While their political and economic interests have become so closely interdependent, cultural ties between the United States and Central America have also grown far stronger in the last quarter century as a result of the increasing prosperity of the coffee-producing countries and the improvement in means of communication. The wealthier families of the Isthmus travel more and more in the United States, and a very large proportion of them send their children to be educated in our schools and colleges. English has taken the place formerly held by French as the most widely spoken foreign language, and North American news services and periodicals are the principal sources of information on events occurring in the outside world. The creation of ties of this kind will have more influence than treaties and diplomatic conferences in determining whether our relations with Central America shall be friendly and mutually profitable rather than characterized by dictation and compulsion on the one side and bitter resentment on the other.

The influence of North American civilization in the Isthmus, which is daily becoming stronger under present conditions, could be greatly increased if the missionary educational enterprise which has been so successful in the Orient could be turned in some measure to these countries at our own doors. The establishment by American philanthropic societies of institutions for higher education and for technical training in agriculture and engineering would perhaps do more than any other one factor could to improve both the economic and the political conditions of the Isthmus. Many of the governments have advanced far in the primary instruction of their people, but they have been prevented from making corresponding progress in higher education by the expense involved and by the lack of properly trained teachers. There is no form of assistance which the people of the Isthmus would appreciate more, and which would do more to convince them of the friendly intentions of their great neighbor.

The political stability and the prosperity of the Central American countries have been the one great object which the United States has sought in its relations with their governments. Modern conditions have made the maintenance of peace and the development of commerce and natural resources in the Isthmus far more important to the American people than ever before. It is inevitable, therefore, that the United States should exert a decided influence in the internal affairs of the five republics, so long as disorder and insolvency expose them to aggression by European powers. But it should never be forgotten that the ultimate purpose of the American policy is to enable the countries of the Isthmus to attain a position where they can manage their own affairs without outside interference. Careless talk about the ultimate absorption of these countries by the United States is as unwarranted as it is mischievous, for none of the measures thus far taken in any Central American state have had as their object or their logical outcome permanent political domination. If the efforts of our government to assist its weaker neighbors are to attain any measure of success, its sincerity and its freedom from any desire for territorial expansion must be placed beyond all doubt.

The present political condition of the Isthmus is a transitory one, which is changing rapidly with the economic development of the country and the spread of education among the common people. If they are given a fair chance, the five republics will work out their own salvation, but they will not be aided in doing so either by the establishment of foreign protectorates over them or by the attempt of a foreign government to impose upon their people responsibilities of self-government for which they are not as yet ready. The ultimate solution of their political problems must be sought in making a reality the democratic institutions which each of them already possesses on paper, by preparing their people for the intelligent exercise of the suffrage. When the people are fitted to take an active part in choosing their own officials, as they already do in Costa Rica, and when they have learned the respect for the constitution and for the will of the majority which can only come with experience in self-government, there will be no need for foreign intervention to protect life and property from destruction at the hands of revolutionary armies. To aid in bringing that time nearer should be one of the primary aims of the foreign policy of the United States.

BIBLIOGRAPHY

of the more important historical and descriptive material dealing with Central America

A. OFFICIAL DOCUMENTS.
1. Publications of the United States Government, especially:
Foreign Relations of the United States.
Commerce Reports.
Congressional Documents.
Congressional Record.
Annual Reports of the Navy Department.
Treaties and Conventions of the United States.
2. Publications of Central American governments.
Each of the Central American Republics publishes the annual reports of the principal executive departments, under the titles *Memoria de Relaciones Exteriores, Memoria de Hacienda y Crédito Público,* etc. Most of them also have statistical bureaus, which publish annual reports containing interesting although too often inaccurate material. They also publish official gazettes, collections of laws and treaties, and other material.

B. HISTORICAL WORKS.
1. General histories of Central America.
Bancroft, Hubert Howe: History of Central America. (3 vols.) San Francisco, 1883-90.
Fortier, A., and Ficklen, J. R.: Central America and Mexico. (Vol. IX of G. C. Lee's History of North America.) Philadelphia, 1907.
Fuentes y Guzman, Francisco Antonio de: Historia de Guatemala, ó Recordación Florida. (Deals only with the sixteenth century.) Madrid, 1882-83.
Gómez Carillo, Augustín: Estudio Histórico de la América Central. San Salvador, 1884.
———— ————: Compendio de Historia de la América Central. Guatemala, 1906.

BIBLIOGRAPHY

Jaurros, Domingo: History of Guatemala. (Translated from the Spanish.) London, 1823.
Milla, José: Historia de la América Central, 1502-1821. (2 vols.) Guatemala, 1879-82.
Montúfar, Lorenzo: Reseña Histórica de Centro América. (A collection of source material in 7 volumes.) Guatemala, 1878-87.
Montúfar, Manuel: Memorias para la Historia de la Revolución de Centro América. San Salvador, 1905.
Squier, Ephraim G. Historia Política de Centro América. Paris, 1856.

2. Nicaragua.

Gámez, José Dolores: Historia de Nicaragua. Managua, 1889.

3. Costa Rica.

Mora, Manuel Argüello: Páginas de Historia, Recuerdos é Impresiones. San José, 1898.
Fernández Guardia, Ricardo: Historia de Costa Rica: El Descubrimiento y la Conquista. San José, 1905.
―――― ――――: Same, translated into English. New York, 1913.
―――― ――――: Cartilla Histórica de Costa Rica. San José, 1909.
Fernández, León. Historia de Costa Rica durante la Dominación Española, 1502-1821. Madrid, 1889.
―――― ――――: Colección de Documentos para la Historia de Costa Rica. San José, 1881-83.
Montero Barrantes, Francisco: Elementos de Historia de Costa Rica. (2 vols.) San José, 1892-94.

4. The Mosquito Coast and the Nicaragua Canal.

Keasbey, L. M.: Early Diplomatic History of the Nicaragua Canal. Newark, 1890. (Columbia Ph.D. dissertation.)
―――― ――――: The Nicaragua Canal and the Monroe Doctrine. New York, 1896.
Peralta, Manuel M. de: Costa Rica y Costa de Mosquitos. Paris, 1898.
Travis, Ira D.: History of the Clayton-Bulwer Treaty. Ann Arbor, 1900.
―――― ――――: British Rule in Central America. Ann Arbor, 1895.
Williams, Mary W.: Anglo-American Isthmian · Diplomacy, 1815-1915. Washington, 1916.

5. Walker's expeditions to Nicaragua.
> Doubleday, Charles William: The Filibusters' War in Nicaragua. New York, 1886.
> Lucas, D. B.: Nicaragua: War of the Filibusters. Richmond, Va., 1896.
> Montúfar, Lorenzo: Walker en Centro América. Guatemala, 1887.
> Nicaise, Auguste: Les Filibustiers Américains. Paris, 1861.
> Scroggs, William O.: Filibusters and Financiers. New York, 1916.
> Wells, William V.: Walker's Expedition to Nicaragua. New York, 1856.

6. Miscellaneous material for more recent history.
> Buchanan, William I.: Report of the Central American Peace Conference, 1907. Washington (U. S. State Department), 1908.
> Corte de Justicia Centroamericana. Sentencia en el Juicio promovido por la Republica de Honduras contra las Republicas de El Salvador y Guatemala, 1908. San José, Costa Rica, 1908.
> ———— ————: Anales. San José, 1911–
> Council of the Corporation of Foreign Bondholders; Annual Reports. London.
> Crichfield, Geo. W.: American Supremacy. New York, 1908.
> Espinoza, Rudolfo: Nicaraguan Affairs. Memorial to the U. S. Senate. San José, Costa Rica, 1912.
> Harrison, F. C., and Conant, C. A.: Report Presenting a Plan of Monetary Reform for Nicaragua. Presented to Messrs. Brown Brothers and Company and Messrs. J. and W. Seligman and Company. New York, 1912.
> Knox, Philander C.: Speeches in the Countries of the Caribbean. Washington, 1912.
> Kraus, Herbert: Die Monroedoktrin. Berlin, 1913.
> Jones, Chester Lloyd: Caribbean Interests of the United States. New York, 1916.
> Legation of Salvador in Washington: Before the Central American Court of Justice. The Republic of El Salvador vs. the Republic of Nicaragua. Complaint of the Republic of El Salvador. (Translated.) Washington, 1916.

Legation of Costa Rica in Washington: Before the Central American Court of Justice. The Republic of Costa Rica vs. the Republic of Nicaragua. Complaint of Costa Rica. Washington, 1916.

——— ———: Same title. Decision of the Court in the Case of Costa Rica vs. Nicaragua. Washington, 1916.

Moncada, José María: Cosas de Centro América. Madrid, 1908.

——— ———: The Social and Political Influence of the United States in Central America. New York, 1911.

Oficina Internacional Centroamericana: Centro América. (Quarterly organ of the Bureau.) Published in Guatemala City.

——— ———: El Arreglo de la Deuda Externa de Costa Rica. Guatemala, 1911.

——— ———: Informes de las Conferencias Centroamericanas. Guatemala, 1908-13.

Rojas Corrales, Ramón: El Tratado Chamorro-Weitzel ante Centro América y ante El Derecho Internacional. San José, 1914.

World Peace Foundation: The New Panamericanism. Pt. III. (Pamphlet series.) The Central American League of Nations, Boston, February, 1917.

Zelaya, José Santos: La Revolución de Nicaragua y los Estados Unidos. Madrid, 1910.

C. DESCRIPTIVE WORKS, TRAVELERS' ACCOUNTS, ETC.

1. Central America in general.

Bailey, John: Central America. London, 1850.

Bates, H. W.: Central America, the West Indies, and South America. (In Stanford's Compendium of Geography and Travel.) London, 1878.

Batres, Luís: Centro América. San José, 1879.

Dunlap, Robert G.: Travels in Central America. London, 1847.

Dunn, Henry: Guatemala, or the United Provinces of Central America in 1827-28. New York, 1828.

Froebel, Julius. Seven Years' Travel in Central America, Northern Mexico, and the Far West of the United States. London, 1859.

Keane, A. H.: Central and South America. London, 1901.

Morelet, Arthur: Travels in Central America. New York, 1871.
Palmer, Frederick: Central America and its Problems. New York, 1910.
Perigny, Maurice de: Les Cinq Republiques de l'Amerique Centrale. Paris, 1911.
Sapper, Karl: Mittelamerikanische Reisen und Studien aus den Jahren 1888 bis 1900. Braunschweig, 1902.
―――― ――――: Das Noerdliche Mittel-Amerika. Braunschweig, 1897.
Squier, Ephraim G.: Notes on Central America. New York, 1855.
―――― ――――: States of Central America. New York, 1858.
Stephens, John Lloyd: Incidents of Travel in Central America, Chiapas, and Yúcatan. London, 1854.

2. Guatemala.
Brigham, W. T.: Guatemala, the Land of the Quetzal. New York, 1887.
Crowe, F.: The Gospel in Central America. London, 1850.
Domville-Fife, C. W.: Guatemala and the Central States of America. London, 1910.
Maudsley, A. C. and A. P.: Glimpse at Guatemala. London, 1899.
Pepper, C. M.: Guatemala, the Country of the Future. Washington (Legation of Guatemala), 1906.
Winter, N. O.: Guatemala and her People of Today. Boston, 1909.

3. Salvador.
Martin, Percy F.: Salvador of the Twentieth Century. London, 1911.

4. Honduras.
Belot, Gustave de: La Verité sur le Honduras. Paris, 1869.
Squier, Ephraim G.: Honduras, Descriptive, Historical, and Statistical. London, 1870.
Wells, William V.: Explorations and Adventures in Honduras. New York, 1857.

5. Nicaragua.
Belt, Thomas: The Naturalist in Nicaragua. London, 1874. (Now published in the Everyman's Library.)

BIBLIOGRAPHY

 Government of Nicaragua. La República de Nicaragua. Managua, 1906.
 Lévy, Pablo; Nicaragua. Paris, 1873.
 Niederlein, Gustavo: The State of Nicaragua in the Greater Republic of Central America. Philadelphia (Philadelphia Commercial Museum), 1898.
 Pector, Desiré: Étude Économique sur la Republique de Nicaragua. Neûchatel, 1893.
 Squier, Ephraim G.: Nicaragua, its People, Scenery, Monuments, and the Proposed Nicaragua Canal. New York, 1852.
 Stout, Peter F.: Nicaragua, Past, Present, and Future. Philadelphia, 1859.

6. Costa Rica.
 Calvo, Joaquín Bernardo: The Republic of Costa Rica. Chicago and New York, 1890.
 Government of Costa Rica: Revista de Costa Rica en el Siglo XIX. San José, 1900.
 Molina, Felipe: Bosquejo de Costa Rica. New York, 1851.
 Niederlein, Gustavo: The Republic of Costa Rica. Philadelphia (Philadelphia Commercial Museum), 1898.

7. Publications of the United States Department of Commerce, Bureau of Foreign and Domestic Commerce.
 Central America as an Export Field. (By Garrard Harris.) Special Agents' Series, no. 113. 1916.
 Trade Directory of Central America and the West Indies. Miscellaneous series, no. 22. 1915.

INDEX

A

Acajutla, port of, 115
Accessory Transit Company, 83 f.
Agriculture,
  methods of, 16; Costa Rica, 138, 159, 163; Guatemala, 66 ff; Honduras, 126, 129 ff., 132 ff.; Nicaragua, 91 ff.; Salvador, 100, 106, 112
Aguardiente, 10, 15, 67, 246
  influence of, on people, 48, 66, 71; monopoly in, 285, 292
Alajuela, 138, 144
Alfaro, Prudencio, 217
Alta Verapaz,
  labor conditions in, 59; products of, 70
Amapala, 128,
  capture of, 208; Treaty of (1895), 103, 170; Treaty of (1907), 209
American International Corporation, 281
American investments in Central America. *See* Capital
American Phalanx, 82 f.
Amusements, 4, 10
Araujo, Manuel Enrique, 103
Arbitration. *See* Central American Court of Justice
Arce, Manuel José, 29
Army, 42 f., 188 f., 196,
  Costa Rica, 154; Guatemala, 57; Nicaragua, 73 f.; Salvador, 108 f.
Ayuntamientos. *See* Government, Municipal

B

Balsam of Peru,
  export of, 112 f., 273
Bananas, 20, 133 f., 204,
  blight, 270; export trade in, 268 ff.; Costa Rica, 138, 160 f.; Guatemala, 70; Honduras, 120, 133 f.; Nicaragua, 97
Banks. *See* Finance
Barillas, Manuel Lísandro, 52
Barrios, Gerardo, 102
Barrios, José María Reyna, 52
Barrios, Justo Rufino, 52, 102, 123, 171 f.

Beneficios, 18, 266 f.
Bertrand, Francisco, 124
Blaine, Secretary, policy of, 181 f.
Blanco, General, 145 f.
Bluefields, 96 f.,
  blockade of, 230; revolution at (1909), 227 ff.
Bográn, Luis, 123
Bonilla, Manuel, 123 f.; 172, 207 f.
Bonilla, Policarpo, 123
Brown Brothers and Company,
  loans to Nicaragua, 235 ff., 259 ff., 292 f.
Buchanan, President,
  restoration of Central American Union favored by, 181
Buchanan, William I., 210
Bureau, Central American. *See* Central American Bureau

C

Cabañas, Trinidad, 122
Cabinets. *See* Government
Cabrera, Manuel Estrada. *See* Estrada Cabrera, Manuel
Cacao, export of, 17, 92, 273
Cannon, Lee Roy, execution of, 228 f.
Capital, foreign,
  influence of, 98, 183, 267 f.; in Central America, 281 f., 288 f.; in Honduras, 127, 132; in Nicaragua, 235 ff., 259 ff. *See also* Finance
Carazo, Evaristo, 87 f.
Caribbean Coast,
  importance of, 20, 70; in Costa Rica, 160 f.; in Honduras, 132 ff.; in Nicaragua, 95 ff.
Carillo, Braulio, 141, 144 f.
Carrera, Rafael, 32, 51, 101 f., 122, 168, 198
Cartago, 138 f., 144
Castellón, Francisco, 81
Castro, José María, 146
Catholic Church, influence of, 13, 131, 196, 198
Cattle, 16 f., 67, 78, 92,
  export of, 273; Costa Rica, 142; Honduras, 120, 126 f., 135; Salvador, 112

327

328 INDEX

Central America,
  progress retarded in, 14 f., 185 ff.; export trade of, 265 ff.; import trade of, 275 ff.; revenue, sources of, 284 f.; expenditures of each republic (1913), 286 f.; foreign debts, origin of, 288 f.; currencies, depreciation of, 296 ff.; foreign capital, need of, 302; investments, opportunities for, 303 f.; United States, opposition to, 306 f.; financial assistance, need of, 311 ff.
Central American Bureau,
  San José Conference establishes (1906), 206 f.; Washington Conference establishes (1907), 212; convention establishing, 215; work of, 225 f.
Central American Court of Justice, 213 ff.
  case of Nicaragua and Honduras vs. Guatemala and Salvador, 218 f.; work of, 221 ff.; case of Nicaragua and United States Canal Treaty, 254 ff.
Central American Federal Republic. See Central American Union.
Central American Federation. See Central American Union
Central American Public Works Company, 290
Central American Union, 28 ff., 144; need of, 164 f.; advantages of, 179 ff.; difficult to form, 171 f., 174 ff.; attempts to renew, 102, 168 ff.; Union of 1842, 168; Union of 1849, 169; Union of 1895, 170
Centro Americo, 226
Cerna, Vicente, 52
Chalchuapa, battle of (1885), 105, 172
Chamorro, Emiliano, 231 f., 234, 243, 245, 250 ff.
Chamorro, Frutos, 169
Chinandega, treaty of (1842), 168 f.
Christmas, General Lee, 218
Cities. See Government, municipal
Civil Wars. See Revolutions
Claims. See Investments, foreign
Clayton-Bulwer Treaty, 82, 96
Climate,
  Costa Rica, 138 f.; Guatemala, 67 f.; Nicaragua, 92; Salvador, 100
Coban, 70
Cochineal, export of, 17
Cocoanuts, export of, 273

Coffee, 5, 17 ff., 274 f.
  cultivation, methods of, 265 ff.; export of, 266 ff., 275; Costa Rica, 142, 144, 160 ff.; Guatemala, 66 f.; Honduras, 136; Nicaragua, 93; Salvador, 100, 112, 115
Colonos, 59
Commerce, 265 ff.,
  development retarded, 14 f.; foreign control of, 21, 276 ff.; exports, 17, 265 ff.; imports, 275 f.; United States trade with Central America, 276 ff.; Costa Rica, 159 ff., 274; Guatemala, 67 f., 274; Honduras, 135 f., 274; Nicaragua, 92 ff., 274; Salvador, 114 ff., 274
Communication, means of. See Transportation
Concessions, 22, 313 ff.,
  Honduras, 134 f.; Nicaragua, 89 f., 97. See also Investments, foreign
Conferences, 176,
  U. S. S. Marblehead (1906), 206; San José (1906), 206 ff.; Washington Conference, 216, 220 f.; annual, 216, 225
Congress. See Government.
Conservatives. See Political Parties
Contract labor system. See Labor
Contreras brothers, 192
Corinto, 87, 244 f.
Corn, 112
Corporations, foreign,
  influence of, 22, 83 f., 132, 134, 202, 269 ff.; need of government control of, 313 ff. See also Brown Brothers and Co.; Ethelburga Syndicate; Seligman, J. & W. and Co.; Finance
Corral, General, 81 f.
Costa Rica,
  agriculture, 138, 159 f., 162 f.; area and population, 1, 138 ff., 162 f.; army, 154; bananas, 138, 160 f., 268 ff.; cattle, 142; coffee, 142, 144, 160 ff., 275; commerce, 159 ff., 266, 268, 274 f., 277 f.; Court of Justice, decisions of, 224, 253 ff.; education, 147, 158 f.; finance, 285 ff., 290 ff., 301; government, 143 f.; 147 ff., 154 ff., 159; history, 144 ff.; labor, 139 ff., 163; land, ownership of, 141 f.; peace, internal, 148 ff., 194, 200; politics, 148 ff.; transportation, facilities of, 157, 160 f., 291; United Fruit Co., 160 f.
Court of Justice. See Central American Court of Justice

INDEX

Courts, corruption of, 36, 46 ff.
Creel, Señor, 210
Creoles, 3 ff., 25, 56, 78, 191 f.
Crops. See Agriculture
Cuadra family, 232,
Dr. Carlos Cuadra Pasos, 250 ff.
Currency systems, 296 ff.,
Costa Rica, 301; Guatemala, 54, 297 ff.; Honduras, 300; Nicaragua, 236 ff., 248 f., 263, 299; Salvador, 300 f.
Customs, collection of, 238 f., 312

D

Dávila, Miguel, 123 f., 172, 208 ff., 217
Dawson, Thomas C., 233
Dawson agreement, The, 233 f., 243
Delgado, Father, 29
Díaz, Adolfo, 232, 234, 243 ff.
Díaz, Porfirio, 173, 206, 210, 229
Diseases. See Sanitation
Dueñas, Francisco, 102

E

East Coast. See Caribbean Coast
Education, 11, 199, 317 f.,
Costa Rica, 147, 158 f.; Guatemala, 55, 61; Honduras, 131; Nicaragua, 89; Salvador, 110 f.
Elections, 30 f., 34 f.,
Costa Rica, 148 ff.; Guatemala, 55 f.; Nicaragua, 74, 245, 249 ff.
El Triunfo, 116
Emery claim, 228
Encomiendas. See Repartimientos
Escalón, José Pedro, 103
Esquivel, Ascensión, 147
Estrada, Juan J., 227, 230 f., 234 f.
Estrada Cabrera, Manuel, 53, 74, 206, 297
Ethelburga Syndicate, 237 f., 240, 292 f.
European War, effect of, 115, 135, 247 ff., 274 f., 279, 281 ff., 290, 296, 298 ff.
Exchange, rates of, 296, 298 ff.
Export trade. See Commerce
Ezeta brothers, 102

F

Fernández, Mauro, 147
Fernández, Próspero, 146
Ferrer, Francisco, 122
Fiallos, Señor, 173
Figueroa, Fernando, 103, 209
Filibusters and filibustering, 81 ff., 217 f.

Filísola, General, 28
Finance, 21 f., 235 ff., 259 ff., 279 ff., 284 ff. See also Capital Corporation Investment Loans
Fonseca, Casto, 80
Fonseca, Gulf of, 115, 117, 119, naval base on, 252 ff.
Fruit trade. See Commerce

G

Gainza, Governor-general of Guatemala (1821), 24, 80
Germany,
Central American commerce with, 274 ff., 277 f.
Gold, 120, 272
González, Alfredo, 148
González, Santiago, 102
González Víquez, Cleto. See Víquez, Cleto González
Government, 25, 41 f.,
Executive, powers of, 33 ff., 37, 39 ff., 286 f.; Cabinets, 37; Legislatures, 36; Judiciary, 36 f., 46 ff., 111, 155 f.; Costa Rica, 143, 147 ff., 154 ff.; Guatemala, 53 ff.; Honduras, 124 f.; Nicaragua, 73 ff.; Salvador, 105, 107 ff. See also Political Parties, Politics
Government, municipal, 27, 37 f., 66, 156
Grace and Company, 281
Graft. See Politics
Granada,
Leon, rivalry with, 77 ff.; capture of (1855), 81
Granados, Miguel García, 52
Great Britain,
bondholders in Guatemala supported by, 289; bondholders in Honduras supported by, 294; bondholders in Nicaragua supported by, 240; Central American commerce with, 274 f., 277 ff., 282; protectorate on Mosquito Coast, 95 f., 168 f.
Greytown, 82, 95 f.
Groce, Leonard, execution of, 228 f.
Guardia, General Tomás, 33, 146, 291
Guardia Civil, 109
Guardiola, Santos, 122
Guatemala,
agriculture, 66 ff.; area and population, 1, 50, 57 ff., 67, 70, 198; army, 57 f., bananas, 70, 268 f.; cattle, 67; Central American Union and, 168, 178; coffee, 66 ff., 266 ff., 275; commerce,

INDEX

67 f., 274, 277 f.; education, 55, 61; finance, 54, 285 f., 288 f., 297 f.; government, 53 ff.; labor, 58 ff., 62 ff.; land, ownership of, 64; politics, 54 f.; transportation, facilities of, 68 ff.; United Fruit Co., 69 f.
Gutiérrez, Rafael, 102 f.

H

Habilitadores, 62, 64
Ham, Colonel Clifford D., 238 f.
Health. *See* Sanitation
Heredia, 138, 144
Herrera, Dionisio de, 80
Highways. *See* Transportation
Honduras,
 agriculture, 119 f., 126, 129 ff., 132 f.; area and population, 1, 120, 129 f., 133; bananas, 120, 133, 268; capital, foreign, 127 f., 132, 134 f.; Caribbean Coast, importance of, 132 ff.; Central American Union and, 167 f.; cattle, 120, 126 f., 135, 273; coffee, 136, 266, 275; commerce, 133 ff., 273 f., 277; economic development of, retarded, 126 ff.; education, 131; finance, 285 f., 288, 293 ff., 300; foreign relations, 121, 123, 168 f., 172, 207 f.; government, 124 f.; living, standards of, 129 ff.; mines, 120, 127; transportation, facilities of, 127 f., 134 f., 293; United Fruit Co., 134 f.; Washington conventions, 211 f.

I

Immigration, foreign, 21
Import trade. *See* Commerce
Indians, 2, 58, 178,
 Costa Rica, 138 ff.; Guatemala, 57 ff., 64, 198; Honduras, 120; Nicaragua, 72, 93 f.; Salvador, 100
Indigo, 17, 92, 273
Industries. *See* Manufacturing
International Health Commission. *See* Sanitation
Investments, foreign, 21 ff., 265 ff., 271, 301 f., 311 ff. *See also* Finance
Irías, Dr. Julián, 251 f.
Iturbide, Augustin, 28 f.

J

Jeréz, Maximo, 81 f., 85 f.
Jiménez, Jesús, 146
Jiménez, Ricardo, 148
Jinotega, 93
Joint Claims Commission. *See* Nicaraguan Joint Claims Commission
Jornaleros, 59 ff.
Judiciary. *See* Government
Junta Consultiva, 24
Justice, Central American Court of. *See* Central American Court of Justice

K

Keith, Minor C., 160, 269, 291, interests, 271
Knox, Secretary, note of, to Zelaya, 228 f.

L

Labor, 7 f., 10 f.,
 Costa Rica, 139 f., 163; Guatemala, 59 ff., 62 ff.; Nicaragua, 93 ff.; Salvador, 114
La Ceiba, 133
Ladinos, 6, 57, 72, 195
La Libertad, 116
Land, ownership of, 3, 6, 64, 93 f., 141 f., 267 f.
La Union, 115, 117
Legislatures. *See* Government
Leíva, Ponciano, 123
Lempa River, 100, 115
Leon,
 Granada, rivalry with, 77 ff.
Ley de Trabajadores (1894), 59 ff.
Liberals. *See* Political Parties
Living, conditions of, 4 ff., 8 ff., 113 f., 129 ff., 161 ff.
Loans, foreign, 235 ff., 241 ff., 294. *See also* Finance
Local Government. *See* Government, municipal
Localismo, 43 f., 73, 76 f., 196 f.
Lumber, 17, 70, 135, 273

M

Madriz, José, 229 f.
Mahogany. *See* Lumber
Malespín, Francisco, 101 f.
Managua, 80, 86 ff.
Mandamientos, 59
Manufacturing, 15, 114
Marblehead (U. S. S.), 206
Martínez, Tomás, 85 f.
Matagalpa, 92 ff., 236

INDEX 331

Medina, José María, 122
Meléndez, Don Carlos, 103
Mena, General Luís, 231, 234, 242 ff.
Menéndez, Francisco, 102
Mestizos. See Ladinos
Metals, precious. See Mines
Mexico, 28, 123, 206 ff., 218, 229. See also Díaz, Porfirio
Mines, 120, 126 f., 272 f.
Missionaries, influence of, 13
Moncada, General José María, 231, 234
Monroe Doctrine, 204 ff., 302, 304 f.
Montealegre, José María, 145
Mora, Juan, 144
Mora, Juan Rafael, 145, 181
Morazán, Francisco, 29 f., 80, 101, 122, 145, 167
Morgan, J. P. & Co., 294
Mosquito Coast, 95 ff., 169
Municipal government. See Government, municipal
Muñoz, Trinidad, 80

N

Namasigne, battle of (1907), 208
National Constituent Assembly, 28 ff., 166
Negroes. See Population
New York and Honduras Rosario Mining Co., 127
Nicaragua,
  agriculture, 91 ff.; area and population, 1, 72, 76, 93 f.; army, 73 f.; bananas, 97, 268; canal route in, 75 f., 252, 254 ff.; capital, foreign, 89 f., 97, 235 ff., 259 ff.; Caribbean Coast, 95 ff.; cattle, 78, 92, 273; Central American Union and, 167 f.; Claims Commission, 240 f.; commerce, 92 f., 238, 274, 277; coffee, 93, 266, 275; Court of Justice, decision of, 223 f.; education, 89; finance, 232 ff., 239 f., 246 ff., 248 f., 259 ff., 263, 285 f., 288, 292, 299 f.; foreign influence in, 95 ff., 169; government, 73; history, 81 ff., 89 ff.; labor, 93 ff.; politics, 74, 76 ff., 89, 245, 249 ff.; transportation, facilities of, 97 f., 237, 246, 261, 292; United States, intervention of, 182, 228 ff., 244, 306
Nicaragua, Lake, 75
Nicaraguan Joint Claims Commission, 240 f.

O

Oficina Internacional Centroamericana. See Central American Bureau

P

Pan American Financial Conference (1915), 294 f.
Panama Canal, 161, 204
Paper money. See Currency
Pasos, Dr. Carlos Cuadra, 250 ff.
Peonage. See Labor
Personalismo, 43 f., 76 f., 196 f.
Peten, 70
Police, 53, 108 f., 157
Political Parties, 26, 29, 31 ff., 43 ff., 149 ff., 165,
  Conservatives, 29, 32 f., 167 f.; Guatemala, 51 ff.; Honduras, 122; Nicaragua, 78 ff., 85 ff., 169 f., 231, 233, 250; Salvador, 102 f.,
  Liberals, 29, 32 f., 167 f.; Guatemala, 50 ff.; Honduras, 122; Nicaragua, 78, 85 ff., 228 ff., 233, 250 f., 260; Salvador, 101 f.
Politics, corruption in, 45 ff., 186 ff., 286 ff., 291 ff.,
  Costa Rica, 159; Guatemala, 54; Honduras, 125; Nicaragua, 76 ff., 89; Salvador, 111 f.; foreign influence on, 132, 135, 161, 200 ff., 227, 314 f.
Population, 2, 50, 72, 100, 120, 138 ff., Negro, 20, 120 f., 133, 160. See also Indians
Ports, 68 f., 87, 97, 115 f., 128 f., 132, 160 f. See also Transportation
President, power of. See Government
Press, influence of, 48, 149 f.
Protectorates. See Great Britain, United States
Puerto Barrios, 68 f.
Puerto Cortez, 133
Puerto Limón, 160
Puntarenas, 160 f.

R

Railways. See Transportation
Regalado, Tomás, 103
Religion. See Catholic Church
Repartimientos, 7, 58, 139 f.
Revolutions, causes of, 49, 185 ff.
Rivas, Patricio, 81
Roads. See Transportation
Rockefeller Foundation. See Sanitation
Rodríguez, José Joaquín, 147

332 INDEX

Roosevelt, Theodore, 173, 205 ff., 210
Root, Elihu, 210
Rum. *See* Aguardiente

S

Sacasa, Roberto, 88
Salazar, General, 145 f.
Salvador,
  agriculture, 100, 106, 112; area and population, 1, 99 f., 113 f.; army, 108 f.; cattle, 112; Central American Union and, 167 f.; coffee, 100, 112, 115, 266, 275; commerce, 114 f., 274, 277; Court of Justice, decision of, 224; education, 110 f.; finance, 285 f., 288, 290, 300 f.; foreign relations, 104 ff., 117; Guatemala and, 29; government, 107 ff.; labor, 114; manufactures, 114; Nicaraguan Canal Treaty, protest against, 253 ff.; peace, internal, 194; politics, 105 f., 111 f.; transportation, facilities of, 109, 115 ff., 290
Sanitation, 9, 157 f.
San José, 138, 144, 160,
  conference at, 206 f.
San Salvador, 99, 115 f.
Santa Ana, 102, 115 f.
San Vicente, 115
Schools. *See* Education
Seligman, J. & W. and Co., 235, 242, 246 ff., 259 ff., 292 ff.
Sierra, General Terencio, 123, 209
Silver, 127, 272 f.
Social conditions, 5, 10, 12, 22 f.
Sonsonate, 115
Soto, Bernardo, 146
Soto, Marco Aurelio, 123
Spain, influence of colonial system of, 14
Spoils system. *See* Politics
Steamship lines, 19, 69, 97, 116, 132, 269. *See also* Transportation
Sugar, 112

T

Taft, William H., 217, 228
Tegucigalpa, 19, 122, 128 f., 208
Tinoco, Federico, 148
Trade. *See* Commerce
Transportation, 19, 177,
  Costa Rica, 157, 160, 291; Guatemala, 68 ff.; Honduras, 127 f., 134 f., 293; Nicaragua, 97, 237, 246, 261, 292; Salvador, 109, 115 ff., 290. *See also* Steamship lines

U

Union, Central American. *See* Central American Union
United Fruit Company, 19 ff., 269 ff., 281
  Costa Rica, 160 f.; Guatemala, 69 f.; Honduras, 134 f.
United States,
  Central American Union, 171, 181 ff.; commerce with Central America, 269, 274 ff., 279 ff.; commercial and financial interests of, 180 ff., 204 f., 303 ff.; financial assistance of, needed in Central America, 279 f., 302; Honduras, intervention in, 123, 294; influence of, in Central America, 203, 220 f.; intervention in Central America, 304 ff.; intervention, results of, 307 ff.; Mexico and, intervention of, 207 ff.; Monroe Doctrine, maintenance of, 205 f.; Mosquito Coast, British control of, 95; Nicaragua, relations with, 98, 182, 228 ff., 233 f., 235 ff., 244, 250, 253 f., 258; relations with Central America, 105, 171; Salvador, relations with, 117; trade, opportunities for, 282 f.; trade retarded, 279; Walker, attitude toward, 82 f.

V

Valle, Andrés, 102
Vásquez, Domingo, 123
Víquez, Cleto González, 148

W

Wages, 10, 299. *See also* Labor
Walker, William, 81 ff., 85 f., 145, 189
Washington Conference (1907), 123, 173, 210 ff., 216 f., 226, 305; conventions of, 105, 176, 211 ff., 220 f., 315

Y

Yglesias, Rafael, 147, 301

Z

Zacapa, 116
Zaldívar, Rafael, 102, 172
Zelaya, José Santos, 88 ff., 96 f., 103, 123 f., 170, 172, 193, 207 ff., 217 ff., 227 ff., 299, 306
Zeledón, Benjamin, 243 f.